CRUSADER

CRUSADER

THE HELL-RAISING
POLICE CAREER OF
DETECTIVE DAVID DURK

JAMES LARDNER

RANDOM HOUSE   NEW YORK

A portion of this work was originally published in *The New Yorker*.

Library of Congress Cataloging-in-Publication Data

Lardner, James.
Crusader: the hell-raising police career of Detective David Durk/
James Lardner.—1st ed.
p.   cm.
Includes index.
ISBN 0-394-57648-9
1. Durk, David.   2. Detectives—New York (N.Y.)—Biography.
3. Police corruption—New York (N.Y.).   4. Whistle blowing—New York
(N.Y.).   5. New York (N.Y.).   Knapp Commission.—History.   I. Title.
HV7911.D923L37   1996
364.1'323—dc20   95-25431
[B]

Printed in the United States of America on acid-free paper
2   4   6   8   9   7   5   3
First Edition

Book design by Lilly Langotsky

TO DIANE CLEAVER

CRUSADER

PROLOGUE

———⟫●⟪———

Late one night, a wounded young man bursts into a hole-in-the-wall of a restaurant in Manhattan's Chinatown with the three companions of a double date. He is bleeding from the nose, an ear, and the palms of both hands—injuries suffered when he verbally intervened in defense of a woman who was being beaten on a nearby street corner and, as a reward for his chivalry, had a trash can smashed across his face. He wants to call the police.

The manager of the restaurant coldly informs him that the telephone is for patrons only.

The patrons of the moment sit and stare, mesmerized by another installment in the soap opera of New York City circa 1995. All but one patron. The exception is a man in his late fifties, tall and sturdily built, with downy silver-gray hair of the kind favored in the U.S. Senate, droopily handsome features, and spider tracks that radiate out from the corners of his eyes. He is wearing a frayed jacket that was purchased, perhaps a decade ago, from Brooks Brothers, and a tie, shirt, and trousers of the same general vintage.

"Well, I'm eating here," David Durk pipes up. "What if I make the phone call?"

On his way to the phone, he glances out the window and spots a uniformed cop in a doorway across the street—a cop not obviously engaged in any mission more pressing than counting the minutes until the end of his shift. Durk goes out to get him. He tells the cop the story and points out the perpetrators, who are still standing on the sidewalk, right where the incident occurred. But the cop declines to act, citing the fact that his radio is broken. Without a working radio, he explains, he will have no way of calling for backup.

"Look," Durk says. "I used to be on the job. I'll help you."

The cop is adamant: the most he can do for the young man is help him and his friends find a taxi.

Durk gives up on the cop and calls 911—another obstacle course. The police operator says she can't send a car to the corner of Mott and Bayard, as Durk has requested, because her computer has determined that there is no such intersection. Even after he convinces her of its existence, he has to resort to artful exaggeration to get her to send help. "There's a cop here who's trying to make an arrest, and it looks like he's not doing too well," he says. For good measure, he invokes the radio code 10-85—a police officer in need of assistance.

Within a few minutes, several police cars are on the scene, the assailants are in custody (pending further police deliberations), and the ranking official—a captain—is asking, "Where's the wise guy?"

"I guess you mean me," Durk says.

"What's with the ten–eighty-five?" says the captain.

"Well, you had an officer here who was reluctant to take some perps who had committed a felony until he had a backup, and I was simply trying to get a backup," Durk says. "Under the circumstances, I thought a ten–eighty-five was appropriate."

The captain requests Durk's ID.

"Look, why don't we just call it a day?" Durk says.

"You know, you could be locked up for obstruction of justice," the captain points out.

"Obstruction of justice!" Durk protests. "I thought it was enhancement of justice!"

"Let me see some ID," the captain repeats.

"Okay, I'll show you mine, you show me yours," Durk says.

Of the two IDs, Durk's makes the bigger impression. "I don't need this," the captain says with a sigh. "I'm going to be retiring in three weeks. Why are you doing this to me?"

———————

Few events of the last generation have seized New York City's attention as did the hearings of the Knapp Commission, in the fall of 1971, and mentioning them is still a good way to tell a native from a transient. For two weeks in October and one in December, New Yorkers came to work every morning with a compulsion to talk about the latest appalling testimony, broadcast live on radio and TV the day before. Only crime stories and sports stories, as a rule, have the capacity to transfix a city. Here was a crime story with a vengeance. The Knapp Commission—formally the Commission to Investigate Allegations of Police Corruption and the City's Anti-Corruption Procedures—had compiled evidence of crimes beyond counting, committed by the agency that was supposed to protect citizens against crime.

A scandal is usually the result of events spiraling out of control. This one was planned. It happened because three people—a plainclothes cop named Frank Serpico, a reporter named David Burnham, and a young detective sergeant named David Durk—made it happen. And it was Durk who summoned Serpico and Burnham to the task. He laid out the strategy, set it into motion, and provided the greater share of the outrage and the determination for a campaign that ultimately compelled Mayor John Lindsay and the rest of the city's leaders to do something about a pattern of corruption that went back more than a century.

The journalist Jack Newfield has called him one of the "few genuine heroes" in the history of New York City government.

"You kind of forget that there are moments in the world that have massive potential for good and evil," Robert McGuire, a former New York City police commissioner, has said. "We have an honest police department today, by and large, and that's a memorial to David Durk and Frank Serpico." As a young lawyer, McGuire briefly represented both men in their dealings with the Knapp Commission. Durk was "the driving force," and Serpico "a vehicle," according to McGuire. "You could say that David was responsible for the decriminalization of the police department," he says.

He was one of the last witnesses to appear before the Knapp Commission. While most of those who preceded him concentrated on minutiae—the grisly chapter and verse of who had done (or failed to do) what—Durk's testimony was a cry from the heart. He spoke with ferocious earnestness about the cost of corruption, to the city and to cops themselves; about the hopes with which recruits entered the police department; and about the chipping away of those hopes followed by a slow descent into cynicism. He asked his listeners to look at cops as people with good and bad impulses, and to imagine a police department and a criminal justice system that encouraged the best in them—and what that would mean to New York as a whole. At the end of his testimony, fighting back tears, he rushed from the room, leaving the audience to applaud the empty chair in which he had been sitting.

The spectacle of a young cop weeping because his job hadn't turned out as advertised was one that New Yorkers, a famously hard-nosed people, found appealing. So much had Durk stirred the popular imagination that the police commissioner, Patrick V. Murphy, put out a confidential memo. Durk had credibility with the public, the memo observed. Murphy's own credibility would be enhanced if the public could be encouraged to associate him with Durk. How might this be arranged?

The producer of *Butch Cassidy and the Sundance Kid* had the inspiration of making a movie about him, with Paul Newman in the lead role. The editors of *The New York Times* followed his career with tabloidlike devotion, to the point of running irate editorials defending him against criticism or mistreatment. One evening in July 1972, as Durk was bringing a pizza home for dinner, he was attacked by a pair of muggers, one of whom came at him with a stiletto. (Durk was wearing a blue shirt and white pants, and newspapers later theorized that he had been mistaken for a pizza deliveryman.) The story found its way onto page one of the *Times* under the catchy headline SGT. DURK, OUT FOR PIZZA, SHOOTS A MUGGER AND SEIZES ANOTHER. DURK'S PIZZAZZ FOILS MUGGERS was the headline in the *Daily News*, which played the whole affair, more temperately, on page three.

The writer Robert Daley visited Durk soon after his Knapp Commission testimony and asked his wife, Arlene, about his plans for the future.

"He can do anything he wants," she replied—and this sounded to Daley at the time like a fairly accurate assessment of the possibilities.

"David could have made a lot of money," Thomas Reppetto, a former Chicago police officer who now runs New York's Citizens Crime Commission, has said. "In the early seventies, when he entered the room, he was *the* celebrity. If I had done what he had done, I'd dine out on it for the rest of my life."

People who are not fond of David Durk—a plentiful group in the higher ranks of New York City law enforcement—like to make it clear that they have nothing against whistle-blowers or whistle-blowing in general. What they object to, they want it understood, isn't his whistle-blowing, but his manners. Why is it, they ask, that in ordinary, non-whistle-blowing times, he cannot manage to be more gracious? Why does he always press his case with the same irritating intensity? Why can't he be more like the whistle-blower hero of countless celebratory articles, movies, and TV shows: a quietly virtuous employee, content to be a cog in the bureaucratic machine until, one day, he stumbles across evidence of wrongdoing so monstrous that it cannot be ignored?

The notion of the reluctant whistle-blower is attractive but (as most of us would acknowledge if we just looked around our workplaces) fantastic. Few institutions suffer from a shortage of polite, circumspect, collegial people, and when such people come across great outrages—conditions that cry out for exposure—they generally go right on being polite, circumspect, and collegial, and say nothing. The people who rise to these occasions tend to be suspicious, obsessive, and cantankerous, in bad and good times alike.

"David has always got his eye out for somebody who's playing the slightest game," David Garth, a long-time friend of Durk's (and the media strategist behind the political careers of John Lindsay, Ed Koch, Mario Cuomo, and Rudy Giuliani, among others), has said. "He isn't just somebody who rocks the boat—he'll put a fucking hole through the boat to rock it. And he's always got his eye out for somebody who may be playing the slightest game. David takes audacity to the nth degree."

"If you've ever seen saints in museums, they always have arrows sticking out of them, or they've been set on fire by somebody," Clark Whelton, a former reporter who later worked as a speechwriter for Koch, has observed. "It's because they live life by absolute rules. The average person lives from day to day—tries to get along as best he can. I don't mean to imply that David is a saint, but he has a lot of arrows sticking out of him."

"He's manipulative, and impossible to understand, and he's a huge pain in the ass," David Burnham says. "But his nose is very keen—he sees truth with great clarity."

His nose has been at its keenest when sniffing in the vicinity of a class of high-ranking officials whom he calls "the people with flags in their offices." He takes the position that they have a unique obligation to do right. Not very many such people, in Durk's experience, have ever lived up to this obligation, but he expects them to, just the same. "David has got a hang-up about people with flags in their offices," says Harold Hess, a retired assistant chief who used to run the NYPD's Intelligence Division. "Anybody with a flag in his office is in trouble—David doesn't even have to know the guy. He had an interesting career—a crisis a day."

Twenty-five years have passed since Durk made his dramatic entrance onto the city's stage. They have been unexpectedly difficult years, for him and the city alike. He lives upstate now and does not often visit the ground of his former exploits. When old associates catch sight of him, they sometimes have the feeling they are seeing a ghost, or a curiosity—a living link to an era of what it is now fashionable to regard as foolish optimism about public institutions and the future of urban life.

Many of the younger cops of the 1990s have no idea who Durk is. (The police academy curriculum does not include a course in NYPD history.) Yet among the dwindling corps of veterans who haven't forgotten him, his name still elicits fear.

———⟫•⟪———

"I'm really not looking to give you a hard time," Durk assures the captain in Chinatown. "I just want these people treated with some concern. They're victims. You're supposed to help them. I presume everyone here is getting paid."

"Well, you know there are problems about overtime," the captain confides in a low voice, alluding to the reluctance of cops to make arrests at the end of a shift.

Durk nods. He knows, but as he points out, a serious assault has been committed, and some sort of police action would seem to be warranted.

The captain reluctantly agrees.

"I hope you have a wonderful retirement," Durk tells him.

PART
ONE

CHAPTER

ONE

Like many revolutionaries, David Durk had a comfortable childhood. The shtetls of Eastern Europe lay a couple of generations back on either side of his family, but by the time he arrived on the scene his parents and most of his relatives lived in well-kept Manhattan apartment buildings with doormen and high ceilings.

His father was an eye surgeon with an office on Park Avenue, where David, the elder of two sons, had a standing invitation to hang around and tinker with the scalpel, the microscope, and the other tools of the trade. His mother volunteered at this and that, but her life's work (or so it seemed to her firstborn) was to feed and clothe him and make sure he never left the house without at least one more layer of clothing than he could bear. She was, in David's words, "attentive to the point of being intrusive." Yet his friends were always staying for dinner, and sometimes, afterward, they would lament that *their* mothers were not as close to them as his obviously was to him.

Another large presence in David's life was his maternal grandmother—a pioneering figure in the fund-raising world, who saw, before others, the financial potential of charitable evenings in honor of rich people. A small but formidable woman, she would slice her way through groups of menacing youths, umbrella outstretched. As a teenager, David once offered to carry a shopping bag for her, only to be told, "No, you mustn't strain yourself." Years later, after he had become a cop, they shared a taxi back from a family gathering. As he headed toward his front door, he heard his grandmother—by now in her late seventies—telling the cabdriver to stand by until he was safely inside.

While far from rich, the Durks had a spacious apartment on West End Avenue, a housekeeper, a car, and a freedom from financial anxiety that is rare among professional, single-earner households these days. Nor was crime much of a concern on the Upper West Side of Manhattan in the forties and early fifties. Grade-school children played on the sidewalks, did errands, and traveled from home to school to Riverside Park, all without adult supervision. The worst thing that ever happened to David as a child was being relieved of his spare change a few times by a gang of Irish kids who hung out in front of a Catholic school along the route to the St. Agnes branch library. Once or twice he was called a Christ-killer, for good measure.

Growing up in New York in the postwar years, a boy had more than the usual grounds for thinking that fate had placed him at the center of the universe. The United States was not just the richest country in the world but was the focus of the world's envy and hope as no other country had ever been, and New York was a spectacular symbol of the nation's strength, skill, and artistic and intellectual vigor.

The melting pot was on high flame. David's maternal grandfather—who was also in the vision business, designing and manufacturing aviator glasses for the Air Force—considered it a privilege to be allowed to pay taxes to the U.S. government. At his funeral, one of his employees told David, who was eight or so, that "if every boss was like your grandfather there wouldn't have to be any unions." In the Durk family, Memorial Day wasn't just an excuse for a long weekend, it was a for-real holiday when everybody would go down to Riverside Drive to cheer the veterans. In grade school, David collected scrap metal for the war effort and lobbied his relatives to buy war bonds. At PS 9, he was the school flag-bearer.

Although his mother sometimes worried that David spent too much time in his room reading, he played the required New York City sports of baseball, stickball, and handball, knew his scout manuals from cover to cover, went to the movies at Loew's 83rd Street and the RKO 81st Street with small gangs of his friends on weekends, and threw Good & Plentys at the girls when the matron wasn't watching. He developed a taste for pirate movies and swordsplay, and for one of his birthdays, his father gave him an authentic sword, with its edges ground down. Later, David joined the fencing team at Stuyvesant High School—one of a handful of elite public high schools that admitted students by competitive examination.

The memory of Franklin Roosevelt shone brightly in the lives of Dr. and Mrs. Durk; after his passing and that of another family hero, Mayor Fiorello LaGuardia, they never entered a voting booth with quite the same enthusiasm. But, in contrast to many liberals—and on the Upper West Side, almost everybody *was* a liberal—they practiced their politics in everyday ways. David's mother taught him that *schvartze* was an ugly word, and encouraged him to recruit black kids into his Boy Scout troop—to the consternation of the scoutmaster. His father gave up a successful private practice in order to devote himself to a network of free eye clinics he had established, with city funds, for slum children, and, in his fifties, taught himself Spanish in order to communicate better with the growing number of his patients (and their parents) who came from Puerto Rico.

How does someone come by a conspicuous talent for agitation? The question is no less worthy of study than the origins of genius in painting or math, and no easier to answer. In David's case, an examination of his family, his community, and the times explains a lot; it also leaves a lot unexplained—why, for instance, did his brother, Robert, manifest none of his passion either for public service or for making trouble? Robert Durk, four years younger than David, was a quiet child, more skilled with his hands than in conversation (and in that respect more like their father than David was). He grew up to be a dentist.

David was a boy who had to figure things out for himself; peer pressure carried no weight with him. At PS 9 one day a group of students was called out of class and sent back in, one by one, to examine a number of visual conundrums on the blackboard. Asked to compare two parallel lines, David confidently declared that one was shorter than the other—only to be told by his fellow students en masse that the two lines were the same length. His answer, he learned later, had been correct; it was the answer that everybody had given at first, but, like the boy in Hans Christian Andersen's fable of the emperor and his new suit, only David had refused to budge from the truth as his own eyes had told it. This act of obstinacy aroused the scientific interest of the testers, who, to his indignation—and that of his parents, when he complained to them—had him removed from class on two successive days in order to study him further.

His subversive tendencies flowered in earnest at Amherst, where David arrived in the fall of 1954. Amherst was a city kid's dream of a college: a place where you could leave your books on a table in the library and find them, unmoved, a day later, and where the professors were happy to linger after class and volley arguments back and forth with their students. Amherst prided itself not so much on the renown of its teachers as on the fact that they really taught—stood face-to-face with their students, lectured to them, engaged them in conversation, and read and graded their papers. (Amherst had no graduate program, hence no graduate students to do the dirty work.)

Most of his classmates were white Anglo-Saxon Protestants (a quota kept the number of Jews in check), and many were the children of alumni who had made successful careers for themselves in business or law. It was the rare member of the Amherst community who went further out on a political limb than to wear a button of support for Adlai Stevenson—the loser in straw polls of the student body both times he ran for president against Dwight Eisenhower. On the faculty, the economist Colston Warne, who had founded Consumers Union, was the closest thing to a radical that the school could offer. Amherst was scarcely a breeding ground of social reform, and yet, in its comparatively egalitarian ways and its cloistered devotion to learning for its own sake, it was a convivial setting for someone with a strong commitment to liberal values and a large capacity for outrage when he saw them flouted.

David's outrage quickly homed in on the fraternity system. Disgusted with the macho antics of the fraternity he had joined, he quit after a few months, and found himself assigned by default to something called the Lord Jeffrey Amherst Club—a separate but unequal pseudofraternity whose members were widely regarded as "turkeys" by their classmates and were subject to stricter rules of behavior when it came to female visitors. "If you got caught in a dormitory with a girl, they'd arrest you," David said later. "If you were in a fraternity, it was fine." In his junior year, David helped organize a revolt that led to the transformation of the Lord Jeff Club into an independent house, and after winning a seat on the house management committee he successfully pushed for new rules giving himself and his fellow residents the full privileges of fraternity members.

David was tall and dark, broad in the shoulders and lean in the waist, with a thick head of wavy gray-black hair, an aquiline nose, high cheekbones, and lively brown eyes that seemed to pop out at you when he was excited about anything—his general condition. Amherst was an enclave of a thousand young males surrounded by the four thousand females of Smith and Mount Holyoke, and he was a frequent commuter to those campuses; unlike many of his contemporaries when they came to look back on their college years, David did not have to lament that the sexual revolution had come too late. But when other students boasted (as many did) of their sexual exploits, he steered clear of the conversation. Years later, Peter Kline, a classmate of his, recalled that he had never encountered anyone who was so self-confident and, at the same time, so free of undergraduate braggadocio. Sometimes late at night in David's room, as they sipped Cointreau or some other genteel intoxicant, David would dispense advice about the importance of treating every relationship with a woman seriously, and of never forgetting that sex had emotional consequences. He was on a quest for "genuineness in every relationship," Kline recalled.

He didn't make friends in the careless way most young men do when they get to college. He sized up everybody he met and, casting aside those who struck him as superficial, zeroed in on a handful in whom he perceived a readiness to go against convention. He had a sharp eye, sometimes detecting in others rebellious impulses that they had not yet noticed in themselves.

He was determined to avoid what he called (borrowing from Byron) "the living lie." "He quoted that phrase all the time," Kline said. "He meant the tendency of social conventions to trap you into being something other than who you were. We kind of bonded together against the culture of the college, which was a culture of trying to impress your fraternity brothers. We stayed out of that. David had a big impact on my whole perception of life. I had never before met anyone who was willing to say 'What I perceive to be right is the thing I'm going to do—I can't do anything else.' That became a beacon for me."

David had been discouraged from thoughts of a medical career by his father. Dr. Durk, having grown up poor in Brooklyn—the son of a tailor—liked to point out that eye surgery was, in a way, a form of manual labor, since, like his father, he worked with a pair of scissors and a needle and thread. To him, being a doctor meant caring for people in need regardless of their resources, and that was often exceedingly difficult. He advised his son to become a lawyer.

In an obliging moment, David entered Columbia Law School, and he was in his first year there (his first and only year, it turned out) when he met the woman he would marry. They had gone, separately, to hear a lecture—"Must Men Hate?"—by the psychoanalyst Erich Fromm. Arlene Lepow, a senior at Barnard College, was a buxom, no-nonsense young woman with large eyes, shoulder-length brown hair, and a face no painter of the Italian Renaissance could have passed by. She was sitting by herself in an almost empty hall when David took a seat next to her and breezily asked, "What time does this thing break up?" He was twenty-one, and as sure as he had ever been sure of anything that he would not be getting married for years yet. Before the evening was over, he had decided that a man could not expect to meet two such women in one lifetime.

He was driving a cab at night to help pay his law school tuition, and sometimes during their courtship Arlene would sit in the front seat with him. Passengers seemed to like the idea of a cabdriver who cruised the city with his fiancée by his side ("It always got good tips," David recalled). Arlene, like him, was someone who took great pleasure in New York—in the parks, the museums, and the political and intellectual life of the city. They went for long walks around Manhattan and spent many hours talking about books and ideas and plans for the future. They debated the meaning of the Grand Inquisitor story from Dostoyevsky's *The Brothers Karamazov,* in which organized religion is indicted for a litany of false claims. Hypocrisy, they agreed, was the preeminent vice of modern times. Their marriage was going to embody the values they revered: directness, honesty, and social involvement. "You only have one life," David liked to say.

The life they chose for themselves was something of a puzzlement to Arlene's parents, especially her mother, who had grown up in Johannesburg, South Africa, and liked to go out at night "slathered in diamonds," as David put it. She and her husband had rigorous standards of domestic propriety—standards that David and Arlene were continually failing to meet. Mrs. Lepow could not abide breast-feeding (a practice adopted by Arlene after the birth of their first child, Joan) or the clutter of books, newspapers, and toys in their apartment. Arlene's father, for his part, could not understand how they could maintain a home without sugar, and when they left the shades open in their ninth-floor apartment (where no one could have peeked in without binoculars), he instinctively pulled them down.

David hit it off with his father-in-law, just the same. Benjamin Lepow was an outgoing and adventurous man who had journeyed in his youth to East Africa, where he had built a business capturing and importing exotic animals for circuses, zoos, medical laboratories, movies, and TV shows, including *Bring 'Em Back Alive,* a popular pseudodocumentary series. He was, in David's words, "the real Frank Buck."

As an animal importer, Mr. Lepow was a considerate businessman who paid his employees generously and cared about their well-being. As a sideline, however, he had taken to investing in New York City real estate—a field that brought out a less appealing side of his character. He associated New York with wheeler-dealers and sharp-edged practices. When a delivery arrived in Brooklyn or on the Jersey waterfront, Mr. Lepow felt compelled to give the customs inspectors a sizable gratuity; otherwise, he told David, they could seize on a technicality and order his animals into a quarantine that they might not survive. New York, he had concluded, was a place where there was no room for the softhearted.

When David and Arlene announced their intention to wed, Mr. Lepow took him aside to inform him that he was marrying into a family of some wealth, and David became his father-in-law's protégé. He was made the manager of an apartment building (a job that came with a rent-free apartment) and was given to understand that he might wind up running a small real estate empire if he proved himself worthy. With this shot at the easy life, however, also came the opportunity to foul it up.

Before long, David and his father-in-law had a running quarrel involving the city's rent-control law, which had divided New York— and individual buildings—into two classes of tenants: those who paid something like what the market would bear, and those who paid a lot less. Like many landlords, Mr. Lepow found it hard to think of a rent-controlled apartment without thinking of the additional rent it *wasn't* producing and of how nice it would be if the tenant should happen to move out. These meditations encouraged a certain stinginess when it came to expenditures on upkeep. David, on the other hand, was an ardent believer in prompt repairs for all the apartments under his jurisdiction, and he encouraged tenants to call or knock on his door whenever they had a problem.

It was one of those disagreements that start small and, almost unnoticed by the parties, get serious. The lawyers and accountants who did Mr. Lepow's paperwork pleaded with David not to make such a fuss. "He likes you—he's not going to live forever" was the gist of their argument, but it made no headway with him. Matters came to a climax when an old woman who lived next door to the Durks asked for a month's grace with the rent, owing to the recent death of her husband. David and Arlene, seeing no other way to protect her from the danger of eviction, decided to pay her rent for her. David announced that he was bowing out of the real estate business, and he and Arlene moved into another family-owned building, this time as tenants pure and simple—tenants who then had to threaten to go to housing court in order to get radiator covers installed for their daughter's protection.

Thus ended not only David's career as a budding real estate mogul, but pretty much all contact between the Durks and the Lepows. The bad feeling was particularly intense on the part of Arlene's mother, who remained steadfast in her low opinion of David (and of Arlene, for marrying him) for the rest of her life. When she died, after many years of widowhood, in 1992, David and Arlene and their children went conspicuously unmentioned in her will.

Real estate wasn't the only profession that didn't agree with David. After dropping out of law school, he went into business—profitably but restlessly—as an importer of African carvings. At the end of 1962, he was married, the father of a two-year-old girl, and still on the lookout for a livelihood. Then he came across an article (in *Daedalus* magazine) that cast his indecision in a new light. It was called "Social Change and Youth in America." Its author, the psychologist Kenneth Keniston, noted the quiet distaste with which many young people, "even those who appear at first glance to be chiefly concerned with getting ahead and making a place for themselves," viewed the lives that lay before them. "The adult world into which they are headed," Keniston wrote, "is seen as a cold, mechanical, abstract, specialized, and emotionally meaningless place in which one simply goes through the motions, but without conviction that the motions are worthy, humane, dignified, relevant, or exciting." Many college students were not optimistic about being able to change "the great corporations, bureaucracies, and academies for which most of them will work," Keniston observed.

It was a period when young Americans were free, as they hadn't been before (and haven't been since), to consider such issues—a time when, as a character in Michael Weller's play *Loose Ends* commented, "If you are white, middle class and American, you've got to work twenty-four hours a day to *not* make it." In later years, David liked to point out that he could afford to be a whistle-blower because, unlike most cops, he knew he could make a decent living in the outside world. But he was also one of those who, in that era of plenty, didn't think very much about money or financial security. Material needs would take care of themselves, it almost seemed—the idea was liberating to the soul. Not coincidentally, the fifties were a decade that produced an extraordinary cadre of nose-to-the-grindstone American rebels (Ralph Nader and Allard Lowenstein, to mention two) who dressed right, spoke well, and were tireless in their efforts to make the nation, at the pinnacle of its good fortune, live up to its ideals.

David was vaguely planning to reenter law school that autumn, but he didn't relish the prospect. The Peace Corps—an obvious escape—was, unfortunately, not a practical choice for a family man. So he started looking closer to home. New York City, in the early sixties, had started to worry about itself. Suburbanization had assumed the not-so-nice dimensions of "white flight," and jobs (for all but the privileged) were also flying. Frighteningly high rates of unemployment and single motherhood among blacks and Puerto Ricans had begun to cast doubt on the city's ability to absorb its two great waves of postwar migration as it had absorbed the earlier waves of Irish, Italians, and Eastern European Jews. In some neighborhoods, older residents were sealing themselves in at night rather than find out what awaited them on the streets. David's father was robbed repeatedly going to or from his clinics in Harlem. (He refused to call the police on these occasions; he couldn't believe that anything good would come of it. His only precaution was to carry his instruments in a paper bag, since the traditional black leather bag had plainly become too much of an invitation.)

In New York and other cities, academics, editorial writers, and political activists were starting to talk about an "urban crisis," although many of the problems that concerned them would later seem almost quaint. They were problems that middle-class and professional New Yorkers were not necessarily aware of. Poor people had yet to take up residence in the city's parks or subway stations; derelicts and panhandlers were largely confined to areas like the Bowery. By the standards of the nineties, the crime situation, too, was tame. Three quarters of the city's murders involved disputes between people who knew each other (a fraction that had declined to less than one half by the nineties), and most were committed with knives rather than guns. In 1963 New York had 549 homicides. In 1990 the murder tally was 2,245.

The notion of an urban crisis, like that of a "war on poverty," reflected a sense of opportunity as well as alarm. The city, with its neighborhoods, its parks, its landmarks, and its amalgamation of races and nationalities, was a great human achievement. It was worth saving, and there might even be some fun to be had in saving it. In the fervor of the moment, people made career moves that would later appear bizarre. John Lindsay, an unusually smart and strikingly good-looking member of Congress who had no quarrel with those who sized him up as a future president, decided to think about running for mayor of New York—a notorious political dead end. David Durk, determined not to become ensnared in one of those terrible bureaucracies that Keniston had warned about, entered the New York City police department.

CHAPTER

TWO

———⟶⬤⟵———

It's your last chance to be a knight errant," David would say when, at the end of the 1960s, he set out with a grant from the United States Justice Department to recruit police officers on the nation's college campuses. His audiences were largely composed of the sort of young men and women Kenneth Keniston had described—well prepared for careers that they dreaded. Police work, David insisted, was the perfect cure for what ailed them: it was "a socially critical job" and "the best graduate course you could possibly take." In case anyone wasn't satisfied with that argument, he added, "That siren and those red lights are fun. It's a job where self-interest merges with the public interest."

The profession could not have asked for a better champion, as I can testify, for I was one of the wide-eyed kids who heard him and were moved to follow his example. In February 1970, less than a year out of college, I joined the Washington, D.C., police department, which had gone into a hiring frenzy as a result of President Richard Nixon's little-remembered promise to make Washington a law enforcement model for the nation. My two-year stint as a patrolman in a riot-scarred inner-city precinct confirmed much of what David had said. Police work filled my waking and dreaming hours as no other job ever has; nor has any other job given me the satisfaction I got from swooping into people's lives at moments of distress and setting things, if not right, a little righter than they had been. And the siren and red lights *were* fun.

There were also aspects of the job that I found hard to take, such as clerical duty (I had made the mistake of letting my superiors know I could type); fixed posts (nights spent as a bodyguard on the porch of the mayor's house, for example); and long hours of sitting in court, only to be told, as often as not, that my services as a witness would not be needed that day. Police departments are organized on the military model. They are hierarchical and rule-ridden, and they don't place a high value on the time of those at the bottom. The NYPD was like that, only more so. The nation's oldest and most tradition-encrusted police department went to considerable lengths to make newcomers feel their unimportance. "Kid" was the standard form of address for a young cop. Many frontline supervisors seemed to have sworn their lives to the cause of discouraging youthful energy and initiative.

David, in his recruiting pitch, skipped over all that. But he wasn't being deliberately deceptive. For him, getting around the rules and the hierarchy was part of the fun: officious superiors were just another set of dragons to slay.

One night early in his career, he was asked to transfer a prisoner—a prostitute who had complained of internal injuries—from one hospital to another. At St. Clare's Hospital, on West Fiftieth Street, he found his charge lying in a cubicle, nude, with her feet in stirrups, a rubber tube attached to her nose, and a doctor and a couple of nurses hovering over her. While David stood outside the drawn curtain of the cubicle, two ambulance attendants and a cop from another precinct came through a door escorting a gurney to which a large male prisoner had been securely tied at five points. When the attendants released his wrists, the prisoner grabbed the cop by the throat and yanked him down with the ferocity that only the deranged are capable of.

David and the two attendants came to the cop's rescue right away, but several minutes passed before they managed to free him and get

his attacker safely rearcuffed and installed in a body bag—a process
that attracted an audience of orderlies, nurses, and doctors, including (it turned out) the team that had been preparing David's prisoner
for her trip. When calm had been fully restored, David glanced back
at the cubicle in which the prostitute had been lying—and saw that it
was empty.

The duty captain, when he heard the story, assured David that he
had behaved properly. (The cop he had helped rescue felt the same
way.) A few hours later, though, the captain came up to David as
he was going off duty and, with profuse apologies, said he had no
choice but to enter a complaint—"a small one"—on David's record.

"But there was a greater crime being committed in my presence!"
David objected. "The pross was a violation—not even a misde-
meanor. This was a felony."

"Look, kid, it's an automatic," the captain explained. David had
committed the high crime of "losing a prisoner," and, as the captain
put it, "When a prisoner gets lost, someone has to get a complaint."

The captain, in a friendly spirit, advised David to take his complaint
calmly, but it was not in David's nature to take such things calmly. He
insisted on the hearing to which he was entitled and prepared for it
with the thoroughness of a lawyer defending a capital case. He interviewed the admitting psychiatrist at Bellevue, who offered to testify to
the homicidal inclinations of the prisoner David had helped sub-
due—an assessment borne out by the prisoner's criminal record,
which featured two prior charges of assault on a police officer. David
came to his hearing armed not only with this evidence, but with the
names of eleven witnesses to the struggle. Two of them were nuns.

When he entered the hearing room, he found himself facing a tri-
bunal headed by the division administrator, Inspector Alfred Anger,
who was widely known for his dedication to discipline and for his
erect posture.

"Don't even bother to say anything," Inspector Anger said. "It's
automatic. Just accept it."

But David was a born arguer, who argued with a zest like that of
the heroes of the movie swashbucklers he had loved as a boy. In ver-

bal confrontations with his superiors, as in physical confrontations with suspected criminals, his style was full-speed-ahead. "I'm not accepting this—this is crazy," he declared. (Years later, in retirement, Chief Anger—the last title of a long climb through the ranks—could no longer recall his part in this three-decade-old episode; for David, every thrust and counterthrust remained vivid.) "We're talking about a violent psycho. I spoke to the psychiatrist at Bellevue, and he said he would testify that the guy was definitely homicidal. I checked his record. He had attacked two cops prior—one on 42nd Street and one on 125th Street. Both times, he tried to grab their guns."

"When he was strangling your fellow officer, you did not know his prior record," Inspector Anger observed.

David had to acknowledge the point, but asked the inspector to suggest an alternate course of action that would have been acceptable under the circumstances.

Inspector Anger mulled the question over. "Before you went to that cop's aid," he said at last, "you should have stopped and handcuffed your prisoner to her bed."

"But the cop had already turned blue!" David objected. "There was no time."

The inspector fell back on his original argument—that losing a prisoner was an automatic complaint.

"I find it hard to believe that this is the way, in 1963, you run a police department," David said. "The more I think about it, Inspector, the more I think I should apply for a medal. Not a high medal, but certainly an EPD." The letters stood for excellent police duty.

Inspector Anger told David he was insubordinate.

"I don't think I'm being insubordinate," David said. "I think you resent the fact that I happen to know the priorities of my job."

In the end, David was told that he would not be receiving a complaint after all. "But you're not putting in for any medal," Inspector Anger added.

Although David's record remained untarnished, the complaint that he was spared had to be given to another cop, because the complaint number had already been issued, and once issued, it could not be withdrawn without a tangle of paperwork and explanations. Thus, a footman whom I will call Greene* received a complaint that day for failing to be alert at his post—specifically, for not hearing the desperate cries of an ice-cream deliveryman who had inadvertently locked himself in the back of his refrigerated truck. Greene insisted that the ice-cream man's cries were inaudible, but being more reconciled to the workings of the department's disciplinary machinery than David, he made no attempt to appeal the judgment against him. Nor did he forget David's place in the sequence of events leading to his complaint. Greene had a permanent post on Ninth Avenue. His post was heavily populated by prostitutes, and he was known to be on familiar terms with some of them. A number of weeks after the hearing, David was sitting in a car with a group of cops, and they started laughing uncontrollably. Finally, one of them said, "David Durk, I'd like you to meet David Durk."

"What are you talking about?" David said.

The other cop pointed to Greene. "This guy has been telling every prostitute on Ninth Avenue that *his* name is David Durk. One of these days, a pross is going to be arrested, and she'll say, 'You can't arrest me—I'm giving it to David Durk for nothing.'"

———⟶◆⟵———

Policing was a career that ran in families, especially Irish-American families. As a Jew, David was part of a statistically insignificant minority in the NYPD, and as a doctor's son and a graduate of an Ivy League college, he was unique. It was obvious to his mother, and equally obvious to his superiors in the 18th Precinct—the command to which he reported, fresh out of the police academy, in the fall of 1963—that such a young man had no business being a cop. And yet, there he was.

Others in such a situation might have decided to lie low. David did not lie low. One Sunday morning, he showed up for an early roll call

* Not his real name. Henceforth, the introduction of a character by last name only will be a signal to the reader that the person's identity has been disguised.

and learned that his duties for the day were to wax the floor and water the plants in the borough commander's office. The sergeant who issued these instructions was a goodhearted sort, and he thoughtfully added that David would be free to go home as soon as he had finished waxing and watering—a fringe benefit that in the sergeant's mind more than made up for the indignity of the mission.

"You're asking me to do something that is not within the civil service specs for the job of patrolman," David replied unhesitatingly.

Inspector Anger—a frequent adversary—happened to be in earshot. Responsible, as he was, for roughly fifteen hundred subordinates, the inspector did not normally involve himself in the problems of an individual patrolman. For Patrolman Durk, however, he made an exception. He had David called out of roll-call formation, and with the entire shift looking on, told the sergeant to give him a butter knife and have him remove every wad of chewing gum from all five floors of the station house.

When Inspector Anger had departed, David declared that this, too, was an illegal order.

Rather than debate the merits of the question, the sergeant got down on his hands and knees in order to demonstrate how simple it really was to remove a piece of chewing gum with a butter knife.

The spectacle of the sergeant kneeling in front of him softened David's resolve. He took the knife and made a show of removing a single piece of gum from the side of a desk. Then he disappeared into the borough commander's office, remained there for a couple of hours, and went home, leaving everyone to assume that he had performed his mission. The next morning, he was given a five-hour school crossing, and on his return to the precinct was summoned into Inspector Anger's presence for a lecture on the twin themes of discipline and cleanliness, and the close connection of the latter to godliness.

David remarked that the precinct had civilian employees for that sort of work. A civilian cleaner cost the city $7,000 a year, he added, while a cop, on average, cost the city $11,000.

Inspector Anger eyed him closely. "You're the one who went to college, aren't you?"

"Are you holding that against me?" David said. "Is that something bad? Let's talk straight, Inspector. The bottom line is, people are screaming for more police protection. I've got an article here." Out of his pocket came a copy of a journal called *Police Management Review*, opened to an article on "Seven Reasons Why You Can't Get a Cop When You Need One." "How would you feel," David continued, "if you read in a newspaper that you couldn't get a cop because they're watering plants and waxing floors and picking up gum?"

The inspector—by now caught up in the surreal experience of arguing department policy with a nobody—made a disparaging comment about the work of the civilian cleaners.

"Well, that's not my problem—*you're* management," David retorted.

The 18th Precinct was a busy slice of midtown Manhattan that covered the economic spectrum from Hell's Kitchen to Cartier's. On the late tour, Patrolman Durk was often assigned to either of two footposts along Fifth Avenue—"glass posts," they were called, because of the need to protect the many display windows to be found there. One day, well after midnight, David was standing in a doorway near the corner of Fifth Avenue and Fifty-fifth Street when he saw a couple of men in laborers' garb enter an elegant brownstone. Soon a third man went in, carrying what looked like an acetylene torch. Struck by the fact that the building remained dark although it was obviously now occupied, David decided to get some backup. He went to a nearby call box, rang up the station, and declared that he had come across a possible burglary-in-progress.

One of the big surprises of the job, for David and for other recruits, was the department's ambivalent attitude toward its presumed mission of fighting crime. "Cooping," or holing up in some hideaway, was not only expected but virtually demanded between, say, 1:30 and 6:00 A.M., when most of the footmen of the 18th Precinct could be found in an inner chamber of the Gotham Hotel or the University Club, while the radio-car cops—all but the handful engaged at any moment in assignments so serious that they could not be ignored—would be parked over on the piers that lined the Hudson River in the

Fifties and, if not asleep, would be drinking coffee, playing cards, reading newspapers, or (on nights when the moon was full) getting in some target practice at passing rats. The sergeants and lieutenants also had their coops, where DO NOT DISTURB SHORT OF MURDER was the generally understood rule.

It was about 2:00 A.M. when David reported his burglary, and his call brought a sergeant—a hardened veteran whom I will call Pagnotti—and three radio cars. "This better be good," Sergeant Pagnotti said to David by way of greeting. After listening to David's explanation of the circumstances, Pagnotti agreed to search the building, but voiced his opinion in advance that the burglary would prove to be a figment of David's imagination. The search that ensued, under the sergeant's direction, was swift, loud, and fruitless. When it was over, Sergeant Pagnotti told his driver to report back that the call had been unfounded. Four of the six radio-car cops departed with him. But the two who remained—a Mutt-and-Jeff pair named Gallagher and Carduccio—agreed, at David's urging, to conduct a second search, this time on tiptoe, and room by room.

David apprehended one of the presumed burglars in a basement closet, holding a flashlight in one hand and a newspaper in the other. "What are you doing here?" David demanded.

The suspect replied, with no apparent irony intended, that he was studying the *Racing Form.*

Gallagher and Carduccio came across four more intruders hiding upstairs, and a fifth man was later found waiting in a van on Madison Avenue. Sergeant Pagnotti was anything but contrite, however, when the arrests were brought to his attention. The burglary, he pointed out, had occurred half a block off David's post. What had David been doing there in the first place?

"I've got these guys cold," David protested. "I got them for burglary, criminal receiving, parole violations, you name it."

Hearing this enumeration of the charges, and the further fact that the leaders of the group owned a used-car lot and junkyard on Coney Island Avenue and were wanted in connection with a string of office burglaries, Sergeant Pagnotti changed his tack. He would recommend the arrest for a medal, he said, provided that David, in his paperwork, mention the sergeant as having been present at the scene. (This was standard practice. "Put me in at the collar," sergeants and lieutenants would tell their subordinates.)

David said he would skip the medal.

One afternoon he was looking out his living-room window and saw a Hell's Angels type in a black leather jacket going from parked car to parked car, checking for property worth stealing. Grabbing his gun and a pair of handcuffs, David ran downstairs and followed the suspect as far as Sixty-ninth and Columbus, where he saw him jimmy open the butterfly window of a station wagon and then innocently cross the street and loiter on the opposite sidewalk for a while, in order to be sure that it was safe to proceed further.

While David watched from the corner, the suspect returned to the car to remove what turned out to be a tape recorder—a full-sized old-fashioned reel-to-reel model—and walked off cradling it in his arms. When David caught up with him, he put the tape recorder down, reached under his shirt, and pulled out a long knife—a Sabatier chef's knife—which had been taped to his chest.

David drew his revolver, and the man's expression abruptly changed into a grin. "Hey, this is a brand-new Sony," he said. "It's a real good machine. Why don't you take it, and we'll split?"

"Listen, pal, this is for real," David replied.

The man gave him a skeptical look. "If you're a cop, where's your car? Where's your backup?"

David explained that he was off duty.

"If you're off duty, why the fuck are you looking to lock me up?"

The scene was witnessed by a state assemblyman, Richard Gottfried, who had been standing on the corner gathering signatures for a petition. Realizing by now that apprehending a criminal in the act was not always an adequate reason in the department's eyes for making an arrest, David took the precaution, after searching and cuffing the suspect, to march him back to the corner and ask Assemblyman Gottfried if he would mind joining them for the trip to the station.

David then hailed a cab and informed the driver that his vehicle was being commandeered for a police emergency—a provision of the law that he had not previously attempted to exercise. The cabdriver just laughed and turned the meter on. When they were all inside, the arrestee asked if they could make an extra stop on Central Park West; his girlfriend was waiting for him there, he explained, and he didn't want her to worry. David said he would be glad to oblige, and after she had been informed of the situation, they continued to the 20th Precinct, on Sixty-eighth Street.

There David encountered the usual hostility toward off-duty arrests, and the usual inclination to minimize the offense or let the suspect go. (The NYPD's tendency to downgrade crimes was so pronounced at the time that the FBI had publicly declared New York's crime statistics to be unworthy of belief.) For once, though, he had an explanation that made sense in the police department's scheme of things. Pointing to Gottfried, David explained that he had been forced to make the arrest because the crime had been witnessed by a public official. He got no more guff after that—except from the suspect, who demanded, "What's he doing arresting me on his day off?"

"A good question," the desk officer agreed.

In New York, as in other cities, police officers were sworn to uphold the law twenty-four hours a day, seven days a week. Few cops took this vow so much to heart. Escorting his daughter Joan to a friend's birthday party, David saw no reason why he should give anything less than his usual close attention to the passing scene, and if he happened to see someone breaking into a parked car as they set out, he would send Joan upstairs with the message "Tell Mommy to call 911" and, once she was safely indoors, take appropriate action. When Joan was ten, she announced that she would no longer accept lifts from her father. "I don't want to go in the car with Daddy anymore, because he's always arresting people," she explained.

Quite a few of David's off-duty collars occurred in the vicinity of 18 West Seventieth Street, his address through most of the sixties and seventies. Sometimes, after cornering a suspect, he would shout up to his wife—they lived on the fifth floor—and she would call the police dispatcher before returning to the living-room window to see how the situation had been resolved. On one of these occasions, she gave the operator her usual concise explanation of the circumstances ("Off-duty cop holding one") and heard an alarmed voice say, "Lawdy, lawdy, it's that Sergeant Durk again."

Most people, when they see trouble, pause for at least a moment of cost-benefit analysis before they take action. That synapse was missing from David's nervous system. In a sense, his police badge merely conferred an official status on a fact of his nature: once he had alighted on an injustice or a scene of distress, nothing could stop him from intervening.

Returning from a shopping expedition to Zabar's one day, David stopped to observe a quarrel between a prostitute and a pimp who were getting out of a yellow Cadillac on Seventy-second Street. The prostitute was trying to leave, but the pimp slapped her sharply across the face and pulled her back. Drawing closer, David saw that she was bleeding.

"This is a private matter—she's my old lady," the pimp told him.

"Take your hands off her, and we can talk about it," David said, putting his shopping on the sidewalk.

"You're only messing with me because I'm black and she's white," the pimp said.

"Is he your husband?" David asked the prostitute.

"No," she said hesitantly.

Three more pimps (all dressed in improbable, electric-blue, green, and yellow jumpsuits) were standing next to the Cadillac, and one of them remarked that since David was "just one honky" it would not be difficult to "get him."

David drew his gun and held it against his right leg—and heard a cry of "Police brutality!" from somewhere in a semicircle of college-age West Siders who had gathered behind him.

"What's the matter with you people?" he said. "Don't you see the blood? *I* didn't hit her. *They* hit her."

Sirens heralded the arrival of a fleet of police cars. The owner of the corner newsstand had phoned, and the call had gone out as a 10-13—a police officer in trouble. (This was one notch more urgent than a 10-85—a request for assistance.)

"Whatcha got, kid?" David was asked by a captain, who showed up about six cars from the head of the parade.

David listed the applicable charges: attempted kidnapping, assault, attempted assault on a police officer, and "you can throw in incitement to riot."

The captain looked at him as if he was out of his mind. "What the hell's the matter with you?" he said. "She's only a pross."

The victim, as it happened, decided not to press charges. "They'll kill me," she explained. "This way, I'm only going to get a beating." She blew him a kiss as she headed off in the Cadillac.

———

David had taken the police entrance exam on a lark, thinking of the job as something he might do for a while, until he returned to law school. Unlike many cops, he had reason to think he could make as good a living outside the department, and this thought was a source of courage. After all, what was the worst thing that his superiors could do to him? They could fire him—and cut his short career a little shorter. But the truth was, they couldn't fire him. Civil service rules made it next to impossible to dismiss a police officer. What the bosses could and did do was give him a series of thankless assignments: sports events, school crossings, and when they could think of nothing else, a footpost that amounted to guard duty for a clothing store called Martin Burns, on the Central Park South end of Columbus Circle. (Although departmental maps showed the post stretching a few blocks to the north and south, the cops who worked it understood that if the sergeant came looking for them he expected to find them in front of Martin Burns.)

As a footman, David had no radio. An armed robbery could happen nearby, he could see radio cars whiz past with sirens blasting and lights flashing, and he had to watch, dumbfounded, like a character out of a slapstick comedy. Or he could approach a radio car and ask the cops in it to tell him what was going on—a humiliating request that often got a response along the lines of "Don't worry about it, kid. We'll take care of it."

The Martin Burns beat, where David spent many a tour of duty in late 1963, was the least popular footpost in the precinct. Winter had arrived, accompanied by a mean wind blowing in off the Hudson. On Fifth Avenue and its cross streets, where the greatest concentration of footmen were assigned, there were other cops to talk to, and you could warm yourself inside the Plaza or the Gotham Hotel. Here, even if you took the risk of leaving Martin Burns unattended, there was only a Horn & Hardart automat, the Huntington Hartford Museum, and a couple of liquor stores; and when those places shut down for the night, there was nothing at all.

Martin Burns had become a sitting duck for break-ins, partly because Central Park—just across the street—was a convenient place to disappear into, and partly because (as David noted with annoyance) the owner refused to install grates over his windows, preferring to rely on the police for protection. David could see no good reason for Martin Burns to get so much police attention, or for the assignment to fall to him with such regularity. But burglars were burglars, and when he realized they were making a practice of striking during his meal break—that he was being outfoxed—it became the burning desire of his life to catch them in the act. He decided, in effect, to go undercover. He took to hiding behind the park wall, hoping to spot a burglar before the burglar spotted him.

One night, the scenario unfolded just as he had imagined it. He heard the crash of glass and the wail of the alarm, and waited behind the wall until two men, each carrying an armful of clothes, walked into the barrel of his drawn revolver. Once again, Sergeant Pagnotti pointed out that David had been off-post. (Central Park was a precinct unto itself.) But the cops with the radio car that covered Martin Burns—Gallagher and Carduccio, the same two who had helped him arrest the burglars on Fifty-fifth Street—were greatly amused by his latest display of zeal. They had been suspicious of

David. They had been unable to think of a good reason for someone like him to become a cop, and they had surmised that he was a spy who had been planted in their midst by Internal Affairs. Now their suspicions gave way to concern for his safety. A lone footman could get killed, they said, if he kept on engaging in high jinks of this sort. "You're not getting paid enough for this stuff," Gallagher observed. "What are you trying to prove?"

David responded that he wasn't going to "stand out here like a penguin."

The Martin Burns beat had enjoyed a reputation for tranquillity. After David's arrival, it became one of the precinct's hot spots. A few weeks later, standing in front of Martin Burns, David had an intuition about two men he had spotted on the park side of Columbus Circle. He crossed the street and, with his right hand resting on the butt of his revolver, asked them to produce some identification. While he politely awaited a response, a radio car—Gallagher and Carduccio's car—came barreling onto the sidewalk, practically pinning the two men against the park wall.

Gallagher, who was so tall that he had to hunch over to fit in a police car, picked up the smaller of the two suspects by his feet, turned him upside down, and started shaking him by his ankles— causing a knife to come tumbling out of his pocket. Carduccio, who had barely met the department's height requirement of five feet eight, stuck a gun in the ear of the other suspect, and told him, "If you move, I'll fucking kill you." In the same spirit, he advised David to "get out of the fucking way."

"Hey, kid, you got to be more careful," Gallagher said when things had calmed down. "Didn't you know there was an alarm out for these two?"

"How would I know?" David said. "I don't have a radio. Nobody came by and told me."

They were wanted for holding up a liquor store. A description of the suspects had gone out over the radio earlier, and Gallagher apologized profusely for not having passed this news on to David. At the same time, he took David to task for the demure manner in which he had approached the two holdup men. "You don't walk up to people and say, 'Excuse me,' " Gallagher explained. "These people will shoot you without blinking. They don't play by the rules."

David promised to be more careful in the future.

"You want the collar?" Gallagher asked. "I mean, you stopped them."

David declined the offer, so he did not receive credit for the arrest in the eyes of his superiors. But the incident had a strongly positive effect on his reputation with Gallagher and Carduccio. They took to paying him regular visits and letting him warm his extremities in the backseat of their car. First they would roll the window down a quarter of an inch and talk to him through the crack, complaining loudly about the draft as they did so. Then one of them would say, "Hey, kid, get in the car—you're making us cold." After a series of such visits, David decided to raise a question that had been nagging at him: "How come the other rookies aren't getting the same crazy posts I'm getting?"

"Well, it's simple," Gallagher told him. "You didn't see the roll-call guy."

So he went to the roll-call guy—a patrolman who made up the daily list of assignments in consultation with his superiors. "What does a person have to do to get a decent post?" David asked.

The roll-call guy opened a desk drawer and pointed inside. It was full of crumpled bills.

CHAPTER

THREE

As long as New York City has had police, it has had police corruption. In fact, the tradition dates back to the years before the city had a formal police department. In the early nineteenth century, public safety was the responsibility of night watchmen, who were permitted to act only if they witnessed a crime, and constables and marshals, who were paid by the arrest and tended to regard themselves more as entrepreneurs than as civil servants. Many of them got embarrassingly rich. The *New York Herald,* at one point, complained of their "inaction and supineness," adding, "Not a step will be taken without a reward—and even if they possess a clue to the mystery, still they would keep the secret intact, like a capital in trade, till public indignation has raised a sum sufficient" to motivate them.

The reformers who fought to create a police force for New York—a goal realized in 1845—had as a model London's Metropolitan Police, but there were profound differences between the two from the start. In London, the constables were chosen by police commissioners, who reported to the British home secretary. In New York, local aldermen controlled the hiring, and police officers had to be reappointed at regular intervals—an arrangement that insured loyalty to their sponsors. London had a homogeneous and stable population; New York's grew by more than a third between 1845 and 1855, and by the end of that decade, a majority of New Yorkers were foreign born. London's police wore uniforms and saw themselves as public servants; ten years after New York set up a police force, its members were still resisting the idea of a uniform, which they considered degrading. Or so they said. A greater worry may have been the thought that in uniform they would be too easy to find.

Even in its earliest days, the NYPD paid official homage to a set of rules and objectives very different from those that police officers actually followed day to day—a gulf that would still exist when David Durk entered the department a century later. In London there was fairly general support for the laws the police were charged with enforcing. The police of New York—many of them German or Irish immigrants not long off the boat—were supposed to impose a code of behavior devised largely by native-born upstaters. One of the major duties of the city's police officers was to keep saloons closed on Sundays. Torn between their personal convictions and the law, they compromised by charging saloonkeepers for the privilege of violating it.

In the 1850s the Yankee establishment of New York was horrified to discover that the police had become graft-collecting agents for the urban immigrant political machine, Tammany Hall, which had a notably lax attitude toward gambling, prostitution, drunkenness, and violations of the Sabbath. The state legislature declared the existing police force illegitimate and established a new one; when members of the new force, who were known as the Mets, tried to arrest the mayor for crooked dealings, the two law enforcement agencies fought a bloody battle at City Hall, and for months afterward (until the Mets finally prevailed), the city experienced a sort of gang war between the two rival police forces, each claiming that the other had no legal standing.

New York in the late nineteenth century was a town wide open to gambling, prostitution, and the illegal sale of liquor, all of these enterprises thriving with the paid assistance of the police. In the 1890s the veil was lifted by a hell-raising Presbyterian minister, the Reverend Charles H. Parkhurst, who in a series of public diatribes accused the mayor, the district attorney, and the police department of turning the city into "a very hotbed of knavery, debauchery, and bestiality." When the irate DA called Parkhurst before a grand jury, he meekly confessed that he had relied for his information on newspaper accounts and other secondhand sources, and the jurors denounced him as a rumormonger. But he would not be silenced. Determined to compile a body of evidence that the world could not ignore, he disguised himself as a man of loose morals and, accompanied by a private detective and a reform-minded young parishioner, cruised the city in search of organized sin.

Parkhurst's activities, along with the work of the muckraking journalists Jacob Riis and Lincoln Steffens, created a clamor for action, and the police sought to satisfy it with a ritual sacrifice of prostitutes and madams. "I'd be glad to know just what Dr. Parkhurst would like me to do," Captain Max Schmittberger—one of the department's leading bagmen, or collectors of payoffs—complained after conducting a series of lightning raids on brothels. "I've cleaned out the Tenderloin until it looks like a Connecticut village." But the pressure continued to mount until, in 1894, the Republican boss of New York State, Thomas Platt, saw an opportunity to wrest control of the city from Tammany Hall, and arranged for the creation of a committee of inquiry headed by a state senator named Clarence Lexow. With Dr. Parkhurst looking over its shoulder, the Lexow Committee conducted an unexpectedly meaty investigation, culminating in a series of hearings whose star witness was none other than Captain Schmittberger—his conscience having been pricked when, at dinner one night, his oldest son insisted on knowing if certain newspaper stories about him were true.

According to Schmittberger's testimony, every rank was for sale at a price set by Tammany Hall. To join the force, you paid $300; to get promoted to sergeant, $1,600. Captains were charged according to the value of their commands—that is, the added income they were expected to bring. A lucrative precinct could cost $15,000 or more. Another memorable witness was Captain Alexander "Clubber" Williams, famed both for his poetic pronouncement that there was more law at the end of a policeman's club than in any courtroom and for practicing what he preached. In 1876 Williams had rejoiced at the news of his transfer to the nightlife district, north of Fourteenth Street. "All my life I've never had anything but chuck steak," he had said at the time. "Now I'm going to get me some tenderloin." In his testimony before the Lexow Committee, Williams acknowledged a personal fortune of $300,000 in cash, plus an estate in Cos Cob and a steam-powered yacht. He claimed to have accumulated his wealth through real estate speculation in Japan—an explanation so fantastic that no one could disprove it.

The Lexow Committee issued a chilling report on brutality and corruption, and such was the outrage of the citizenry that the reigning boss of Tammany Hall, Richard Croker, abruptly left for England on a vacation that wound up lasting three years. While he was away, the electorate took the extreme step (for New Yorkers) of choosing a Republican, William Strong, as mayor, and he, in turn, placed the police department under the cleansing influence of Theodore Roosevelt, who had presided over an earlier investigation of police misdeeds while serving in the state legislature.

Returning to New York from Washington, where he had been employed as a member of the Civil Service Commission, Roosevelt hurled himself into his new responsibilities with childlike abandon. "I have the most important, and the most corrupt department in New York on my hands . . . and I know well how hard the task ahead of me is," he wrote to his sister. "Yet, in spite of the nervous strain and worry, I am glad I undertook it; for it is man's work." He hired the first Jewish cops, created a call-box system and a bicycle squad, instituted formal training of recruits, and ran around catching errant cops in saloons. The *New York World* published an ecstatic prose poem soon after he got going: "We have a real Police Commissioner. His teeth are big and white, his eyes are small and piercing, his voice is rasping. He makes our policemen feel as the little froggies did when the stork came to rule them."

Like others who have tried to get a handle on the NYPD, however, Roosevelt ultimately found it a vexing experience. He decided that he had no choice but to rigorously enforce the Sunday-closing, or blue, laws, and the public—thoroughly charmed by him at first—turned against him. "I do not deal with public sentiment—I deal with the law," Roosevelt declared when he was questioned about the need for such extreme measures as shutting down soda parlors. Later he described what appeared to be an inviolable pattern of New York political life: "If a reform administration honestly endeavors to carry out reform, it makes an end of itself at the end of its term and insures the return of Tammany to power." After less than two years of policing the police, Roosevelt, as one chronicler put it, beat a "glorious retreat" to the simpler post of assistant secretary of the Navy.

———⟶❦⟵———

The cause of police reform, to which Roosevelt first drew America's attention, got going in earnest a generation later, and three thousand miles to the west. In the 1920s and '30s, the center of innovative policing was California, under the influence of August Vollmer, who ran the departments of Berkeley and, briefly, Los Angeles, and his ally Earl Warren, who served variously as district attorney of Alameda County and attorney general and governor of California. The NYPD, basking in its venerability, remained squarely in the rearguard of American law enforcement. It was a setting in which even a "reform" commissioner—Lewis Valentine, who was appointed by Mayor LaGuardia in 1934—could chastise his men for bringing in a murderer without "mussing him up."

The leaders of the department in the postwar years talked a good deal about professionalism. What they had in mind, however, was different from what the West Coast champions of the concept understood by it. In California it incorporated such notions as norms of performance, scientific deployment, and rigorous standards of hiring and training. In New York, the term meant the pursuit of higher status and pay, and freedom from what came to be known as "political interference"—not only the attempts of machine politicians to manipulate the police for ignoble purposes, but almost any efforts by any elected officials to have a say in police policies. The NYPD defined professionalism to mean—as one police scholar has put it—"a business free of outside control."

In the 1940s—a time of consolidation in enterprises legal and illegal—a pudgy little man with a Flatbush accent, wavy hair, and a nervous tic in his right eye built a $20-million-a-year gambling empire. Harry Gross presided over an organization that, at its peak, included over thirty-five betting parlors and a staff of four hundred bookies, runners, accountants, and phone handlers, to say nothing of the hundreds of police officers and police bosses who were on his payroll. He and the police brass were so thoroughly entangled that at one stage of his career, according to Miles McDonald, the Brooklyn district attorney who eventually brought him down, Gross lost big on basketball betting and retired to California, only to be lured back to New York by a group of his police cronies, who gave him a fresh stake of $50,000. "They weren't making any money without him," McDonald explained.

McDonald's investigation was sparked by a series of articles that appeared in the *Brooklyn Eagle*, beginning in December 1949. (The *Eagle*'s investigation, in turn, originated in some barroom gossip—overheard by a reporter named Ed Reid—concerning a certain "Mr. G." who had taken over most of the bookie joints in town after having been "put in business by three top coppers.")

With forty rookie cops as undercovers, McDonald and his deputies got the goods on Gross and had him arrested on September 15, 1950. "I got a hunch there's going to be a lot of worried people in the city soon," Gross told the arresting officers. He proceeded to implicate, before a grand jury, some two hundred police officers of various ranks, of whom twenty-one were indicted and fifty-seven others named as coconspirators. Gross had been spending a million dollars a year on police graft, and he seemed to remember every transaction. Milton Mollen, a young city attorney who debriefed him (and who, nearly forty years later, would lead a commission of inquiry into another police-corruption scandal), remembered Gross as "a beautiful witness."

But on the eve of his scheduled appearance at the criminal trials of some of the police officers, Gross escaped his police guard during a visit with his wife in Atlantic Beach, New Jersey. Found two days later at the $100 betting window of the Atlantic City racetrack, he explained that he had felt a need for fresh air. Circumstantial evidence, however, led many observers to suspect that there had been a rendezvous—and a bargain—between Gross and some of his old police associates. Upon his return, he delivered just enough testimony to get the trial under way, and to give the defendants a double-jeopardy claim against retrial; then he dramatically announced that he could not continue. The judge—Samuel Leibowitz, the famed defender of the Scottsboro Boys—was furious but felt compelled to let the accused cops go free. Leibowitz later sentenced Gross to twelve consecutive one-year sentences for gambling and contempt of court.

The mayor of New York City at the time, William O'Dwyer, was an ex-cop who had spent much of his police career in plainclothes vice units. O'Dwyer had gone on to obtain a law degree, and became celebrated as the gangbusting district attorney who had nailed a Brooklyn mob-enforcement ring known as Murder, Inc. That reputation, and the ardent backing of Tammany Hall (which had suffered through twelve years of "fusion" government under LaGuardia, a Republican), had catapulted him to the mayoralty, the voters choosing to overlook his failure to pursue an investigation of waterfront racketeering charges against Mafia boss Albert Anastasia, and also the death, while in the custody of a police detail led by a close friend of O'Dwyer's, of a mob assassin who had agreed to testify against Anastasia. (Two other troublesome pieces of O'Dwyer's life story were later to come to light: a clandestine wartime meeting with the "prime minister of the underworld," Frank Costello, and $20,000 contributions from Harry Gross during each of O'Dwyer's two successful campaigns for mayor.) When the Gross investigation's net began snagging prominent figures in the police department, O'Dwyer tried to arouse public sympathy for them as innocent victims of a Joe McCarthy–style witchhunt. But the voters were unmoved, and sensing that the tide had turned against him, O'Dwyer abruptly resigned, accepting a convenient appointment from President Harry Truman as ambassador to Mexico. Thus the Gross scandal had unseated a mayor, in addition to causing the imprisonment or dismissal of scores of cops, and a few suicides as well. But that was pretty much the toll of its effects. Milton Mollen—when he was asked four decades later just what had changed in the police department as a result of the scandal— replied, "I don't think very much did."

CHAPTER

FOUR

On his first day out of the police academy, David had been assigned to a footbeat that included the "21" Club and Toots Shor's, two celebrated gathering places of the well known and the well-to-do. "I can see you're new on the post," the doorman at the "21" Club told him. "You go in here." He pointed to the service entrance.

"What do you mean, I go in here?" David said.

"That's where you go in," the doorman explained, sounding like a character out of *Alice in Wonderland.* So David went in, and found himself in a basement hallway where several Puerto Rican employees were absent-mindedly smashing wine bottles and shoveling the crushed remains into trash bins. Proceeding further, he encountered a group of kitchen hands who were splitting loaves of bread, carving hollows in them, and placing quails in the hollows. Finally, he arrived in the kitchen proper, and a chef—one of many—told him, "I'll cut you a steak. How do you want your potatoes?"

David said he didn't want a steak, or potatoes. "A steak I can have at home. What do you recommend?" He wound up eating shrimp creole in an anteroom off the main kitchen, along with the head chef, the sommelier, and the maître d'. When he had finished, he made an attempt to pay.

"Don't worry about it," the maitre d' told him. "The top people at headquarters all eat upstairs—nobody pays."

The next day, standing near the entrance of Toots Shor's, David saw a Cadillac pull up and park next to a fire hydrant. "Watch it for me, kid," said the driver—a big, broad-shouldered man in a double-breasted jacket—as he breezed on in.

David was in the process of writing a parking ticket when the doorman approached and, in an agitated voice, called his attention to the identity of the driver: it was Toots Shor himself. David thanked the doorman for the information and, reasoning that he would surely be in trouble if a sergeant came by and saw that he had failed to act against so flagrant a violation, placed the filled-out summons on the Cadillac's windshield.

A sergeant *did* come by. "Hey, kid, get in the back—you've got a post change," he told David. The sergeant drove him over to a deserted park next to the West Side Highway, where David completed his tour of duty under "intense supervision": hourly visits to make sure he stayed on his post. After a few days of patrolling the park, David was brought back to civilization, and he promptly ticketed another Cadillac, this time in front of the Carnegie Delicatessen, on Seventh Avenue at Fifty-fifth Street. The car turned out to belong to a local gambler—a habitué of the Carnegie. Again, word of David's action quickly reached his superiors. "Are you nuts? This place is good to us," a sergeant said to him. When David began to explain that he had made a diligent attempt to find the car's owner before writing the summons, the sergeant cut him off, saying, "You're the one who went to college, aren't you?" The next day, David got word that he was going "flying."

"What does 'flying' mean?" he inquired.

"Kid, you're going to grow wings after what you did," he was told.

To fly was to be assigned, on a temporary basis, to another unit—in his case, to the 28th Precinct, in central Harlem. When David reported there for his first roll call, a sergeant with a broad, well-wrinkled face entered the muster room, carrying a clipboard. "All right," he said. "All you new men who haven't been here before, step forward!"

Although the department had done its best to put black cops into black precincts, it did not have many black cops to work with, so the great majority of the recruits were white (the same was true of the old-timers), and many of them had never set foot in a black neighborhood. With that fact in mind, someone had prepared a sort of primer on Harlem and cultural diversity, from which the sergeant began reading. He quoted the legendary (and incumbent) congressman Adam Clayton Powell III on the subject of the Harlem arrest rate, which was eight times that of the city as a whole—proof, in Powell's view, of police racism. "This is a vibrant, vital community," the sergeant read, without much conviction. He put down the clipboard and looked his men in the eye. "All right, I'll skip the rest of this bullshit. I want you to go out there. Don't lose sight of your partner, don't go down any block alone, don't go into any buildings, and no arrests unless you're personally assaulted."

David's partner for the night, a cop named McManus, was no more than thirty-five but exuded the belief that life was downhill from there. (Cops of his sort, who had long since abandoned the idea of doing any policing, were referred to in the department as "hairbags.") David and McManus were assigned to walk a post on Lenox Avenue. "Kid, if you need me, I'll be in the Alhambra," McManus announced, not long after they had left the stationhouse. The Alhambra was the RKO Alhambra Theater, on Lenox at 126th Street.

Strolling down Lenox, David saw a crowd of black men in front of Sugar Ray's, a bar partly owned by former middleweight champion Sugar Ray Robinson. David had an idea that something illegal was going on in the center of that galaxy of bodies, and he didn't see how one lone cop could do anything about it. On the other hand, he figured it would look bad if he changed direction ("I had never seen a police movie in which the cop ran away," he said later), so he strode forward, swinging his nightstick with what he hoped was an air of élan, while doing his best not to hit himself in the knee with it. When he crossed 123rd Street—at the very instant, in fact, that his foot touched the curb—the activity ceased, and a tiny man with a hospitable smile sallied forth to meet him. "I can see you're new, chief," he said, examining David's well-pressed uniform and youthful figure. "You get four dollars a half hour."

David responded with a look of incomprehension.

"For the game," the little man told him.

David was stunned. "No, no, it's okay—it's on me," he said at last.

The game resumed as soon as he left the block, and stopped when he came strolling uptown again a quarter of an hour later. Although gambling was against the law, David wasn't about to make an issue of it with this large and peaceable assemblage. But he didn't like the inconvenience he was causing just by his presence, and since his beat was only three blocks long he could see that there would be many more of these encounters over the course of an eight-hour tour of duty. He decided to seek advice from his supposed partner and found him in the balcony of the Alhambra, watching a Tarzan movie along with a fair number of the cops David had seen at roll call. Some of them had their hats off, their jackets unbuttoned, and their feet stretched across the seats in front of them. David imagined, with horror, the arrival of some straitlaced superior who would report every man in the place. Then the lights went up, and he saw a throng of cockroaches crawling over the floors, the seats, and the cops.

"They're harmless," McManus said, detecting David's anxiety.

David related what had happened in front of Sugar Ray's and asked how he should handle the situation.

McManus gave the question a moment's thought before declaring that it was up to David whether to take the money or not. "But, whatever you do, don't break up that game," he added.

David said he had no intention of breaking up the game. His problem was the consternation he was causing every time he walked past it.

"Hey, kid, the movie's over," McManus said. "I'll show you somewhere you can go." He escorted David to a garage on 122nd Street, where a poker game was in progress. The players were happy to have a couple of cops on the premises, and equally happy to have them partake of the communal refreshments. McManus poured himself a paper cup full of bourbon and offered to do the same for David (who declined). When David asked how he would explain himself if a superior should check his post and not find him anywhere on it, McManus told him to take out his notebook. "Write down what I tell you to write: 'Heard screams—went to investigate,' " McManus said. "That's good for half an hour," he added.

David looked unconvinced.

"You don't hear screams?" McManus said. "I hear screams. We're in a dangerous neighborhood. People are getting hurt here all the time."

David was twenty-eight when he became a police officer, and he had seen enough of the adult world to know that the official earnings of those in positions of authority were sometimes supplemented by cash or in-kind contributions from persons seeking some form of preferential treatment. His father-in-law had regarded tips to customs officers as a routine cost of the animal-import business. David himself, as a dealer in African carvings, had discovered that it was the rare buyer for a department store who would agree to carry a product (especially a nonessential product like his) without a gratuity, which was usually paid in the form of free samples. David didn't consider himself naïve. He had been prepared to find corruption in the New York City police department. What startled him was the openness of it.

The police of the 1890s had been engaged, according to the Lexow Committee, in selling protection for (or extorting payoffs from) gamblers, "disorderly houses," and "all classes of persons whose business is subject to the observation of the police, or who may be reported as violating ordinances, or who may require the aid of the police." More than half a century (and three big police-corruption scandals) later, the situation was essentially unchanged. Experts on police corruption sometimes mentioned a "code of silence" that supposedly made crooked cops all but invulnerable to exposure, and it was true that most cops, in the face of a direct question from a superior or an outsider, would deny all. Among themselves, however, they were anything but circumspect.

Free meals, free drinks, free movies (with free cockroaches)—such practices were a matter of course throughout the department. In most units, police officers also received regular payments of cash. In the 18th Precinct, for example, merchants large and small contributed on a monthly basis to a kitty that was divided up, according to a prescribed formula, among the members of the command. Different places paid for different reasons. The owners of bars and restaurants fretted about their liquor licenses, which could be snatched away if a cop caught them serving a drink to a minor. Contractors worried about being cited for failure to follow the multifarious regulations governing safety and traffic flow at construction sites. Parking lot managers paid for the privilege of annexing portions of the surrounding sidewalk or street when they had more cars than they could handle within their rightful boundaries. (On occasion, a parking lot employee would toss a ten- or twenty-dollar bill into a passing radio car.) Still other merchants paid in the expectation that when an emergency arose the police would respond with unusual dispatch—or without unusual delay.

The monthly payments were known as the pad, and most of the money went to radio-car cops and their supervisors. But the same merchants, and others, also compensated cops on a day-to-day basis for, say, the freedom to do business on Sunday, in violation of the all-but-unenforced (but still unrepealed) blue laws. This practice became evident to David after a couple of occasions when, as he strolled past a grocery, the owner or manager came running out with a couple of dollars in his outstretched hand. (David would wave the money away, telling the man not to worry.) And beat cops, as he was to discover, were expected to pay the roll-call officer a few dollars whenever they got assigned to a post on which such benefactors were unusually numerous or generous.

Returning to the precinct one afternoon, David was approached by a buddy of the roll-call officer, who demanded ten dollars—the usual commission on the fifty dollars that the post was believed to be "worth."

"But I didn't take anything," David said.

"How do I know you didn't take anything?" the other cop said.

"You can go out and ask," David said.

"But you had the post—you owe us for the post," he was told.

"*You* go out and collect the money—I don't do that," David said.

The price of his nonparticipation was many more cold nights in Columbus Circle. Just before Christmas of 1963, however, there was a robbery at a nearby liquor store, and the son of the owner got pistol-whipped. As the first cop on the scene, David stayed with the owner's son (who seemed more worried about his father's reaction to the theft than about his own injuries) while a number of radio cars searched unsuccessfully for the perpetrators. When David was about to leave, the kid thanked him, and added, "By the way, did you get yours?"

"My what?" David asked.

"Your Christmas present. Your name's Durk, right?" The kid consulted a sheet of paper he had stowed under the counter. "They picked it up for you."

"Can I see that?" David said quickly. What he saw was a list of the sector-car cops and the footmen who worked the area, and their superiors. One of the names on the list, with a check mark next to it, was his own.

David asked the kid who had made the pickup, and he described a pot-bellied cop with thinning hair, whom David knew by face but not by name. He was a clerical man, but, unaccountably, he seemed to have the run of the precinct. The kid wanted only to know if David had received his money—twenty dollars. David assured him that he hadn't received it, and didn't want it.

"What *can* I do for you, then?" he was asked.

"Why do you want to do *anything* for me?" David said. "I haven't done anything for you. I got here too late." But the kid persisted, and David finally said, "I'll tell you what—I know nothing about wine. What you can do for me is give me your advice about what's good and cheap."

The next day, he returned to buy a case of Beaujolais—on special because of water damage to the labels—and he made a point of getting to the station early in order to confront the clerical man. David found him in a basement office, alone. "You've been picking up money in my name!" he exclaimed.

The clerical man tried out a number of responses to the charge, ranging from "It's got to be a mistake" to "Why are you being such an asshole?" After he ceased disputing the basic facts, he said to David, "So what do you want me to do about it? We can't give the money back. Do you want me to donate it to charity?" To return David's share of the money was impossible, the clerical man explained, because such a gesture would jeopardize longstanding arrangements that involved the entire precinct, not just David. "If you don't take it, *someone* has to take it. You can't screw it up for everyone else."

"You don't pick up *any* money in my name!" David insisted.

When the next Christmas season rolled around, the keepers of the pad took preemptive action. David spent nearly the whole month of December flying. "If there was a parade somewhere, I went to it," he recalled. He had been assured that there would be no further pickups in his name, but he managed to get a look at the current Christmas list, and there was his name all over again. This time, he ordered the clerical man to give the money back. Otherwise, David said, he would put out the word that the clerical man had been taking a double share.

The option of reporting what he knew to higher authorities went unmentioned in these conversations, because David considered it out of the question. To whom would he have made such a report? To the precinct commanders? That could have been awkward, since the names of several of them were on the list that David had seen at the liquor store, and he had other reasons to suppose that they did not generally thumb their noses at supplementary income. The men of the 18th Precinct were often put on security details for play or movie premieres, sports events, concerts, and the like. On the four-to-twelve evening shift, when violent crime was highest, the precinct was somehow never too busy to send a complement of cops to the old Madison Square Garden for basketball or hockey games. (The cops would file into the arena and check their nightsticks at a Nedick's hot dog stand, so as not to spoil the sporting atmosphere.) Rumor had it that the Garden was paying some of the top people in the division for these services. If so, the proceeds were not shared with the cops on the scene. For them, the pleasure of seeing the game was evidently considered compensation enough.

Detachments of cops were also regularly made available to Radio City Music Hall for crowd control. David took a dim view of these assignments; he figured that Radio City could control its own crowds. When he showed up for one such detail, at the height of the Christmas shopping season, and learned that his mission was to assume custody of a velvet rope and let the line of ticketholders advance on instructions from a Radio City usher—a teenager in white tie, wing collar, and tails—he rebelled, angrily throwing the rope in the gutter.

Later that afternoon, he was manning a nearby police barricade when the familiar figure of Inspector Anger approached.

The inspector asked David to explain himself.

"You mean the incident with the kid?" David replied.

"With the employee of Radio City—that's right," Anger said. "Do you have any idea what you did?"

"No," David said.

"Don't you know Radio City is good?" Anger said.

"Good?" David asked, pretending he didn't understand the term.

"You work here, you hold the rope, you get two free tickets and a free lunch," Anger explained.

"You've got to be kidding," David said. "The Radio City cafeteria? You consider that lunch?"

Inspector Anger studied him for a moment. "So what else don't you like?"

"Well, since when did we start working for Madison Square Garden?" David asked. "Since when did they become a charitable institution?"

———

For someone fated to be known as a crusader against corruption, David was initially anything but a zealot on the subject. He wouldn't take money himself, but he was more than a little sympathetic to the justification many of his colleagues offered for doing so. Business executives and politicians had their perks; why not cops? The starting salary, when David joined the department, was about $8,000 a year, and the pad money was widely regarded as an unofficial supplement that did no more than bring cops' pay a little closer to what it should have been. In midtown, to compound matters, not many eating establishments fell within a police officer's means, and cops were forbidden to carry paper bags, including lunchbags.

The department's response to allegations of corrupt acts—on those infrequent occasions when it felt a need to respond—was to go after individuals, and nearly always after rank-and-file cops. (The Internal Affairs Division was much feared, because it had a reputation for never concluding an investigation without bringing charges, even if for an offense—doing a personal errand while on duty, for instance—that had nothing to do with the original accusation.) Yet corruption wasn't an individual thing. Gratuities and payoffs were virtually a departmentwide practice, which thrived with the active or tacit support of much of the hierarchy.

Even bosses who disliked the whole business were resigned to it. "I don't tell you to take bribes," said a well-meaning lieutenant in the course of a send-off lecture to David's class at the police academy. "But if you're gonna do this, carry a stamped, self-addressed envelope, and mail the money to yourself first chance you get." Evidently convinced that abstinence was an unrealistic objective, the lieutenant made a plea for moderation: "Never go back for more—don't leave them barefoot and pregnant."

Beat cops would be told of restaurants where they could eat on the arm (for free)—and of other restaurants that had to be avoided, because they were "headquarters places." One day, David struck up a conversation with the manager of the Carnegie Delicatessen, who told him, "I don't mind feeding the radio cars—I don't mind feeding the guy who has the post. I don't even mind the division or the borough. But those pigs at headquarters—they don't even send a *car* up anymore. They send a *van*. I'm spending over four thousand dollars a month feeding cops!"

This kind of information went into a special file in David's brain, for it confirmed his emerging view of the world. The heavy-duty corruption, it seemed to him, was engaged in by people with far more power and money than cops. To punish the rank and file for their relatively petty crimes while letting the other kind of corruption go untouched (as it generally did go) would be unconscionable.

The kind of police corruption he had so far observed was, in any case, not terribly heinous. It was just one of many stains on the department's honor, and not perhaps the worst. Had he been in a reporting mood, he might equally well have reported the partner who, on one of David's rare early days in a sector car, chewed him out for picking up the microphone to acknowledge a burglary-in-progress call. "What the fuck are you answering the radio for?" his partner complained, reluctantly accelerating toward the scene. "Didn't they teach you anything in the academy? If you're the car that answers, you're the one that has to do the paperwork. Never answer the radio first. Wait awhile. Let somebody else answer."

Cynicism, not corruption, was the underlying malady, and the cynicism of rank-and-file cops was abundantly justified, David thought, by the department's disciplinary procedures and personnel practices. In the summer of 1964, while he was in Harlem on antiriot duty, one of his fellow cops was fined five days' pay for losing his shield, although he had lost it when his shirt was ripped from his back during a struggle with a group of demonstrators. Car accidents, no matter where the blame lay, were guaranteed bad news from a disciplinary standpoint, so cops often would pay for repairs out of their own pockets rather than make an official report. Veteran cops advised rookies to carry throwaway knives—knives intended for planting on people—because, it was said, a cop who used his nightstick or revolver to defend himself against an unarmed assailant would be in deep trouble unless he could show that he had been at risk of losing consciousness. The standard police jacket had a concealed breast pocket that was widely thought to have been put there for a throwaway knife.

Gun battles, on the other hand, were a reliable ticket to advancement; indeed, they were a standard path to a detective's shield—they made headlines, and the department rarely wished to imply that a headline-making incident reflected anything but credit on the men involved. In 1959 an off-duty lieutenant, Mario Biaggi, was stopped at a red light with a friend of his—a contractor—when, according to Biaggi, a gunman forced his way into their car and told him to continue driving. "I see this guy in the rearview mirror and I read him as a killer," Biaggi recalled. He discreetly drew his gun, whirled around, and started firing. Bullets flew both ways. When they stopped flying, the gunman lay dead. The fact that Biaggi had been at the wheel of his friend's car, along with what *The New York Times* later called "unverified reports" of associations with members of organized crime, fed suspicions among the police brass that there was more to the incident than he had disclosed. But a long official inquiry failed to prove anything unsavory, and the department—seemingly unable to find a middle ground between disciplining Biaggi and celebrating him—decided to give him the medal of honor. Five years later, Biaggi took a disability retirement, and three years after that (billed as New York's "most decorated cop") he won election to Congress. His political career ended in 1988, when he was sent to prison in the Wedtech scandal.

When cops talked about the dos and don'ts of a career in the NYPD, it was stories like these, more than any official department policies, that guided them. Advancement was clearly a whimsical business at best, many cops told themselves, so why bother to try? Instead, long before they had the twenty years' service that entitled them to a pension, they would begin mapping out their postpolice careers, when, with two sources of income, they would be sitting pretty. Gray hair in a cop was considered a sign of not much on the ball. "Twenty and gone" was the department's unofficial motto.

When a desirable job fell vacant, cops expected it to go to someone with a well-placed friend—known as a hook or a rabbi. "You got a hook? Good for you" was the customary response to the news that a brother officer had received a cushy assignment.

When a cop came on the scene of a serious crime, his thoughts turned automatically to the matter of notifications: which bosses to call, and in what order. "You could mess up the fingerprints, you could forget to secure the crime scene, you could let the suspect get away—everything could be forgiven—as long as you remembered to make the proper notifications," David has said. The point was to ensure that if one of the bosses downtown got a call from a reporter, the boss would not be placed in the embarrassing position of knowing less than the reporter knew—"which was always a danger," according to David, "because the reporters monitored the police radio."

One of the older members of his squad—a slight but physically assertive cop named Ames—had, as a rookie, been jumped and beaten over the head with his own nightstick. According to Ames's account, the incident had left him with a middle ear problem, which caused dizzy spells. More than once, he had passed out while on foot patrol. But the department had failed to acknowledge his condition, and Ames had determined never again to do anything that would put him at risk of either physical injury or administrative scrutiny.

By the time David met him, Ames was a confirmed believer in curbstone justice, or, as David put it, in "controlling his post with a certain amount of violence." His first principle of policing was to keep everything unofficial. As long as you didn't leave a record, he reasoned, you couldn't get in trouble. Ames was sometimes guilty of conduct that ran counter to the spirit of due process or verged on what a layperson might have called brutality; yet he had a strong, elemental sense of fairness. One night, he and David were asked to accompany a pair of female prisoners to Bellevue for psychiatric examination. In the ambulance, one of the two women complained about a paramedic who was fondling her breasts. "If you don't take your hands off her, I'm going to break your arm," Ames said. The paramedic tried to laugh the incident off but soon touched the woman again, inspiring Ames to follow through on his threat. Later, with David's help, Ames drew up a formal complaint, and the paramedic filed a countercomplaint, and the issue was fought to a bureaucratic standstill between their agencies—an outcome that so far exceeded Ames's dismal expectations that he was forever grateful to David for his support. To repay the debt, he offered to teach David how to fight dirty. When David questioned the need for this knowledge, Ames asked him, hypothetically, how he would respond if a large and menacing individual were about to assault him.

David said he would draw his gun and tell the man to back off.

Ames shook his head. The department, he said, would never support a cop who used his revolver against an unarmed suspect. So it was essential to know how to administer a beating without leaving a mark.

Maltby, a black cop who wore his hair in a one-sided Afro, returned from court in a rage one night and told David the story of an arrest he had made. While secreted in a doorway, he had seen a man knock a hole in the butterfly window of a heavily loaded station wagon. Once before, Maltby had made a collar under similar circumstances—only to be chewed out by a judge for moving too quickly. (How could anyone be sure of the suspect's intentions, the judge had wanted to know. Perhaps the man had merely fallen against the window.) This time, Maltby had deliberately waited until the suspect removed several pieces of luggage and walked down the street with them. Again, however, the case had been thrown out—on the basis of a defense lawyer's argument that (as Maltby understood it) by standing and watching he had encouraged the commission of a crime he was legally obliged to prevent. There were a number of theaters on Maltby's post, and thefts from parked cars had been getting out of hand. The moral of this story, according to Maltby, was that he should never have bothered to concern himself with the problem.

Maltby had enough seniority to get almost any assignment he wanted, but he preferred walking to riding. As a footman, he explained, he could be his own master; he didn't have to deal with partners, sergeants, or (since he had vowed not to do any further policing) lawyers or judges.

In such an institution, the act of taking money was not necessarily a sign of faulty character, it seemed to David. "Cynicism is the flip side of pride," he has said. "When they take away your pride, it's the only way you can look at yourself in the mirror." The precinct pad and the Christmas list were traditions observed throughout the city. For the rank and file, the sums of money involved were comparatively modest. Most cops participated, but many did so halfheartedly, seeing no easy alternative. Gallagher's participation in the pad, for example, did not prevent him from being one of the more idealistic and hard-working members of the squad. As the son of a detective who had been killed in the line of duty, Gallagher had connections that he could have exploited to get started on the road to becoming a detective himself. The first step down that road, however, was to go into one of the plainclothes gambling or prostitution units, where a far worse order of corruption reigned. Gallagher had ruled out that option. "I'm not going to get a B-number," he explained. (A B-number was a criminal arrest number.) "I'm not going to be a rat, either."

David's tenderheartedness toward his peers extended to some who did not always give the job 100 percent of their attention. He and a round-faced rookie named Frank Schiele—a self-described pacifist who moonlighted as a folksinger—often walked parallel posts along Fifth Avenue. Schiele (pronounced *Sheel*ey) disliked the cold with a passion. He told David that if there was such a thing as reincarnation he hoped to come back as a cockroach and live under a radiator. As it was, he carried hand-warmers in his pockets and wore battery-heated socks, multiple layers of winter underwear, and a customized police overcoat that was a foot longer than anybody else's. Schiele was blessed with a physique that allowed him to conceal large objects on his person, and when he had the midnight tour he sometimes carried a pillow and an alarm clock and, in the small hours of the morning, would retire to a darkened lounge in the Gotham.

If there had been a crackdown on cooping, Schiele would have been a natural target, and yet in other respects, David observed, he was a commendable police officer. During his waking hours, he treated people—crime victims, tourists requesting directions, pretty much anyone in need—with great consideration. "What was to be taken serious, I took serious," Schiele recalled thirty years later. "But if it was a useless post—if it was like, 'Where can we put this guy where he won't mess anything up?'—I went to sleep." Schiele viewed it as part of his job to charm and entertain the public, especially children, and when it seemed safe to do so, he wore his cap backward. He liked to refer to his overcoat as his "cloak of impartiality." "And now I don my cloak of impartiality," he would say as he headed out of the locker room.

"Few young people are deliberately cynical or calculating," Kenneth Keniston had written in *Daedalus;* the article was about college kids—the children of professionals—but to David its observations seemed equally true of his fellow cops. "Rather, many feel forced into detachment and premature cynicism because society seems to offer them so little that is relevant, stable, and meaningful. They wish there were values, goals, or institutions to which they could be genuinely committed. . . . But when society as a whole appears to offer them few challenging or exciting opportunities . . . 'playing it cool' seems to many the only way to avoid a damaging commitment to false life styles or goals."

In this context, David came to see, corruption was an insidious fact of police life that made it impossible for cops to respect the job. He viewed it, however, not basically as a crime committed *by* cops but as one committed *against* them. So he did not do what he was required to do under the rules of the department: he did not report the corruption he had witnessed. What he did instead was launch a campaign of guerrilla warfare against it.

———>•<———

Of all the divisions of the police department, the uniformed division got the least respect. Of all the cops who worked in uniform, footmen got the least. The uniform was known as the "bag." The ambition of almost every rookie cop who had any was to "get a seat"—a regularly assigned place in a sector car—and then, if possible, to "get out of the bag." By early 1965, most of the rookies who had come out of the academy with David were riding as fill-ins, if not permanently, and David was getting impatient. But the normal route to a seat was closed to him, what with his refusal to take money or give the roll-call guy his expected commission. David went to the commander of the 18th Precinct, Captain John Schawaroch, and pointed out that, of all the rookies in the precinct, he had made the most collars, had issued the most summonses, and had been, in general, the busiest. "How come I haven't been given a chance to ride?" he asked. Schawaroch had a reputation as a straight shooter; he wasn't necessarily out looking for opportunities to buck the system, but if a victim of injustice appeared on his doorstep, he was prepared to lend a hand. He promised to look into the matter, and a few weeks later David was informed that he had been assigned to Sector Four. This meant that he would be patrolling the area west of Central Park from Fifty-ninth Street to Sixty-sixth, teamed with a tall, blond, concave-chested cop named Boyd.

It was no coincidence that Sector Four had a vacancy. Boyd was— in the phrase employed by the more generous of his coworkers—"an odd one." For example, he seemed to regard his police shield as a license to pursue a personal war against cabdrivers. It was a point of pride with Boyd that he had never issued a summons to anyone other than a cabdriver.

The task of collecting the pad money was shared by the cops regularly assigned to the sector. At the outset of the new partnership, Boyd informed David that he would have to "honor all the contracts" if he wanted a permanent seat. David promised to honor them—and set out to subvert them. As a starting point, he chose Stampler's, an expensive steakhouse in the Mayflower Hotel, at Sixty-second Street and Central Park West. Stampler's had an unusual understanding with the police. In return for payments that added up to several hundred dollars a month, the restaurant got the right to use Central Park West as a valet parking lot, reducing the flow of traffic, at times, to one lane in each direction. David was incensed by the practice, and more so by advertisements in *The New York Times* and *The Village Voice* in which Stampler's listed free parking as one of its attractions.

When the pickup day arrived, David casually inquired whether Boyd ever worried about being photographed by Internal Affairs. Rumors of such surveillance had been circulating, and David helpfully pointed out a rooftop across from Stampler's that would make an ideal observation station. "You know, they could be up there right now," he added. Boyd dismissed the idea, but to David he looked uneasy.

His next step was to send an anonymous letter to the police commissioner describing the situation outside Stampler's, alluding to its
ads, and identifying the sender as "An Irate Citizen." Ten days after he
mailed it, the letter—now stamped with a police commissioner's
number, a chief inspector's number, and borough division, and
precinct numbers, reflecting its descent through the chain of command—was handed to David by a patrol sergeant, who told him,
"Take care of this. Hand out a few tickets, do what's necessary, but
make sure you don't hurt anybody."

That afternoon, David showed the letter to Boyd and suggested
that they ticket every illegally parked car on the block.

"You did this," Boyd said.

"Relax, we're covered," David told him. "The sergeant told us to
take action."

"Well, you know what he meant," Boyd said.

"I've seen you go in there to make the pickup," David said. "There
was sweat pouring off your head, you were so afraid. And what did
you get? You got twenty dollars, right? Plus, you got the cop-special
sandwich that the chef probably spit in, if he didn't drop in a dose of
rat poison, too."

Boyd was shocked. "He wouldn't do that."

"He would," David insisted. "He doesn't like you. Why should he
like you? As for the money, let's work it out. Twenty dollars, eight
guys, thirty days—that's ten cents a day per man. If we were talking
about a lot of money I could understand it, but we're talking about ten
cents a day. For ten cents a day you're risking your pension, your job,
everything, and I'm not even counting the sweat and the anxiety."

Invent a vaccine, set an athletic record, make a bundle of money in
business, and the world will shower you with honors. There are no
great prizes for challenging a coworker to live up to his oath of office.
"Thou shalt not interfere in the performance of a fellow employee" is
the rule of most workplaces, and it goes double for cops. (One of the
things I dreaded, during my time on the Washington, D.C., police force,
were partners who liked to stop and frisk people for no good reason. The
fact that I had gone to Harvard and rode a bicycle to work was already

a minor topic of amusement in the precinct, and enough of a distinction, it seemed to me, without my becoming known as someone who lectured other cops about how to conduct themselves—or, worse yet, complained about them to our superiors. Once in awhile I would find a tactful way of expressing my disapproval, and once in awhile I would go to a sergeant and ask, without saying why, to be assigned with someone else. But by and large I showed the deference expected of a rookie and refused to allow my principles to stand in the way of the all-important mission of being accepted by my peers.)

It is hard to convey the pressure that the police are under to conform or, at any rate, to keep their criticisms to themselves. And, as rare as it is for one cop to confront another about some piece of slovenly behavior, it is far rarer that the point of the exercise is to prod and inspire that other cop to do better.

"You're an aggressive cop, right?" David told Boyd. "People stop you all the time and ask you, 'How come there's so many cars double- and triple-parked over here?' The only reason you don't want to do this is you're afraid of what the other guys will think of you. But you're safe—you're protected—this letter will protect you."

David had taken an extra summons book with him, and he proposed to strike at 9:00 P.M., when business at Stampler's would be at its peak. Boyd cursed and fumed, but he didn't do anything to prevent David from executing his plan, and he actually wound up writing a few summonses himself.

As David and Boyd were starting to launch their crackdown, a doorman in full military regalia ran up to them shouting, "What are you doing? We take care of everybody!"

"Yeah? Who do you take care of?" David asked him.

"We take care of the sector," he said. "We take care of Safety B. We take care of the people downtown."

"Oh, really?" David said.

As he continued writing summonses, the doorman opened the door of one of the cars—the chef's car—intending to move it. "If you move that car, you'd better have the license and the registration, or you're going," David warned him.

He and Boyd issued five hundred dollars' worth of ten-dollar summonses that night. The next day, after roll call, a sergeant from the midtown traffic-enforcement unit—known as Safety B—asked David to identify himself and took him to task in front of the other cops in his squad. "You are personally going to pay the tag you put on the chef's Cadillac," the sergeant said.

"Look," said David, waving the anonymous letter in the sergeant's face. "I didn't have any choice. Here's a communication from the commissioner's office ordering me to take action. What do you expect me to do? If I ignore this memo, I'll get a complaint."

A few nights later, he came to work carrying a chart he had prepared of the various pickup spots and the sums of money they were good for. Each of the eight cops who worked the sector was making about a hundred dollars a month from all the contracts put together, David figured, and the tally surprised him. "I had thought the price of selling out would be much higher," he said later.

After sharing this information with Boyd, he folded up the chart and stowed it in the back of his memo book so he could show it to the six other cops when he got a chance. "Look, these are all the pickup spots, and here's what it adds up to," he told them. "We've got the lousiest sector in the precinct."

Now that it was clear that they could ignore the contracts and get away with it, Boyd became an eager convert to David's theory. Together, they persuaded all but two of the eight cops—"the two senior hairbags," as David put it—to stop taking money. "All of a sudden, they were cops again, and they loved it," he said. "Doormen couldn't order them around anymore."

At the 18th Precinct, David's unusual pedigree and his air of naïveté made him an object of general curiosity. The desk lieutenant, a bluff, blond Irishman named Dalton, took delight in acting as his tutor. One night, Dalton called him into the station and asked him to pick up a "flute" at a bar on Amsterdam Avenue. When David said he didn't know what a flute was, Dalton threw his arms in the air and exclaimed, "Oh, my God! What are they hiring for the job these days? Well, just go there. They'll know."

The fact that the bar had a 100 percent black clientele, and the further fact that it was located far from the station house, led David to suspect that some sort of rite of initiation was being administered. "I'm supposed to get a flute for Lieutenant Dalton," he told the bartender. "Can you tell me what a flute is?"

The bartender laughed, filled a Coke bottle with Scotch, sealed it with a cork, and handed it—the flute—to David for delivery.

He was an oddity and, at the same time, a role model. During one of David's classes at the police academy (where he read *The New York Times* while everybody else read the *Daily News*, the *Post*, or the *Mirror*), the instructor queried his students about their reasons for joining the force. "My father was a cop," one of them answered. "For the pension," a second said. "I couldn't get into the fire department," a third chimed in, setting off a wave of appreciative laughter. The answers continued in this vein until David got his chance. He made a long and passionate statement about justice and making a difference in people's lives and what a wonderful and important job being a cop was. When it was the next student's turn, he thought for a moment, pointed toward David, and said, "Same as him."

The radio car was a live-and-let-live environment, in which cops tended to stick to small talk. David treated it as a place to address the big issues of law enforcement and to win converts to his belief that there was no more important or powerful position in the world. He urged his fellow cops to forget the police bureaucracy and its rules, and to be the police officers they had dreamed of being.

The cops who listened to his sermons had a divided reaction. On the one hand, they concluded that there was something not quite right with David upstairs. On the other hand, some of them began acting funny themselves.

Gregory Roth was probably the outstanding success story of David's missionary work in the 18th Precinct. Roth, who succeeded Boyd as his partner, wanted the world to see him as an average guy. He had round features, a chunky build, and slovenly habits. He found it hard to eat a meal without depositing some of it on his uniform, and if he happened to be eating when an emergency call came over the radio, his food usually went flying. (After a few meals together, David asked Roth to eat outside the vehicle, using the fender for a dinner table.) For longer than Roth cared to remember, he had been the man responsible for rounding up drunks in the 18th Precinct. (His policy was to round up the ones who wanted to be rounded up—who wanted an enforced opportunity to go on the wagon—and to leave the others alone.) After months of quiet agitation for a change of assignment, he was called in to see Captain Schawaroch. "I'm giving you a seat," Schawaroch told him, "but you've got to work with Durk."

Roth did not know Durk. Schawaroch described him as an undisciplined rookie who needed the guidance of someone older and wiser—i.e., Roth. As things turned out, it was David who did most of the guiding. Prior to his partnership with David, Roth had tried to take the job as it was. David did not take the job as it was. Because their car didn't have a first-aid kit (hardly any cars did, although, in theory, it was standard equipment), David assembled one by sweet-talking the necessary elements out of nurses and orderlies at a couple of local hospitals. In the same spirit, he persuaded a mortuary to make a wooden box for storing summonses and report forms.

He wrote summonses for air pollution (the actual charge was "emission of noxious fumes") and for other offenses that Roth had never heard of. When business was slow, David offered lifts to people waiting at bus stops—just to get some conversation going. Roth found that a tour of duty passed quickly with David. "He liked action—he was always there, always on the scene," Roth recalled.

The mission of every cop, according to the police manual, was the protection of life and property, in that order. But it seemed to David that he and his fellow cops spent the greater part of their time tending to the needs of the precinct's hotels, department stores, and restaurants, and that certain local merchants regarded the police, not without reason, as "hired muscle." So he made it his business to gum up the works whenever he could.

One day, he was sent to the Plaza Hotel to stand watch over the remains of a guest who had died in residence. The management of the Plaza would deliver breakfast, lunch, dinner, and any amount of alcoholic refreshment that a cop with this taxing assignment desired. All that the Plaza asked of him—and most cops were glad to oblige—was to be discreet when the time came for the morgue wagon crew to remove the body. ("They had to carry it down a service staircase into the basement and back up another staircase and out a side door," David said. "It was a lot of extra work.") When the morgue attendants came for the body, David had them leave through the main entrance, pausing for rest in the middle of the Palm Court—a sort of outdoor café that happens to be situated indoors, in the middle of the lobby. After the maître d' had calmed down sufficiently to put the full force of his feelings into words, David politely explained that he had chosen "the most direct way out of the hotel" and that the attendants had needed a rest. He invited the maître d' to lift the body himself if he wanted to see how heavy it was.

Most of his coworkers would never have pulled such a stunt themselves, but they were by no means incapable of appreciating its charm. Sometimes, when tangling with a cantankerous individual who had wealth or power behind him, they would bring David in as a consultant and ask him to handle the situation. Roth admired the verbiage that poured out of David's mouth in these encounters. "With most cops, it was 'Fuck you, scumbag!' " Roth recalled. "But Dave would really get into it. He would come on like William F. Buckley. If you've never seen him go into a tirade, there's nothing like it. Dave used to get people excited. He could agitate a group of people— for good or evil. He gave us the moxie to go after these guys."

Whenever David left the station house, the Inspector Angers and the Sergeant Pagnottis disappeared from his thoughts, and he answered only to the law and his own sense of justice, which sometimes went a little further than the law. Late one night, he and Roth pulled up alongside the car of a South American diplomat who was parking, as he routinely did, in a crosstown bus stop at Sixty-sixth

Street and Central Park West. David politely explained that buses were being forced to stop in the middle of Sixty-sixth Street, blocking traffic, while passengers got on and off. "I'm not asking you to find a legal parking place," he said. "All you have to do is go around the corner. On Central Park West, you can park your car in any bus stop you like, and the traffic can still get through." The diplomat smiled and walked away.

Legally, diplomats were not required to pay parking tickets; nor could their cars be towed. This was the sort of thing that cops griped about constantly, there being, it seemed, nothing they could do but gripe. But when the same car showed up in the same bus stop the next night, Roth and David were seized by a conviction that something had to be done, immunity or no immunity. Roth jocularly proposed that they slash the car's tires. David suggested—and Roth agreed—that they settle for letting the air out.

The rise of the Lincoln Center for the Performing Arts had set off a real estate boom in the West Sixties, an area whose proximity to midtown and Central Park gave it obvious potential as an upper-income neighborhood. There was only one obstacle: the low-income neighborhood that was already there. On the north side of Sixty-fifth Street between Central Park West and Columbus Avenue was a motley row of five-story walkups that had been experiencing an unusual series of burglaries, thefts, breakdowns, acts of arson, and other troubles that led some tenants to consider moving elsewhere. Stories were making the rounds of the precinct about detectives and commanders who had been paid to look the other way. One day, David and Roth were summoned to one of the Sixty-fifth Street buildings by its manager, whom they found inside, embroiled in a dispute with a tenant organizer. The manager, a round little man wearing a diamond pinky ring, wanted the organizer arrested. When David inquired what the charge might be, the manager answered, "He's a troublemaker. He's telling the tenants not to pay their rent." He produced a ten-dollar bill and extended it in David's direction.

The department had a rule about bribery collars: there had to be two witnesses (although the law contained no such requirement).

Since Roth was busy talking to the organizer, David called him over and asked the manager to repeat the offer—which he did. David informed him that he was under arrest.

The manager protested loudly. His employers, he said, were people whom a mere cop offended at his peril.

Roth was not happy about the turn of events, either. "You can't do this," he told David. "We're going to be shipped to Staten Island tomorrow."

"I'll say it was my idea—you're just a witness," David replied. He ordered the building manager to stand, spread-eagled, with his palms against the wall and handcuffed him before a dumbfounded audience of tenants—an audience that swelled in number and broke into applause as the two cops led the manager down the stairs, out onto the sidewalk, and into the backseat of their car. As the car pulled away with its dome light spinning, shouts of *"Viva la policía!"* trailed after them.

Roth learned from David that it was possible for a cop to treat people of all classes equally. "This precinct had from the wealthiest and most powerful people on the planet to the dregs," Roth recalled. "Once you started treating everybody the same, you did better for yourself and them."

Some of the things that David did made Roth uneasy. "You're batting out of your league," he would say. Sometimes he worried about the career consequences of being associated with David. As time passed, though, he saw that David seemed to know how to make himself immune to retribution, and their run-ins with lawyers, judges, and police bosses began to take on the flavor of a Road Runner cartoon, the suspense lying not as much in the outcome as in the means by which David would frustrate the latest effort to put him in his place.

PART
TWO

CHAPTER

FIVE

———➤●◄———

On the night of March 13, 1964, a young woman named Kitty Genovese parked her car in a railroad station in the Kew Gardens section of Queens and started walking toward her apartment building, a few blocks away. By the time she got there, she was bleeding to death from multiple stab wounds inflicted by a lunatic with a knife. The police later calculated that thirty-seven people had heard her screams or seen some part of her struggle without doing anything to help. A thirty-eighth person—the one who finally telephoned the police—fretted about it and called a friend for advice first.

Four months later, on a hot afternoon in July, an off-duty police lieutenant named Thomas Gilligan was standing in a TV repair shop in the Yorkville section of Manhattan. Looking out the window, he saw a quarrel erupt between a group of black teenagers and a white building superintendent who had sprayed water on them. Accidentally, he said. On purpose, they said. A fifteen-year-old named James Powell got a knife, chased the superintendent into the building, but failed to catch him. He met up with Lieutenant Gilligan on the way out. Still holding the knife in his hand, Powell came at Gilligan with it. Gilligan shot him dead on the sidewalk. There was a peaceful protest march the next day (SAVE US FROM OUR PROTECTORS, one of the picket signs declared), and a group of black leaders issued a fairly temperate statement arguing that an experienced police officer could have found another way of handling the situation. But there were other people, some of them claiming to be eyewitnesses, who portrayed the incident as cold-blooded murder, and this was the consensus of a series of speakers at a protest rally in Harlem a day later—a rally that evolved into an attempt to storm a police precinct, and from there into a full-fledged riot, with Molotov cocktails and garbage cans thrown from rooftops. Five more days of rioting followed, in Harlem and Bedford-Stuyvesant.

New York had never experienced racial violence on such a scale, and the city was taken aback. The inaction of Kitty Genovese's neighbors and the fury of the rioters declared with scary symmetry that a lot of people were no longer prepared to take the responsibilities or follow the rules that bound the city together. It was hard to reconcile these events with the idea—regularly repeated on WNYC radio in the sixties—that New York was a place where "nearly eight million people live together in peace and harmony and enjoy the fruits of democracy." More apropos was a public service announcement that was beginning to be heard on other local radio and TV stations: "It's ten P.M. Do you know where your children are?"

The mayor at the time, Robert F. Wagner—first elected in 1953—had been groomed for the office by Tammany Hall, and he was a product of the urge that occasionally comes over machine politicians to be led by someone better than they are. Personally honest and hard-working, he had annoyed his sponsors at the outset by reserving a few key offices in his administration for people who were actually qualified to hold them. When he came up for reelection, in 1957, the party regulars spurned him and unsuccessfully ran a candidate of their own. Four years later, Wagner allied himself with the reform wing of the party and won a third term by such a wide margin that people began to describe him as "mayor for life."

He was, by some measures, one of the most effective mayors in the city's history. Although black and Hispanic leaders were pressing for police reforms and more minority access to municipal construction work, it was Wagner who had prodded the city council into enacting the first civil rights bill in the nation to bar discrimination by private landlords, and during his years as mayor the city built public housing at an unprecedented (and, since then, unequaled) rate—so much of it that by some estimates Wagner might have been in a position to reach his stated goal of a "slum-free New York" had he only been dealing with a stable population. The city was in the throes of an office-construction boom, too (Sixth Avenue was fast becoming a canyon of skyscrapers), and a World's Fair had opened in the Flushing Meadow area of Queens.

In the tumult of the mid-sixties, however, Wagner did not cut a sharp figure. When the riots broke out, he flew home from a trip to Europe and rushed from the airport to a TV studio to make a none-too-confident-sounding speech in which he described law and order as "the Negro's best friend" and urged the rioters to desist out of concern for—of all things—New York's image in the eyes of the world. Wagner had been mayor for more than ten years, and those years were visible in the lines of his face.

Even after the riots, much of the opposition to Wagner's mayoralty came from groups accustomed to a fringe position in New York City politics. But one of the mayor's critics was a man of singular influence. This was John Hay Whitney, the publisher of the *New York Herald Tribune*. In January 1966, the *Tribune* began running a series of articles under the banner "City in Crisis." "New York is the greatest city in the world, and everything is wrong with it" was the theme, restated in article after article. Intended to last no more than a few weeks, "City in Crisis" met with such a positive reaction from the public (and from Whitney) that the series wound up running for four and a half months. During those months, the movie-star-handsome congressman from the Silk Stocking district of Manhattan's East Side announced (with Whitney's private encouragement) that he would be a candidate for mayor, and Wagner announced that he would not be. The *Tribune*—a dying newspaper—had risen up from its deathbed to deliver a fatal blow to an era in New York City politics.

John Lindsay shared the conviction of the *Tribune* articles that there was nothing wrong with the city that an enlightened new generation of leaders, or, as he put it, "modern men," couldn't solve. The Lindsay administration, even more than the Kennedy administration, would stand for the idea that the worst problems facing government would yield to the efforts of a fresh team of public servants, drawn from the "best and the brightest." "We were young and pure, willing to work twenty-four hours a day," Barry Gottehrer—the principal author of the series, who went on to serve as one of Lindsay's top aides—wrote later. "We really believed that we would change things and make our city livable."

Lindsay invoked the spirit of Fiorello LaGuardia, and David and Arlene Durk had warm childhood memories of LaGuardia. By contrast, New York City government under LaGuardia's successors had been "just the hacks running things," as Arlene put it. David had often heard his father complain about the decline of the city's public health clinics since LaGuardia's day, and about bureaucrats who were more interested in the number of forms he completed than in the number of children he helped. Lindsay was six feet four, blond, graceful, and well spoken, and he had an aristocratic veneer—partly a product of his schooling at St. Paul's and Yale—that made him an unlikely inheritor of LaGuardia's mantle and an unlikely mayor of a city that liked its politicians down-to-earth. But he was not afraid to think for himself. One of the distinctive characteristics of his three-term career as a congressman had been a readiness to be the lone voice in opposition to some proposal (say, a bill giving the postal service new authority to define and intercept obscene mail) that colleagues on both sides of the aisle equated with motherhood and apple pie. When an issue came before him, he read, listened, studied, and made up his own mind—the conventional political wisdom be damned.

To David and Arlene (who was studying to become a social worker), Wagner represented the politics of a bygone era—a politics of personal favors and backroom deals. Lindsay, unlike Wagner, seemed to be attempting to understand the changes that were coming over the city. A Lindsay campaign mailing that came to the Durk household included the text of a speech on "juvenile delinquency" in which Lindsay talked about the despair of inner-city children who spent long hours watching TV shows that depicted homes filled with goodies that they could never realistically hope to own—not by lawful means, that is. That speech so impressed David that he made a point of attending a Lindsay fund-raising party at the apartment of some West Side neighbors. Seeing the candidate up close, his respect grew. Wagner's style as mayor had been to get every building block in place before he announced anything; if an idea seemed unlikely to receive the necessary support, he would follow his favorite maxim (taught him by his father—an influential U.S. senator of the New Deal era), "When in doubt, don't." Lindsay, David noted with pleasure, was not afraid to say, "*I* think," as opposed to "Let's appoint a commission."

More telling than any platform plank or speech was the graceful way Lindsay moved among constituencies. On the news one day was the candidate in a bathing suit diving into a pool at Coney Island. Another day, he was giving a guest sermon at an all-black church. Still another, he was standing at the scene of Kitty Genovese's death, denouncing apathy and promising that "the double padlock on the front door will no longer be the symbol of New York City." Lindsay was a living refutation of the idea that the city was coming apart.

Almost the first position that Lindsay took as a candidate was to endorse a proposal to add four civilians to the police department's three-member board for reviewing complaints of brutality or misconduct. This was another mark of political courage, and Lindsay paid the price for it almost daily during the campaign, as supporters of the Conservative Party candidate, William F. Buckley, Jr.—who had dismissed all concern about police brutality as "the fancied fears of a neurotic population"—showed up at Lindsay events to make trouble, and the police failed to do anything about it.

Just about everything else broke right for Lindsay in 1965. The Democrats did him a large favor by nominating Comptroller Abe

Beame—a candidate so wooden that people couldn't help wondering who was pulling his strings. And Buckley's candidacy, although it attracted much of its support from Republicans who held Lindsay in disdain, was probably also a stroke of good fortune, for Lindsay won the election with 44 percent of the vote, and in a city where Democrats outnumbered Republicans by a ratio of seven to two, it was far from clear how he could have triumphed in a two-way contest.

"He is fresh and everyone else is tired," the columnist Murray Kempton had written, giving Lindsay a campaign slogan. City Hall, with Lindsay in occupancy, became a sort of military command center that strove to stay on top of every problem. Lindsay appointed "night mayors" to tend to crises that developed after hours, and the mayor himself was always ready to visit the scene of some late-breaking emergency. Photo opportunities abounded: Lindsay clearing a vacant lot in the Bronx; picking up litter at Lincoln Center; visiting tenements in East Harlem; shoveling the snow outside Gracie Mansion; and, dressed in black tie because he had ducked out of a dinner party, watching over a four-alarm fire in Brooklyn.

In Washington, if not exactly everywhere in the land, there was a willingness during this period to look on the nation's cities as victims of forces beyond their control, and a readiness to invest in programs intended to give a sense of hope and involvement to the poorest of the poor. Lindsay, more than any other big-city mayor of the time, was determined to capitalize on this mood. While other local politicians scoffed at the rhetoric of Lyndon Johnson's war on poverty—and some opted out of its programs when they realized they couldn't control the money—Lindsay wanted New York to take advantage of every available dollar. His administration played a key role in drafting economic redevelopment plans for Harlem, central Brooklyn, and the South Bronx and, with city money as a supplement to federal antipoverty funds, helped provide summer jobs (clearing lots or helping out at hospitals at $1.50 an hour) for 42,000 teenagers. All this attention to slum-dwellers rubbed a lot of people the wrong way. "What's he done for white people?" became a popular line of inquiry. To many New Yorkers, however, the city seemed to be a more upbeat and hopeful place with John Lindsay as mayor.

Among the people who thought so were David and Arlene Durk. Arlene had been part of a delegation of West Side mothers who, under Wagner, had gone to see the long-time parks commissioner, Robert Moses, in order to plead for safer, more imaginative playgrounds (and ones better designed for smaller children) than the spartan, metal-and-concrete affairs the city had created by the hundreds during the years of Moses's commissionership. Told by Arlene and the other mothers of cases in which children had suffered broken bones and fractured skulls, he responded gruffly: his *own* children had played on those playgrounds without mishap, he noted, so perhaps the failure was not one of design but, rather, of maternal vigilance.

Lindsay summarily dismissed Moses from his last city post (as, in effect, highway commissioner), all but ending the career of a man who had been building roads, bridges, parks, and public housing—and ignoring criticism—for a generation. Under Lindsay and his parks commissioner, Thomas Hoving, the city created playgrounds with wooden mazes, spiral slides, leather-bucket swings, and soft rubber surfaces underfoot. The first "adventure playground," as it was known, was at Sixty-eighth Street and Central Park West, and the Durks, who lived around the corner on Seventieth Street, were regulars there from the day it opened, in the fall of 1966.

Meanwhile, acting on the simple but novel idea that the way to make parks safer was to bring more people into them, the new administration arranged concerts, sports events, and kite-flying and Frisbee-throwing demonstrations. Moses had often put the interests of motorists first. Lindsay and Hoving banned automobiles from the roadways of the city's larger parks on weekends, and runners, bicyclists, and roller skaters poured in to fill the void.

Lindsay's first big decision, as far as the police department was concerned, was the choice of a police commissioner. The incumbent,

Vincent Broderick—a former judge—had put himself out of the running by openly opposing the idea of a civilian review board. When
Lindsay's advisors began scouring the horizon for a replacement,
they discovered that most of the obvious candidates—the police
chiefs and commissioners of other large cities—didn't even regard
brutality as a significant problem, much less see a need to enter into
a dialogue on the subject with outside critics. It was against this
background that Howard Leary of Philadelphia emerged as a top
contender. Leary was a career cop who had put himself through college and law school at night and had nicely incorporated certain
advanced ideas about the police role. He went to the right meetings
and shook the right hands. Philadelphia already had a civilian
review board, and Leary had gotten along with it just fine. "Howard
is intelligent, mild-mannered, cool, and has mature judgment," the
head of the Philadelphia chapter of the NAACP said of him. "I think
he is the most enlightened police commissioner in the United
States—and I'm not one given to praise, especially for a cop."

A few years later, it would become apparent that the Philadelphia
police department was as corrupt as any in the United States, and
that Leary had not done much of anything about it. But the question
hardly came up in the Lindsay administration's selection process.
Corruption was a nonissue.

There were a few people in the Lindsay camp who questioned
whether Leary had the leadership skills for such an important job.
There were others, however, who seemed to see this shortcoming as
a point in his favor—perhaps even his greatest asset. Because Lindsay
was vulnerable to attack as antipolice, they argued, he needed a
police commissioner with impeccable police credentials. But he also
needed one who would take direction—and Leary gave the impression that he would take direction very well.

Robert Wagner, following in a long mayoral tradition, had kept a
wary distance from police affairs. John Lindsay plunged right in. On
July 21, 1966, an eleven-year-old black boy named Eric Dean was
shot to death, apparently by a sniper, in the East New York section of
Brooklyn, where a group of white residents (many of them teenagers)

had banded together under the acronym SPONGE—the Society for the Prevention of Niggers Getting Everything. Determined to avoid the sort of rioting that had followed the Gilligan-Powell incident two years earlier, or, worse, riots on the scale of those that had struck Los Angeles in the summer of 1965, Lindsay rushed to the scene and toured the area. Over the next few days, Barry Gottehrer and another young mayoral aide, Sid Davidoff, worked closely with Leary to fashion what came to be known as the "New York City technique" for averting racial violence. It was a technique that emphasized a massive deployment of police, followed by a great deal of watching and waiting. "The idea was to get as many cops as possible out to an area and form a perimeter," Gottehrer said later. "Whatever was happening, Leary would let it happen for the first evening. When the crowds started to thin out, the perimeter would be moved in, and ultimately— whether it took one night or two or three—the police would regain the neighborhood." There was plenty of criticism (much of it from cops) of the department's failure to meet every criminal act with an aggressive response, and Leary took a lot of flak, personally, for accepting so much guidance from Gottehrer and Davidoff. But the results made the strategy look good.

Lindsay also moved swiftly to keep his promise of a civilian review board—perhaps too swiftly. He established the new board, by executive order, in April 1966, and no sooner had he done so than the Patrolmen's Benevolent Association began gathering signatures to make it a referendum question on the fall election ballot. In Philadelphia and other cities, such boards had proved to be anything but hostile to the police (in fact, their civilian members tended to become police buffs), and resistance to them had faded. Lindsay, by creating his board when he did, gave the PBA an opportunity to make an election issue out of it before the board could establish a record for itself. "I'm sick and tired of giving in to minority groups, with their whims, their shouting, and their gripes," John Cassesse, the president of the PBA, declared. That summer and fall, New Yorkers had many opportunities to view a PBA-produced TV commercial in which a mugger attacked a little girl while a cop stood idly by, his hands tied behind his back. On election day, in a vote that divided largely along racial lines, the civilian review board got thrashed. By a vote of two to one, New Yorkers decided that they preferred to let the police department investigate itself. It was a humiliation that Lindsay and the people around him would never forget.

CHAPTER

SIX

———➤●◄———

On a Sunday afternoon in the early summer of 1965, Patrolman Durk (who had been assigned to a footpost that day) was walking past the statue of Simon Bolivar on Central Park South when he spotted a pint-size political rally. It consisted of a speaker, a few dozen listeners, and a rim of hecklers who were loudly impugning the speaker's patriotism—until David gave them a lecture on the right of dissent. The spectacle of a police officer upholding the First Amendment caught the attention of a passerby, a slight young man with a triangular face, largely hidden by a pair of heavy-duty eyeglasses, and a nest of long, thick brown hair that seemed quite out of proportion to the rest of him. He complimented David on his handling of the situation, and they got to talking. It soon emerged that both of them had gone to Amherst. Both also had a professional interest in law enforcement. David's new acquaintance, Jay Kriegel, had just finished law school, and he was spending the summer as a Lindsay volunteer. His immediate assignment was to draft a campaign white paper on crime.

Kriegel was the embodiment of John Lindsay's faith in youthful intelligence and zeal untarnished by prior government service or political expertise. A year earlier, he had taken time off from law school to work for passage of the Johnson administration's civil rights bill, and he had been dazzled by the effectiveness of Lindsay's efforts on the bill's behalf, as a member of a minority wing of the minority party. A few days after their encounter on Central Park South, Kriegel visited the Durks' apartment. He came equipped with a legal pad and pencil—he would be described as a "walking notebook" during his career at City Hall—and for several hours he scribbled while David rattled off examples of waste, inefficiency, and absurdity in the administration of justice.

Merely to issue a parking summons, he told Kriegel, you had to write the basic information over four times. ("A lot of cops liked that," David said later, "because they would go out and zap a block and then go into a coop and get lost for two hours—and if they got caught they'd say, 'Hey, I'm filling out my paperwork!' ") He showed Kriegel some of the forms—about ten in all—a cop had to complete for an ordinary drug arrest. He described the routine in arraignment court, where cops would stay with their prisoners for hours on end, drawing overtime pay—in order to attend a two-minute hearing.

The meeting with Kriegel yielded quick results. Several of David's ideas were prominently featured in the Lindsay white paper, and at a press conference called to unveil it, the candidate made a show-and-tell exhibit, as David had suggested, of an ordinary patrolman's winter overcoat, which weighed close to fifteen pounds. ("You can practice judo from now till doomsday," he had told Kriegel, "and by the time you get to the fifth floor of a tenement with that overcoat and all the other junk you're supposed to be carrying, they'll just throw you right down the stairs.")

———⋙•⋘———

That fall, Captain Paul Delise, the new commander of the Chief Inspector's Investigating Unit—an elite citywide antigambling squad —offered David a job as a plainclothesman. David had put in for CIIU after learning from a newspaper article that the unit was undergoing a complete overhaul in the wake of one of the minor scandals that rocked small fiefdoms of the department from time to time. Indeed, only a scandal could have elevated someone with Delise's reputation into a position of authority in the NYPD. Not only was he rigorously honest (some of his former subordinates had given him the derisive nickname St. Paul), but—stranger still—he disliked gamblers with a passion. After he took over, important figures in the gambling world discovered that they were vulnerable. David's first assignment was to be part of a six-man team watching the comings and goings outside an apartment house used as a policy drop by Moe Schlitten, a prominent numbers banker in the Bronx. The surveillance was conducted from a vehicle disguised as a telephone company van. This practice was so well known that sometimes, when CIIU ran a surveillance, kids from the neighborhood would take to setting fires under the van in order to have the satisfaction of seeing the doors fly open and the occupants come tumbling out. In Schlitten's case, though, the cover held, and after several days of observations, the CIIU team entered the building with the aid of a sledgehammer and a battering ram. While Schlitten and a couple of his aides looked on, the cops ransacked the premises, searching for "work"—slips of paper recording the bets that smaller gamblers had laid off.

David had never participated in such a search, and having only just reported to his new assignment, he wasn't expected to do anything more than look and learn. But he made a point of watching Schlitten's expression as the other cops inspected this place and that, and he thought he detected a look of anxiety as they were rummaging through the contents of a closet next to the sofa on which Schlitten and his associates were sitting. When the cops moved on, David surveyed the closet, trying to think of a hiding place that might have been neglected. His eye fell on a folded-up ironing board leaning against the wall. He picked it up, examined it, and idly removed the rubber caps from the ends of the legs. Out came the work. It was his first collar as a plainclothesman, and Schlitten was sufficiently impressed to ask David his name.

The CIIU men took their prisoners to the nearest precinct, and there David discovered that his new status made him someone of consequence. The desk lieutenant offered to provide him with any assistance he needed. Since it was a complicated arrest, David requested coffee for himself and the other CIIU men, plus the loan of a couple of precinct detectives to help with the typing. As the paperwork proceeded, he noticed that an unusual number of cops seemed to consider Moe Schlitten's arrest an event worth checking out personally. It dawned on him that they were probably thinking about the money that Schlitten would no longer be paying them, now that his operation had been at least temporarily shut down.

At CIIU, David's stock rose sharply, and he was in on the planning stages of the unit's next big case. This time, the target was Ralph Gigante, who, with his two brothers, the mobster Vincent "The Chin" Gigante and the Reverend Louis Gigante, a street priest and political activist who was known for building and renovating a great deal of low-income housing in the Bronx (and for being willing to give a proper Catholic burial to Mafia figures whom his church peers shunned even in death), constituted one of the city's more powerful, and interesting, families. Ralph Gigante ran his gambling operations out of Googie's, a bar on Thompson Street, in the Village. Plainclothesmen who knew the scene voiced the opinion that Googie's—the whole block, for that matter—was so well guarded by Gigante's people that a police observation team could not escape notice. But David pointed out that New York University Law School, at the end of the block, might provide a good cover. Dressing up to look like a law student, he sat on the sidewalk surrounded by books and snapped pictures with a camera built into his belt.

Without asking anybody for permission, he began to use a faculty lounge in the law school building as an observation point. Inevitably, a time came when a few of the regular occupants noticed the police presence in their midst and raised questions about privacy and academic freedom. David responded by pointing out that the Supreme Court, in the Escobedo case, had urged the police to make more of an effort to gather "extrinsic evidence" before seeking wiretap orders and search warrants. "We're not doing anything illegal," he told a skeptical law professor. "We're just doing what Arthur Goldberg"—the justice who had written the Escobedo decision—"told us to do."

Delise was a commander who liked to be on the front lines, and he and David spent long hours together during the Gigante surveillance. Like David, he could walk down Thompson Street without attracting the notice of Gigante's lookouts. A small, sinewy man with black hair and blacker eyebrows, Delise wore wrinkled clothes that fashion had passed by, and he looked a little like a Neapolitan tradesman out for a Sunday stroll. He was the first boss of David's who was willing to admit he considered police work fun. He was also the first who talked about corruption—a subject that had weighed on him for the whole of his twenty-four-year police career.

Delise had grown up on Arthur Avenue in the Bronx. As a boy, he had often gone shopping with his mother at an open-air market, and she would contemptuously point out uniformed cops who were helping themselves to apples, bananas, and other items. "In a lot of Italian neighborhoods, the cop was considered a scrounger—someone who was always looking for something for nothing," Delise recalled, as a retired deputy chief in the early 1990s. He would probably never have become a cop but for the Depression. When he finished high school, stable jobs were scarce. He got hired as a dishwasher at the 1939 World's Fair, but there was no direct subway service between the Bronx and Queens, and he had to "go all the way down and around, for a lousy twenty-five cents an hour." He was working in the engine room of Montefiore Hospital when it dawned on him that the civil service was the place to be. "But I made up my mind," he said, "that if I became a cop I would be an honest one."

The older cops did not have much to say to Delise when he joined the department in 1942. Day after day, he rode the trolley between the station and his post in the company of a veteran cop who never uttered a word. Finally Delise decided to break the silence. "Well, another day, another dollar," he said, innocently.

The old-timer stirred. "At least you made a dollar—I didn't make anything," he replied.

David learned from Delise that an investigator had to watch for corruption out of the corner of his eye, the way a cautious driver on a highway watches for cars darting in off of side roads. It was standard practice at CIIU for anyone requesting a criminal record to check the files personally; if you made the request over the phone, Delise explained to him, the cop who did the checking for you could turn around and sell the information—the fact of your inquiry—to the target of your investigation.

Delise had picked David for CIIU because, among other things, he didn't look like a cop and he knew next to nothing about gambling. David, he noted, didn't seem to mind looking foolish in the eyes of other cops. Amateurish enthusiasm was a virtue in Delise's book; he was proud to call himself a "door buster" or a "buff." In that spirit, he approved David's proposal to send an attractive blond-haired policewoman named Anne King into Googie's with the object of getting Gigante to incriminate himself on tape. Gigante was a big man—wider than he was tall, it seemed—who did not allow his shape to undermine his self-esteem in relations with the opposite sex. David enjoyed the planning phase of undercover operations, and he gave King an elaborate cover story, casting her as the unhappy wife of an impotent husband. She had come to Googie's to drown her sorrows.

Gigante's sympathy—more than his sympathy—was aroused, but King's first visit exposed a weakness in the plan. Gigante kept plying her with drinks, and by the time she left Googie's she was wobbly on her feet. She needed to be sober in order to stay on top of the situation. Besides, she would be expected to testify in court about her conversations with Gigante, and she would not be a very effective witness if she had to admit that she had been drinking steadily at the time. David remembered a movie in which the vulnerable heroine, in a similar situation, had periodically poured her drink into a plant. There were no plants at Googie's. At his suggestion, however, a small plastic bottle was fitted into King's bra, with a rubber tube leading to her collar, so she could drain her glass when no one was looking. (She emptied the bottle during periodic visits to the ladies' room.) Within several days of her appearance at Googie's, Gigante was transacting illicit business in front of her and boasting of his wealth and accomplishments. A few more days, and King was making excuses about why she couldn't go to the racetrack with him—an invitation that was still on the table when her backup team entered Googie's to inform Gigante that he was under arrest. King was one of those who did the informing, and the realization that he had been taken by a woman sent Gigante into a mighty rage. The prospect of going to prison seemed to be a fairly minor concern, taken in context.

———————

During the election campaign Jay Kriegel had tried to carve out a portion of every evening to ponder the important question of how to get closer to the candidate. A year later, he had moved considerably closer. He was the short, bespectacled, often-unnamed figure who regularly showed up by the mayor's side in newspaper photographs and TV news clips. "Jay doesn't need an apartment—he lives in my husband's ear," the mayor's wife, Mary, commented. He was the third member, along with Gottehrer and Davidoff, of what had come to be known as the Kiddie Corps—a group of junior aides whose influence at City Hall was attracting considerable acerbic comment from old political observers. If you had business with the mayor, and if your business involved the criminal justice system, your destination was likely to be a basement office where two shocks awaited you: first, the boyishness and the rolled-up-sleeve, floppy-haired deportment of your host; and, second, the sense that you were speaking mainly to his feet, which he was in the habit of resting on his desk while the rest of him slouched back in semivisibility. Kriegel was the youngest of the Kiddie Corpsmen, and there were veteran police commanders who did not enjoy pleading their case with a long-haired twenty-six-year-old. Nor could it have been said that he went out of his way to behave with an air of humility and deference befitting someone of his years. But if he lacked diplomacy, he also lacked the formality that went with it. He was excitable—a quality that David could relate to. Sometimes he spat out his words so fast that, as another Lindsay aide remarked, "Talking to Jay Kriegel is like putting your finger in an electric light socket." Barry Gottehrer described him as "one of the most unsophisticated bright people in government."

David, for his part, had moved closer to Kriegel, becoming a kind of closet consultant to City Hall in matters pertaining to the police. Through Kriegel, he met others in the Lindsay inner circle, including Deputy Mayor Robert Price, who gave him an introduction to the new Commissioner of Investigation, Arnold Fraiman. An interview with Fraiman led to an offer of a job as one of his investigators, who were, by tradition, borrowed from the police department. David had enjoyed his time at CIIU, but he had never shared Paul Delise's sense of mission about locking up gamblers. Working at the Department of Investigation (DOI) would mean going after crooks in government. It would also put him on the path to being made a detective. He jumped at the chance.

He had daydreamed of being police commissioner some day. Now, while still a mere patrolman, he was an unofficial member of the Lindsay team, in on the development of criminal justice policy at the highest level. It was an intoxicating role, and a role that astonished some of David's superiors—notably, Captain Philip Foran. David had formed a favorable opinion of Foran (an opinion he would later regret) while the two men worked at CIIU together. When Arnold Fraiman asked David to look over a list of candidates for the post of DOI's chief investigator, David confidently declared that the best candidate was not on the list. That man, he said, was Foran. Shortly thereafter, David informed Foran that the job was his for the asking. Foran—though at first he couldn't quite believe that such news could be coming from such a source—asked, and was duly appointed.

At DOI, David quickly found a niche for himself handling assignments that required "a bit of sophistication," as Robert Ruskin, Fraiman's deputy (and successor), would recall. For undercover purposes, David was typecast as the innocent upper-middle-class youth. One of his first cases involved a couple of health department clerks who were soliciting payoffs for expediting the delivery of death certificates to funeral directors. They were doing this so indiscreetly that David didn't even have to enter the health department building to confirm the charge. Standing outside a first-floor window, he could plainly see the accused clerks taking ten-dollar bills from a series of visitors. Wearing an Edwards Device—the high-priced ancestor of the modern pocket-size audio recorder—David went inside, identified himself as an employee of a fictitious funeral home, and got one of the clerks to hit him up for money. In such situations, many undercover cops would go to great lengths to seem relaxed and with-it; sometimes they were so cool that they never quite managed to get explicit evidence of a crime. David was unashamedly naïve. He insisted on restating the transaction in painstaking detail. "I need change," he said. "I want to be sure I'm paying you the right amount, because I need two death certificates." After the deal had been consummated, he added, "I'm new. I'll be coming on a regular basis. Can we work out a monthly rate?"

Another early assignment involved a landlord who was demanding cash payments before putting tenants into city-subsidized, low-income apartments. The landlord was also the manager of an East Village variety store, and that was where David found him, watching over his employees from a raised booth inside the entrance and, from time to time, barking orders at them. David wanted to be sure that the payment he had been asked to make was illegal, so he identified himself as a graduate student at NYU who was counting on his father to reimburse him for his housing expenses. "I have to tell him what this is for," David said. "Could you explain to me in simple terms, so I can explain it to him?"

"What are you, stupid?" the landlord said.

"Please, I have the money you want," David said. "But if I can't explain what it's for, my father might think I'm pocketing it."

The landlord was getting increasingly annoyed. "Didn't you say you go to graduate school?" he shouted. "I can't believe anyone with so much education could be such an idiot! This is a bribe, for God's sake!"

"All right," David said politely. "That's something I can tell my father." He counted out the money, handed it over, and told the landlord he was under arrest.

Some of his missions called for painstaking surveillance rather than acting talent—a charge of systematic theft by a group of twenty parking-meter collectors, for example. David had to figure out what they were doing at the end of the day with the money they were stealing. He tailed several of the collectors to a bar near City Hall and saw them passing cosmetics pouches (they turned out to contain roughly a hundred dollars' worth of dimes each) to the bartender, who gave them bills in exchange, deducting a commission for his services as money launderer. The investigation concluded with the arrest of the collectors in the counting room of the Parking Violations Bureau. As each collector entered the room and turned in his incomplete take, he was arrested and whisked away, so that the next arrival, seeing nothing awry, would feel free to do the same.

It was during his time at DOI that David first began to exhibit a talent for eliciting provocative information from people who did not normally confide in the police. The typical detective finds his informants in saloons, alleys, and other known criminal habitats. He does his looking during working hours, and concentrates on his assigned area of specialization—narcotics, say, or burglary. David made it a round-the-clock quest, with no setting or subject off-limits. Dinner parties, he discovered, were a particularly rich hunting ground. Finding themselves sitting next to an off-duty detective, with a plentiful supply of food and drink handy, people would say the darndest things: an architect, for example, might talk about rigged bids in the construction of a new city office building; a steel importer about how to get goods through customs without paying duties; a rich matron about the predicament confronting her housekeeper's son, who was wanted for murder.

One Sunday afternoon, on his way to the Museum of Modern Art to see a Picasso exhibit, David chased down a thief who had been fleeing a bookstore on West Fifty-seventh Street with a stash of expensive art books. The suspect, Eddie Cruz, was a good-looking young man with a lot of criminal know-how and presence of mind. These qualities emerged in a helpful suggestion that he made as David, with Cruz in tow, was preparing to take his place at the end of a long line of cops seeking "yellow sheets"—arrest records—at the Bureau of Criminal Identification. "I like you," Cruz said. "You're a nice guy. We don't have to stand in line here. Follow me."

First peering into a captain's office to be sure it was empty, Cruz then marched to the head of the line and asked for the captain by name.

"He's out," said one of the clerks behind the counter.

"I'm in a hurry," said Cruz, who had assumed the persona of a detective. "Here are the prints on Eddie Cruz—I need his record right away." To David, Cruz added, "Give the guy two dollars."

David—thinking, Who's arresting whom?—gave the guy two dollars, and the record was furnished forthwith.

From the Bureau of Criminal Identification, they repaired to the Ban Hung Inn, a noodle shop in Chinatown. Detectives did not normally invite prisoners or informants to dine with them; they regarded mealtime as a precious opportunity to be free of such people. But David would eat with pretty much anybody, and the offer he made to Cruz—a trip to the Ban Hung Inn instead of four hours in a holding cell—was a standard offer in his perpetual effort to cultivate sources and obtain information. Over a heaping order of pepper steak, Cruz announced that his ambition in life was to become a man of consequence in the Mafia, and he boasted of having done time in prison with Joey Gallo, the local mobster, who was later assassinated at Umberto's Clam House in Little Italy.

"Well, you know, the Mafia is not an equal opportunity employer," David pointed out.

Cruz gave him a blank look.

"I mean the Italians are the Italians," David said, "and when it's time to pick a don, blacks and Hispanics need not apply."

"You're very unusual," Cruz said.

"*You're* very unusual," David said.

According to Cruz's yellow sheet, he had been arrested three times, the most serious charge (the one that had landed him in prison with Joey Gallo) being auto theft. This comparatively modest criminal record was part of the reason that the DA's office was, at David's urging, willing to do some negotiating with him. It belatedly occurred to David, however, that Cruz's performance at the Bureau of Criminal Identification and his general air of élan reflected a greater familiarity with the legal system than three minor arrests could account for. So he made another inquiry, which yielded another yellow sheet—this one under the name Eddie Torres. It was four pages long, and the charges were more troubling, as well as more numerous. One of them was assaulting a police officer.

By the time David made this discovery, Cruz had been released in the company of an unarmed civilian investigator from the DA's office with whom he was supposedly making a tour of midtown bookshops where he had been in the habit of selling his stolen goods. To David's relief, Cruz and the investigator returned safely a few hours later.

"You fuck!" David exclaimed, confronting Cruz with his corrected yellow sheet. "I was so nice to you, and you put me in this position."

"I'll make it up to you," Cruz said.

And make it up he did. A few days later, David and two detectives from the DA's office tagged along as Cruz walked through a midtown office building carrying a tray of plastic cups and calling, "Coffee! Who wanted coffee?" It was eight-thirty in the morning, and a fair number of offices were not only empty but unlocked; of these, a few had unattended IBM Selectric typewriters in them. As soon as Cruz identified such an office, he would slip inside, pick up the typewriter, and, with lightning speed, wrap it in a sheet of brown paper he had brought along for the purpose. The whole process took about half a minute, and when Cruz reappeared in the corridor, he looked for all the world like an ordinary deliveryman. With his police accomplices still in tow, he took the train to Yonkers and sold his bounty to an office machinery store there that billed itself as the biggest seller of secondhand IBM typewriters in the world. The store was later indicted for receiving stolen property.

Cruz became a regular source of David's: over a period of years, he supplied information on two homicides and a number of robberies, and he fingered a doctor at Bellevue Hospital who, for a fee, had been helping murderers, holdup men, and other patients designated as criminally insane get transferred to less secure facilities, from which they could easily escape.

———

The secret of good government, John Lindsay believed, was to ignore the power brokers, the interest groups, and the bureaucrats and bring in smart, well-educated, "modern" men and (in considerably smaller numbers) women. He declared his intention to merge some forty-nine city agencies into ten "super-agencies"—a plan promoted as a way of saving millions of dollars, but one that had the added virtue of creating a roster of impressive-sounding new jobs for which Lindsay could recruit appropriately renowned experts, luring them away from prominent positions in business, the academic world, and other city governments. Fearful of the obstructive powers of middle-level officials who were not susceptible to the mayoral axe, Lindsay relied on consultants and special task forces to do work he feared would otherwise be bungled or sabotaged. For example, a committee headed by McGeorge Bundy, the president of the Ford Foundation, examined the New York City school system, and came up with a proposal to create sixty community-controlled school boards that would have primary jurisdiction over curriculum and personnel.

The problems of the police and the criminal justice system, similarly, were submitted for study to the Rand Corporation, a California-based efficiency analysis firm set up by the Air Force at the end of World War II. The people at Rand were trying to broaden their purview by adding social policy to military policy, and they had found a profitable client in the City of New York. Indeed, Rand wound up opening a New York office to handle all the business John Lindsay sent its way. With Rand's help, the Lindsay administration put together a plan to consolidate police precincts, hire civilians, use one-man instead of two-man cars, issue summonses in lieu of making arrests for certain minor offenses, and, by these and other measures, produce a theoretical 40 percent increase in police presence on the streets. Also in the works was a new police communications system that would allow New Yorkers to dial 911 in an emergency, leading to a sharp reduction in police response time.

Kriegel was City Hall's liaison with Rand and, at the same time, with David. He was getting very different signals from these two places. The Rand Corporation's advice was mostly about efficiency and technology; David's was about cops and the things that motivated and troubled them. Rand's insights were often conveyed in the form of data; David communicated in anecdotes and inside dope. Sometimes David cut through to the essence of a situation that had the Rand people bewildered—why, for example, detectives tended to score badly on the promotional exam for sergeant. They had no motivation to do well, David explained, because of all the illicit income that was available to them as detectives; the only reason they even bothered to take the exam was that, by doing so, they got the rest of the day off.

Almost as soon as the Lindsay people took power, David was after them to do something about police corruption, which (now that he had been educated by Delise, Cruz, and others) he saw as the department's most pressing problem. Kriegel was torn. The various city, state, and federal prosecutors weren't particularly worried about the level of corruption; nor, by and large, was the community of recognized outside authorities. Nobody denied that corruption existed, but according to the consensus of informed opinion, it was a phenomenon largely confined to the lowest ranks of the department and involving something close to the irrepressible minimum number of cops who, faced with temptation, were bound to yield. Only David was saying anything else.

In the face of all this contrary testimony (and sensing that Kriegel himself might need some convincing), David decided that he had better strengthen his case. Late in the summer of 1966, he offered to arrange a private briefing for the mayor with a group of cops. If they were given a promise of confidentiality, David told Kriegel, they would gladly talk about their knowledge of corruption and the difficulty of fighting it from inside the department. Kriegel seemed to look favorably on the idea. He said he would speak to Lindsay, and David alerted his briefers (one of whom was Delise) to prepare for a summons to City Hall. No such summons ever came. Instead, a few days later, Kriegel warned David (and asked him to warn the others) not to speak of the proposed meeting, because it was "never planned, never contemplated." Lindsay had already been criticized for over-involvement in the management of the police department, and he was determined, Kriegel explained, to do nothing behind his new police commissioner's back. Kriegel added that the moment might not be right to address the issue of corruption—not with the threat of civil disorders still hanging over East New York, and with City Hall still in the thick of the struggle for a civilian review board. Disappointed, but undeterred, David resolved to go on gathering evidence, and to try again.

CHAPTER

SEVEN

——⟫●⟨——

For Frank Serpico, the decision to become a cop wasn't nearly as complicated as it was for David Durk. Serpico had grown up in a predominantly Italian section of Bedford-Stuyvesant, where, he said later, a boy had two career choices: the police department and organized crime. And they were not as different as they appeared, he liked to add. His parents were devout, hard-working people from a town outside Naples (his father was a shoemaker) who had taught him to regard gangsters as bad guys and cops as good guys—a lesson reinforced by the radio show *Gang Busters*, which Serpico never missed, and by more than one occasion when, as a slighter-than-average teenager with a shoeshine stand, he was robbed by local toughs.

He had embarked on his career in 1959 with a view of the police profession shaped by radio and TV shows, comic books, movies, and a romantic cast of mind. By the mid-sixties, the bloom was off the rose. The reality of life in the trenches of the NYPD—precinct patrol in Bedford-Stuyvesant and Bushwick—had gotten to him, and unlike David he took no pleasure in doing battle with narrow-minded superiors or in debating the big issues of law enforcement with his coworkers. As events undermined his boyhood fantasies, a new dream arose to take the place of the original one: he would become a detective. Then and only then, he told himself, would he be free to do the job as he had first imagined it.

He would eventually prove to be a gifted undercover man. Enforcing the prostitution laws—normally a crude business—became a high art when Serpico applied himself to it. Most prostitutes tried to avoid making the sort of explicit statements the law required; they let their customers do the talking. So most cops simply rounded up the obvious suspects and falsely claimed in their reports (and, if need be, their courtroom testimony) that incriminating words had been spoken. Serpico insisted on observing all the niceties. To allay suspicion and give himself a plausible excuse for the inability to articulate his desires, he would pretend to be a foreigner—José, the factory manager from Madrid, or Pierre, the diamond merchant from Antwerp. He prepared for each role with the thoroughness of a method actor, and in his spare time he collected useful accessories: eyeglasses, hats, pipes, a walking stick, and European labels to sew into his jacket collars.

He brought some of the same theatrical air to his personal life. Although nature had not obviously cut him out for a career as a Don Juan, he seemed to emulate the *Playboy* magazine ideal of the young bachelor, with a different date for every night of the week and, it sometimes appeared, a different persona (rock fan, aficionado of the ballet and the opera, budding Scientologist) for each woman. (David later made a vain attempt to persuade him that he was leaving a trail of emotional havoc by speaking of love with women for whom his feelings were clearly more short-term.) Whether an evening's tryst was investigative or romantic, Serpico could spend hours in front of a mirror getting the look just so.

Even before his police duties included any undercover work, Serpico was preparing himself. He and David met in January of 1966 at the police academy, during a four-week in-service training program—known as plainclothes school—that dealt with prostitution, gambling, drugs, and undercover work. David had recently left the 18th Precinct for CIIU, and Serpico was about to be sent to a Brooklyn plainclothes unit. Riding the Twenty-third Street crosstown bus home from the police academy one day, he expressed shock at the cavalier way

David flashed his police shield as he boarded. Cops could legally ride free to and from work (the idea was to give the citizens added police protection at no cost), but Serpico had carefully cupped his shield in his hand so no one but the driver could see. "You're blowing your cover," he admonished David.

"Frank, you're carrying a manual that says 'Police Department' on it," David replied, "and you've just left the police academy. There are twenty cops on this bus! What cover do you think I'm blowing?"

———————

Plainclothesmen were not CIA agents. They were not expected to conceal their occupations from friends and neighbors. But Serpico told as few people as possible, and when friends and neighbors wondered aloud about his means of support, he often invented fantastic tales. He told some people that he was the child of wealthy parents with whom he had never gotten along—parents who had given him a generous allowance conditioned on his agreeing to stay far away. He told others that he was a remittance man. When asked by his more observant neighbors and his girlfriends why he carried a gun, he said it was for protection. Why did he need protection? Because his real line of work, he implied, was something he hadn't mentioned, something he couldn't mention. Soon the story got around—and Serpico did nothing to dispel it—that he was a hit man for the mob.

One of his reasons for hiding the truth may have been that, after six and a half years on the job, he was far from proud of what he did for a living. David was aware of the distance that divided him from his fellow cops, but it was a gap he wanted to bridge. He believed that his values and theirs were, at heart, the same. Serpico's mental trajectory was carrying him away from the police world. They were about the same age—David was thirty and Serpico twenty-nine when they met—but while one man was a product of the 1950s, the other was molten material for the sixties. Serpico grew long hair and a beard, and he took to wearing exotic clothes—bell bottoms, leather jerkins, lederhosen—on and off duty. Around the time of his transfer to the plainclothes division, he left Brooklyn and moved into a basement apartment on Perry Street, in the West Village—a strange address for a cop, and just as strange on the inside. The wall decor, after Serpico had fixed the place up, included a scowling African mask, a Spanish wineskin, a pair of buffalo horns, and directly over his bed, a scimitar. He had an authentic camel saddle for an armchair. The main source of illumination (or so David would remember) was a twenty-five-watt red lightbulb. Serpico had become a sort of hippie cop.

Occasionally, another cop would compliment him on his "great disguise."

"What disguise?" Serpico would ask, looking nonplussed.

————————

In plainclothes school, young cops learned just how far a prostitute had to go in order to be subject to arrest (she had to offer sex for money, in no uncertain terms) and how far an undercover cop could legally go (not far) in his efforts to induce such an offer. They learned the ins and outs of bookmaking, policy betting (numbers), and such ethnic games of chance as *bokapu* and bolita.

One of their instructors, a bulldog of a lieutenant named Grainey, dispensed useful tips on how not to come on like a cop. A good general rule for anyone working undercover, he advised, was to avoid eye contact; only cops looked people straight in the eye. If your assignment required you to hang out at a neighborhood bar, why not bring a small dog or cat with you, and wear bedroom slippers?

David was delighted with Lieutenant Grainey, and with plainclothes school generally, but he discovered that a lot of his classmates had their minds elsewhere. The predominant topic of hallway conversation was the money everybody would be making as soon as school let out. When older, more knowing cops compared notes on the size of the "nut" (the monthly payoffs that a squad had negotiated with local gamblers) in each command, their younger and more innocent colleagues perked up their ears in the hope of learning which units paid the most. (Seven or eight hundred dollars a month was typical, a thousand dollars or more not unheard of.) Nobody seemed to think that there might be any risk associated with this activity. Only fifteen years had passed since the Gross scandal, but as Robert Daley wrote in his memoir of a year as a deputy commissioner, the NYPD "no more studied its own history than a football team did."

Between Frank Serpico and David Durk lay a considerable class divide. Serpico had grown up in Bedford-Stuyvesant; David, on the Upper West Side. Serpico had taken a few night courses at Brooklyn College; David had a degree from Amherst. Serpico's parents had been thrilled by his decision to be a police officer; David's mother had been aghast. The two men would have been unlikely friends in the outside world. But in the corridors of the police academy, reeling from the cynical talk of their classmates, they gravitated toward each other. They started having lunch together, and having long conversations about the job and what was wrong with it. David talked about the signals that cops got from above—from department superiors who came down on them for honest mistakes or unavoidable mishaps and from lawyers and judges who held them to impossibly rigid standards of conduct while cutting themselves plenty of slack. It was unreasonable, he said, to expect cops to believe in the rule of law if they didn't see it at work in the halls of law.

Serpico was impressed by the ease of David's analysis. He was also impressed by the fact that, after less than three years on the job, David was working at headquarters, for Paul Delise. He couldn't help envying David, and the envy grew when plainclothes school concluded, and Serpico was sent to the 90th Precinct, in the Williamsburg section of Brooklyn. As a fledgling plainclothesman, one of his responsibilities was to follow up on what were called "communications"—letters complaining of gambling operations and other illegal enterprises. Allegations of police corruption were a recurring theme of these letters, and they were usually anonymous and often addressed to the police commissioner, the mayor, the director of the FBI, or some other important personage whom the sender considered trustworthy. Many of the letters either began or ended with a passionate appeal to the addressee that, at all costs, the matter not be referred to the 90th Precinct itself.

Serpico pursued every allegation as far as the evidence led him, and when he could, he made an arrest.

"Hey, Frank, you don't have to kill yourself over these things," his sergeant said to him.

"Why not?" Serpico replied.

Soon after his arrival, he became aware of whispered conversations that tailed off when he entered the room. A plainclothesman from another squad cornered Serpico in a luncheonette and gave him a friendly lecture on the need to fraternize with his coworkers—to reassure them that he was a live-and-let-live kind of guy. And that was, in fact, Serpico's inclination. If the other cops in the squad had been content to let him do his job his way, he would not have said anything about how they did theirs.

Serpico was by now a frequent guest at the Durks' apartment. He would bring presents for Joan Durk and her younger sister, Julie, and sit on the floor and clown around with them. Arlene helped him with term papers for classes he was taking at the John Jay College of Criminal Justice. One afternoon, he and David drove out to Bedford-Stuyvesant to visit Serpico's parents. After a generous lunch served up by his mother, they said their goodbyes and were in the process of leaving—they had scarcely stepped out of the front yard—when they saw two men holding up a third at knifepoint across the street. Without a word of discussion, David and Serpico drew their revolvers, circled wide left and wide right, and called out "Police!" and "Drop the knife!" It was a picture-perfect arrest. Holding the two suspects at gunpoint, they exchanged looks, and the looks became grins. In David's mind, those grins said, This is police work as it ought to be. Still warm from the wine he had been drinking over lunch, he started thinking what a terrific partner Serpico would make, for he was street smart and quick on his feet, and he didn't pause to ask himself what his superiors would say before he took action. And, like David, he loved the job. Not the department, but the job.

Late one night in August 1966—shortly after David had gone to DOI—Serpico called him in panic. Another plainclothesman, he said, had come up to him at the end of a tour of duty, saying, "I've been holding something for you. This is from Jewish Max," and Serpico had unthinkingly accepted an envelope that turned out to contain $300. Jewish Max was one of the bigger gamblers in the area. In Serpico's mind, though, the money didn't really come from Jewish Max. It was a letter of invitation from the other members of his squad to join the club; it was their way of satisfying themselves that he wasn't going to be a threat.

Serpico had put in for the plainclothes division with misgivings, a sympathetic captain having told him that, sadly, there was no other route to take if his goal was to be a detective.

"Well, you hear all these stories and stuff about plainclothes," Serpico had said.

The captain had heard the stories, too. "But, you know," he had replied, "no one can force you to do something you don't want to do."

Serpico wasn't out to launch a crusade—he was just looking for a way to extricate himself. David, listening to Serpico's story, was outraged, not only for Serpico's sake, but for the department's and the city's; he was thinking about the honor of the NYPD and about all the well-meaning cops, then and in the future, who might be subject to similar intimidation. An investigation was called for, he told Serpico. Maybe DOI could conduct it, using Serpico's information but keeping his role under wraps. The man who would know for sure, he added, was his boss, Captain Philip Foran.

Foran was a charming man who reminded Serpico of John F. Kennedy, albeit a shorter and less-polished version. He radiated warmth and good humor—qualities that evaporated quickly, however, as he listened to Serpico's tale. When the envelope with the three hundred dollars was submitted for Foran's perusal, he quickly handed it back, remarking that it had been a foolish move on Serpico's part to take money from someone he didn't know. Recovering his composure, Foran told Serpico he had two choices. One was to make an appointment with Commissioner Fraiman. If he went that route, he would probably be called to testify before a grand jury and, Foran added, could wind up "facedown in the East River." Foran's tone, as he said this, was that of a man conveying useful information, not someone trafficking in threats. The other choice, he said, was to forget that the incident had occurred.

"But what'll I do with the envelope?" Serpico asked. "I don't want anyone to think I kept it."

That, Foran told Serpico, was for him to decide.

"Maybe I'll give it to my sergeant," Serpico suggested.

Foran nodded his approval.

Serpico was not surprised by Foran's analysis, and though he was annoyed with David for giving him a bum steer, the meeting at least left him with the satisfaction of knowing he had tried to do the right thing. He then turned his energies to the task of getting out of the 90th Precinct as fast as possible. When he learned of a chance to transfer to a plainclothes unit in the Bronx, he was mightily relieved to be told by Cornelius Behan, a friendly captain from whom he sought counsel, that the 7th Division—his prospective assignment—was "as clean as a hound's tooth."

He reported to the 7th Division at the end of 1966, and soon was more miserable than ever. Responding to a complaint, Serpico and a tough-talking pseudoworldly plainclothesman named Robert Stanard went to a bar near Yankee Stadium and observed a gambler taking sports action. "Goddammit, we told you to stay the fuck out of here!" Stanard shouted (as Serpico recounted the incident to Peter Maas). "You were told this place was hot. We got a complaint, and now you're going to have to go."

The gambler insisted that the word had never reached him, and he pleaded for mercy, offering $200 as compensation. But Stanard insisted that an arrest was unavoidable, once there had been a complaint. The most he could offer, he said, was "a light one," meaning an arrest in which the paperwork would be rigged to allow any halfway competent defense lawyer to get the case thrown out of court. Serpico withdrew into the background while Stanard worked out his deal. The next morning, Stanard handed him a hundred-dollar bill as his share. When Serpico refused the money, Stanard took him for a ride—and an education.

What Stanard described that day was codified corruption, many years in the making. The nut in the 7th Division was $800 a month, and it was "clean money," Stanard said, because it came from responsible gamblers who were closely monitored. A plainclothesman needn't worry about being implicated in a wiretap, because only Italians had permission to take bets over the telephone, "niggers and the spics" being considered insufficiently discreet. The squad also preferred not to take money from bookmakers, for their business was largely transacted by telephone.

Gamblers who were on the pad were called "cousins." Other gamblers were vulnerable to "scores"—one-time bribes, sometimes highly lucrative, to get them out of a particular brush with the law. "And there's only certain locations they can work," Stanard added. "If they work other locations than what we tell them is okay, we can bust them for that. And if there's any heat on to make an arrest, we make the arrest, and that's it. So we're always covered."

If a gambler had to be arrested at a time he found inconvenient, he would volunteer to present himself at the station a few hours later, complete with incriminating evidence. The squad had monthly meetings to discuss the administration of the pad and to distribute the money in hand. Pickups were made twice a month by three "bagmen," of whom Serpico's regular partner, Gil Zumatto, was one. A new member of the squad, such as Serpico, had to wait six weeks before being put on the pad—"until everybody is satisfied you're okay," Stanard explained. When he left the unit, he got this lost money back as severance pay.

Although David got a blow-by-blow account of all this, Serpico now had a new confidant: Captain Behan, who was an aide in the chief inspector's office and, like Serpico, a night student at John Jay College. Tall, thin, and ascetic—an unofficial priest to cops with a serious Catholic bent, for whom he held weekend retreats—Behan was a classic example of what might be called the altar-boy cop, one who, rather than succumbing to the corruption around him, withdrew from it by getting assigned to some island of relative probity, such as emergency services, community relations, or the police academy.

Behan was not thrilled to be confided in. What Serpico was describing, Behan told him gloomily and repeatedly, was a "real bucket of worms." He entreated Serpico to take his complaint to the commanders of the 7th Division, but when Serpico resisted—how could he know how high the corruption reached?—Behan, guilty over having vouched for the integrity of the unit in the first place (on the say-so of a high-ranking colleague) finally, reluctantly, raised another possibility. He would go see First Deputy Police Commissioner John Walsh.

As first deputy—a post he had held under three successive police commissioners—John Walsh commanded a formidable intradepartmental police force of investigators, or "shoo-flies," who were known for swooping down on errant cops. He had joined the department in 1930, and some people thought that he, rather than Commissioner Leary, really ran things. Walsh was not a tall man, but he had a large, elongated head, sharply etched features, chalk white skin, and in the words of one associate, "the darkest, most piercing eyes I've ever seen." From the neck up, Walsh looked like a plaster bust of himself, and no one could have sat comfortably in a room with such a bust on the mantel.

After his retirement, in 1971, journalists, politicians, and police historians would point out that the department's anticorruption efforts during the Walsh years had been almost exclusively reactive—responses to complaints from people whose complaints could not safely be ignored. Even in those situations, the customary practice was to respond as narrowly as possible: to go after the specific incidents and the specific cops cited. Walsh and his minions never made an effort to turn a cop they had caught, using him to implicate others. "It just wasn't conceived of," William Bonocum, an inspector at Internal Affairs in the late sixties, said later. "The goal was to get rid of the bad apples, and we did it one at a time."

Rarely if ever did Walsh's people attempt to determine—through surveillance, neighborhood interviews, or other means—if an incident fell into a broader pattern. On the contrary, once they had caught a cop in a violation, they made a point of identifying and punishing him as swiftly as possible—a policy that had the effect, intended or unintended, of alerting other cops who might be engaged in the same conduct. Many cops, in any event, had friends in the various anticorruption units on whom they could rely for advance intelligence of an impending crackdown.

Every now and then, it would become impractical for the department to deny the involvement of a number of cops—maybe even an entire unit—in acts of corruption. Mass transfers were the usual remedy in these situations, and if the problem was messy enough, someone with a legitimate reputation for integrity might even be brought in, as Paul Delise was brought in to clean up CIIU in 1965. But such people understood that their role was a circumscribed one. "I think I worked for thirteen different commissioners, and I went through I don't know how many minor scandals," Delise recalled. "The department's reaction was always the same. They caught a few of the underlings, they made a little noise, and then they tried to put their head in the sand. I always felt that the department was more interested in its image than in anything else. Personally, I was never convinced that we had an image. We were trying to protect a nonexistent image."

After the shortcomings of Walsh's administration had become known, it was the virtually unanimous conviction of his colleagues that the former first deputy himself had never taken a dime. If he had let corruption slide, they said, he had done so out of a pessimistic view of human nature. Whatever his motives, he presided over a system that was ideally designed to perpetuate corruption. Following his departure, a memo was unearthed in which his right-hand man, Joseph McGovern—explaining his boss's refusal to act on corruption-related tips from the Federal Bureau of Narcotics and Dangerous Drugs—noted that Walsh "doesn't want to help the feds lock up local police. Let them arrest federal people."

Anthony Bouza, who retired from the NYPD as an assistant chief and went on to run the Minneapolis police department, remembered

Walsh as a "wooden titan—all form and no substance." At the time, however, Walsh was regarded inside and outside the department as "an implacable foe of corruption" and (in Jay Kriegel's phrase) "the most fearsome cop in New York City."

As promised, Behan spoke to Walsh. Serpico, with David accompanying him, was then summoned to a clandestine rendezvous on an exit ramp of the Van Wyck Expressway, near Kennedy Airport. Walsh was not present, but Behan, acting as his representative, reported that the first deputy had expressed great satisfaction on hearing of the existence of a plainclothesman of such high integrity. Informed of Serpico's desire to leave the 7th Division, Walsh had said that he was prepared to satisfy such a request—if Serpico insisted. Walsh's preference, however, was for Serpico to stay where he was, acting as the first deputy's eyes and ears while an investigation of the unit was mounted. Behan added that Walsh was prepared to meet Serpico "at any time of the day or night at the last station of any subway line in the city."

The arrangement appealed to the melodramatic side of Serpico's nature, and for the next six months, at considerable risk, he continued to gather information, telling himself that when his secret mission was over Walsh would undoubtedly bring him to headquarters and reward him with a detective's shield. In early April, however, Serpico's partner, Zumatto, revealed that he was going to be transferred. Serpico, in spelling out his own unorthodox attitude toward money, had said that he didn't care what anyone else did, as long as he, personally, was not involved. In that case, Zumatto had replied, he would "hold" Serpico's share for the present, and "whenever you make up your mind, it'll be there." Zumatto had also been good enough to safeguard Serpico's secret from the other members of the squad, and Serpico now became seized by the fear of being found out. He assumed—correctly—that Zumatto would make off with the money he had been "holding," and that the subterfuge would come to light as soon as his replacement appeared on the scene. The time had come, Serpico decided, to take Walsh up on his offer to meet at the end of a subway line.

He put in a call to Behan, who agreed to speak to Walsh. But when Behan called Serpico back to say that he had done so, it was clear that the conversation had taken a toll. The first deputy commissioner, Behan told Serpico, "often works in strange ways." The important thing was, Walsh was appreciative of Serpico's efforts and would be "reaching out" to him.

"When will that be?" Serpico wanted to know.

Behan suddenly lost his cool. He could not answer any more of Serpico's questions, he declared. His career as an intermediary was over. The first deputy would have to deliver his own messages in the future.

Serpico was in anguish about what would happen when the other members of his squad realized he hadn't been taking money. He was also deeply confused about his status as an undercover agent working for Walsh. "How can you say you're working for Walsh when you've never met Walsh," David had asked him. If Walsh intended to do something about corruption in the 7th Division, David had said, certain practical steps would have to be taken. There would have to be eavesdropping, photographic surveillance, and marked money. To arrange all this, someone would have to consult Serpico about times and places. The fact that no one had contacted him suggested that no such investigation was in the works.

Serpico was beginning to think that David might be right, and though going to see Captain Foran had been a mistake, David had a new idea that sounded far more promising. They would go to City Hall, where Serpico would tell his story to Jay Kriegel, and he, in turn, would tell the mayor. It seemed to David that Lindsay ought to know—would want to know—that the number two man in the department, alerted to a case of heavy-duty corruption, had done nothing. Serpico did not know Kriegel, but, like David, he imagined John Lindsay, from afar, as a sort of good prince who, if only he were made aware of the evil brewing in the farthermost reaches of his domain, would order an end to it.

CHAPTER

EIGHT

"**I** poured out my guts," Serpico said later, referring to the meeting with Kriegel. It took place in Kriegel's basement office at City Hall, on a Sunday afternoon in April 1967. After recounting his experiences in Brooklyn and the Bronx, Serpico spoke of the supposed relationship with Walsh, and of the perilousness of his current situation. From time to time, David prodded him with a reminder along the lines of "Tell him about paying the desk officers." But most of the prodding came from Kriegel, who was plainly horrified. David had not been exaggerating, after all.

What he and Serpico were after was an independent investigation with undercover agents, cameras, and electronic surveillance, and with no involvement of the top police brass, since that would include Walsh. David insisted that the current regime at police headquarters couldn't be trusted, that (as Kriegel later recalled him saying) "no one up there is doing anything—they don't care about corruption." But he also wanted to know whether, if it turned out to be impossible to launch an investigation of that sort, Kriegel or Lindsay couldn't at least take steps to get Serpico out of the South Bronx, since he obviously wasn't safe there.

Several times during the meeting, Kriegel responded with a "Wow!" or some other exclamation of amazement, and he concluded by saying that in view of the seriousness of the charges, the idea of an independent investigation did not seem unreasonable, but he would want to make some inquiries first about what headquarters was already doing in response to Serpico's allegations. The point was, he had to be sure that the new investigation didn't compromise an existing investigation.

David and Serpico left his office with the strong feeling that something was going to happen. By the time of David's next conversation with Kriegel, however, the sense of urgency had faded. Circumstances, David later recalled Kriegel saying, made it impossible to take any action until the fall. Priorities had to be considered. The mayor was struggling with a number of other problems involving the police department. He needed Commissioner Leary's cooperation, and he couldn't afford to "upset the cops."

David interpreted this as a reference to the much-talked-of threat of "a long hot summer" in the slums of New York—an unrelated concern, he told Kriegel, since there was generally no love lost between uniformed cops and plainclothesmen. Kriegel, afterward, denied having made any such connection, but he did not deny that the danger of large-scale ghetto violence was on his mind, and his boss's. That summer, a police raid on an after-hours club in Detroit set off three days of looting and burning that left the northwest quarter of the city looking "like Berlin in 1945," in the words of Mayor Jerome Cavanagh. Rioters and police between them killed thirty-six people, and only an invasion force of national guardsmen and army paratroopers succeeded in restoring order. During the same week, New York experienced a wave of violence in East Harlem that seemed mild by contrast (only two lives lost), and Lindsay and his policies were widely praised. He was becoming nationally known as an urban leader capable of taming the ugly forces that Americans associated with the inner city, and this was a reputation that everyone at City Hall was out to protect.

David had also been pressing the subject of police corruption on his boss, Arnold Fraiman. The Department of Investigation had generally let the police department handle its own corruption cases, but Fraiman had expressed a desire to break with this tradition. He was disappointed, he told David one day in late May 1967, at DOI's failure to make any significant police cases. And when David offered to introduce him to a plainclothesman who was prepared to talk about corruption in the Bronx (as long as his identity was protected), Fraiman responded enthusiastically.

The following Sunday afternoon, David and Serpico went to see Fraiman at his Park Avenue apartment, and Serpico told his story. A tall, broad-shouldered, athletic man—Clark Kent with a crewcut—Fraiman was a former federal prosecutor with a reputation for being "thoroughly incorruptible but very tough," as a piece in *The New York Times* had observed. But, to David's dismay, he unhesitatingly shot down the two investigative strategies that David and Serpico proposed: staking out the pickup spots and bugging the division office. "You're going to have to wear a wire and go out and get conversations for us," Fraiman told Serpico, prescribing the one course of action that he had flatly ruled out. Later, Fraiman explained his reluctance to get involved with Serpico by saying (David recalled) that Serpico had struck him as a "psycho."

David was infuriated by Fraiman's response, as he had been by Kriegel's. He was beginning to suspect that the Lindsay administration was not as different from previous administrations as it claimed to be.

His career at DOI, where he served from the middle of 1966 to the middle of 1969, would be a continuing education in the reluctance of his superiors to tackle difficult problems. It was a plum job, but David couldn't help noticing that the department spent most of its time going after easy targets—"little cases and little people," as he put it. One of his early investigations involved a city sanitation man who had picked up a load of commercial trash on the sly, each time collecting ten dollars for doing so. In another case, the target was a sign painter for the Department of Transportation accused of taking a few gallons of city-owned paint and putting them to personal use. David was ordered to go to Yonkers to remove paint-chip samples from the outside of the sign painter's house and send them to the police lab for analysis, although the sign painter offered a full confession as soon as he was confronted. "We spent hundreds and hundreds of dollars trying to prove the theft of about five dollars' worth of paint," David said later.

DOI was a complaint-driven agency: rather than conceive its own investigations, it responded to complaints. And the point of an investigation, as a rule, was to confirm or deny the original charge—no more and no less. Early in his tenure, David was asked to look into an allegation that cops and firefighters were getting into Broadway shows free. David and an unusually large investigator named Waldron Tidmarsh—"a pure mesomorph, the kind of guy who walked through doors sideways," David recalled—proceeded to the offices of the Shubert Organization, which owned or managed more than half the theaters on Broadway. After hearing them out, a Shubert official did some in-house research and reported that he could find no record of free passes going to cops or firefighters. But if they had any interest in passes for city commissioners, legislators, judges, and officials of the United Nations, he added, there were bountiful records of *that.*

"This case is going to be closed out," Tidmarsh predicted as they left the Shubert offices. When Fraiman heard what Tidmarsh and David had to report, he simply reminded them that the complaint had been about cops and firefighters, not about commissioners, legislators, judges, or UN officials.

In the summer of 1967, David worked on a case involving one of Lindsay's most highly touted programs, the Neighborhood Youth Corps, which ran (among other things) a summer jobs program using federal money. DOI had received tips about kickbacks in the jobs program; in Bedford-Stuyvesant, David found a young man who explained how the scam worked. Each participant in theory drew a salary of $38.38 a week; actually, he was given two checks in that amount, on the understanding that thirty dollars would be kicked back to his supervisor.

Some of the kickback money, according to David's source, was finding its way to high-level officials at 250 Broadway, where the

Neighborhood Youth Corps had its headquarters. He planted an informant there, and before long the informant reported that he had seen thousands of duplicate checks being prepared and placed in cartons, which he had taken the trouble to mark. David, without consulting his superiors, persuaded another DOI investigator, Edward Seidlick, to accompany him to 250 Broadway on an afternoon when the duplicate checks were being readied for distribution. At the door, David and Seidlick were greeted by Willie Smith, an exceedingly well built young black man who was one of Barry Gottehrer's aides. David showed his identification and explained his purpose: to take possession of the cartons he believed to contain the fraudulent checks. But Smith planted himself in the doorway, and deliberately striking the same pose as Arkansas governor Orval Faubus when federal marshals had attempted to take black children into the schools of Little Rock, he told his visitors, "You shall not pass."

While Smith's associates got on the phone to City Hall, David got on the phone to the DOI, explaining what he had reason to believe was afoot and seeking authorization to seize the checks. But the orders that came back from Commissioner Fraiman were for David and Seidlick to depart, leaving the checks where they were. (At such times, David was reminded of the fact that Fraiman, besides being a former prosecutor, had managed Lindsay's campaign operation in Queens.) A few days later, David was removed from the Neighborhood Youth Corps case. His unique talents, he was informed, were urgently needed on an investigation of the theft of chickens and other food supplies from the kitchens of Bellevue Hospital.

What upset him more than the outright fraud was the sort of people who got the most generous funding under these programs. In the course of his interviews in Brooklyn, he came across a middle-aged man who had been running a sports program for years, basically paying for it out of his own pocket. Here was the kind of person the city ought to be supporting, it seemed to David. But the Neighborhood Youth Corps had given the man a flat ninety dollars for the summer—less than two dollars a participant. Around the same time, David went to see Gottehrer, in order to ask him some questions about the program. While David was waiting in a reception area, two young men from a minority theater group walked in to talk about a $44,000 grant. When a secretary began telling them about some forms they would have to complete, one of them called her a bitch and demanded to see Gottehrer.

His attitude changed after Gottehrer appeared. "Are we getting our money, or do we burn the place down?" the man said, jocularly.

Gottehrer assured him that the money would be forthcoming. The paperwork was a necessity, he said, but he would give them any help they needed.

(Gottehrer later made no bones about the fact that a program promoted as benefiting disadvantaged kids had evolved into a structure of arrangements in which city and federal money was used to buy off people who appeared likely to foment trouble. According to Gottehrer, there was a conscious effort to identify "the worst kids in New York" and put them on the payroll.)

Early in the summer of 1968, there were complaints of renewed pilferage from the Neighborhood Youth Corps, and once again David commenced an investigation that was eventually halted on orders from above. This time, however, a fluke revived the case. Later that summer, uniformed cops stopped a car driven by several city employees who turned out to be transporting a stash of fraudulent checks. David was part of a team of DOI investigators who wound up arresting fourteen members of a group known as the Durham mob, because some of them had grown up in Durham, North Carolina. With stolen city and federal money, they had purchased a yacht and opened a nightclub in Trinidad. Their leader drove a silver Porsche.

After getting no action from Kriegel or Fraiman, Serpico went back to his friend Inspector Behan, disgustedly summing up the state of affairs in the 7th Division and adding that he couldn't put up with the place any longer—he would go back to uniform if he had to. Behan was shocked to learn that Serpico had never heard from John

Walsh. He was even more shocked by the news, which emerged almost incidentally in the torrent of Serpico's anger, that "outside agencies" had been made aware of the situation. The department, Behan told Serpico sternly, could "clean our own laundry." Serpico laughed.

The outside agencies to which Serpico had alluded were the Department of Investigation and the mayor's office. Neither of them had in fact evinced any great interest in his story. Nevertheless, he had spoken the magic words. As soon as it got out that "outside agencies" had been alerted, the police department began mobilizing.

The result, for Serpico, was a series of nearly hysterical meetings with high-level supervisors in the 7th Division. The supervisors then went to John Walsh, who, while giving no hint that he had heard any part of Serpico's tale before, ordered the division to launch an investigation of his charges. The division commanders were surprised to be asked to handle such a sensitive inquiry—to investigate themselves, one might have said. But in such matters, Walsh's word was law. Although Serpico refused to wear a wire, he provided the names of a number of gamblers who were subsequently arrested and encouraged to talk about the cops they were paying off. No thought, however, was given to the idea of having the gamblers make further payoffs, under surveillance, in order to secure evidence against cops who might then be turned. Inspector Jules Sachson, the commander of all plainclothes units in the Bronx, said later that there was "no particular reason" for the failure to use such tactics.

In the spring of 1968, the case was handed over to the Bronx district attorney, Burton Roberts, a blustery, cigar-smoking man famed for his theatrical press conferences. Roberts declared that the 7th Division had mishandled the case, and that he, Roberts, should have been brought in sooner. He vowed to leave no stone unturned and spoke of an investigation that would be bigger than the Gross scandal—it would sweep across the Bronx, Manhattan, Brooklyn, and Queens. In the end, Roberts's investigation did not even sweep across the Bronx. It stayed where it had started, in the 7th Division, focused on the handful of cops whose corrupt activities had been witnessed by Serpico personally. Ten plainclothesmen, including one sergeant and one lieutenant, were indicted—not for taking money but for perjury.

For a time, Serpico believed that his role in the investigation might remain confidential. But in December 1968, with the grand jury on the verge of completing its deliberations, he was ordered to report to the Manhattan North plainclothes squad. Soon after Serpico's arrival, one of his new coworkers confronted him with the rumor that he had testified against a group of cops in the Bronx. "The word is you went in there and didn't hold back anything," Serpico was told. Another cop opened a switchblade in his presence, remarking, "We know how to handle guys like you."

Serpico's boss was now Paul Delise. Meeting Serpico for the first time, Delise rose from his desk to shake his hand, and said, "I'm lucky to have you in my command—somebody that I can rely on." When it became apparent that nobody else would work with Serpico, Delise, an inspector, volunteered to be his partner, and explained that he was "still a door-buster." But Delise's hospitality was small compensation for Serpico's discovery that his part in the Bronx investigation—supposedly a secret—was common gossip around the department.

David, who accompanied Serpico to a number of conferences with attorneys from the Bronx DA's office, thought that he needed protection. "Frank's doing this for you—now what are you going to do for Frank?" he asked one of the prosecutors.

"He's got a gun, hasn't he?" the prosecutor said.

When David raised the same question with Roberts himself, he replied, coolly, that he was prepared to look out for Serpico's legal interests in the event that he found it necessary to shoot a fellow cop. He added that Serpico might do well to confine his travels to the Bronx and Manhattan, since Roberts could not guarantee that the DAs of Queens and Brooklyn would be equally supportive.

It soon became apparent that Roberts's people were counting on Serpico as their key witness when the cases came to trial. Serpico was furious when he realized this, and in the months that followed, he frequently implied or said outright that he had no intention of testifying. Roberts looked on him as just another recalcitrant witness. "Frank Serpico was not the overwhelming hero he has been made out to be," Roberts said later. "I suppose it was good that he came forward. No one else was coming forward. But everything he did, you had to pull teeth. 'I want you to testify.' 'Why do I have to testify?' 'Goddamn, you're going to testify!' Everything was a big production." Roberts blamed Serpico for the investigation's meager results. "He never gave us enough to enable us to get a bribery prosecution against any of those guys."

Perhaps Serpico would have been more cooperative (he would certainly have been happier) if anyone in a position of authority had held out the promise of a reward for his services. After his reassignment to Manhattan North, however, Serpico was detailed to antiprostitution duty in Times Square—the "pussy posse," as it was known—and if there was a more exalted assignment in his future, no one said so. The only member of the department's top brass who sought him out was John Walsh's right-hand man, Supervising Assistant Chief Inspector McGovern, who took the occasion of a brief meeting to chastise Serpico for assuming that the problem of corruption reached up through the ranks or out over the boroughs.

It was now 1969, three years since Serpico's first attempt to get some official action, and he was growing more and more bitter. The way to reform the police department, he told David, was to get rid of all the bosses—to "drive them out, like cattle." He spoke of quitting the department, perhaps to teach Spanish in San Francisco, a city that was more to his liking. His career as a corruption fighter was, he hoped, coming to an end, along with his police career.

David, on the other hand, had acquired a new and curiously optimistic outlook. For him, the crusade was just beginning. The batterings that he and Serpico had endured, he argued, only added to the scope of the problem that they would sooner or later succeed in exposing. Serpico's original complaint had been a small one, implicating a handful of plainclothesmen. What made it big, David took to saying, was the reaction. The scandal wasn't the behavior of a group of cops in Brooklyn and the Bronx, or that of the eight hundred plainclothesmen spread out around the city. Nor was it even the likely involvement of many of their superiors. It was the conduct of a succession of public officials who had been told what was going on and, for their various reasons, had failed to act. And, as David pointed out to Serpico, "We're both witnesses to that."

CHAPTER

NINE

———⇒⦿⇐———

A t the Department of Investigation one day in January 1969, the owner of a Greenwich Village antique shop showed up to lodge a complaint. Like many Village merchants, he owned a van, and he was in the habit of parking it in front of his shop. The difference was, he got parking tickets and his neighbors didn't. He had spoken to several cops about his problem, and a sergeant from the local precinct had encouraged him to think about "taking care" of the police.

The teller of this tale was a young man with long hair and a gold tooth with a diamond in it, and he was wearing a tie made out of bird feathers—a fashion statement that was a source of ill-concealed hilarity among the investigators who happened to be in the office at the time. Behind their smiles and snickers, however, there was authentic discomfort. DOI recruited its people from the police department (although the man with the bird-feather tie had no way of knowing this), and most of them wanted no part of a case that would pit them against their fellow cops. So they gave him the runaround, and it was only because he refused to go away—and only after one of the investigators, in desperation, passed him on to David—that he finally got a hearing.

He was David's kind of complainant—someone who, encountering an injustice, became consumed with the need to right it. At

David's suggestion, he telephoned the local sergeant and expressed a desire to work things out. They made a date to meet at his antique shop, and on the appointed day David was there, too, hiding behind a crate. But the sergeant failed to show. (David suspected that he had been warned off by a friend at DOI.) After waiting a few hours, David abandoned the stakeout and told the man with the bird-feather tie that he should keep a log of any parking tickets he received and note the license plate numbers of the unticketed trucks next to his own. Armed with this information, he could go to court and get his tickets canceled, and the cop who wrote them would have some explaining to do. "And if you ever want to make another complaint to a city agency," David added, "take my advice—don't wear that tie."

While they were talking, Frank Serpico happened to walk by the shop, and David invited him in, thinking he might be a useful witness to any further police harassment. It turned out that Serpico, who lived only a few minutes away, was already acquainted with the antique store and its owner. The three men chatted together for a while on the theme of police corruption. The man with the bird-feather tie was indignant about how the local cops had treated him. He made some sweeping statements about the venality of the police—too sweeping to suit David.

"Well, what about Paco here?" David asked, referring to Serpico by his nickname. "You trust him, don't you?"

The man with the bird-feather tie was dumbfounded. "You're a cop?" he asked, staring at Serpico.

Serpico, looking very uncomfortable, acknowledged the truth of the charge.

David knew that Serpico sometimes hid his occupation, but he had regarded this practice as an amusing idiosyncrasy, rather than (as Serpico saw it) a necessity of life for any right-thinking law enforcement officer residing in the heart of the Village, in the full flower of the 1960s. Even now, realizing his mistake, David was not exactly consumed with guilt about it. Serpico, however, was steaming over the loss of what he later called "my cover in the neighborhood."

All the while, in the back of the antique shop, an employee was quietly and methodically stripping the finish from an oak rolltop desk. He was a short, heavyset, exceptionally strong man without much hair; what hair remained was slick and black. He was dressed in a pair of dark trousers and a ribbed undershirt with straps—the sort of undershirt that nobody who was anybody wore anymore. When David left the shop, the "old man," as he would come to refer to him, followed him out the door and caught up with him on the sidewalk.

"You honest cop—I tell you about narcotics," he said, speaking with a slight Italian accent. As they stood together on the curb, the old man began talking about his neighborhood, East Harlem, and about his son Vinnie, who was nineteen. Vinnie had a chance to go to college on a football scholarship, but he had decided that his future lay in "moving packages" for an up-and-coming young drug dealer named "Ernie Boy" Abbamonte. The old man had worn himself out making speeches about the folly of this ambition. Nothing he could say carried as much force as the three to five thousand dollars his son could earn each week as a courier—far more than the father made from three jobs put together. The old man had no credibility with his son. "Here he was, working all the time—he left home at five in the morning," David recalled. "He was constantly exhausted, and his son ridiculed him for working so hard."

He had concluded that only one thing would make Vinnie rethink his choice of a career: the news that his hero Ernie Boy was behind bars. Could David arrange to put him there?

David began to explain some of the obstacles. He would need a lot more information, he said, thinking that he wasn't likely to get it from this obviously upstanding citizen. But the old man insisted that he could provide names, vehicles, addresses—anything David wanted. "I'll take you up there—I'll show you everything," he said.

"When can we start?" David said.

———◆———

Heroin, the illegal drug of greatest concern to Americans in the sixties, was not new. But it might as well have been, so little did most people remember of the alarm it had inspired in the early decades of the century. Drug use has tended to follow a cyclical pattern in our nation's history. A new consciousness-altering compound (or a new method of processing an old compound) is discovered, and people flock to it. Then, gradually, they get wind of its dangers, and its popularity wanes. The restraints on international shipping that came with World War II, following on a period of natural decline, produced an extraordinary trough in the cycle, where heroin was concerned. In the fifties, as incredible as it would subsequently seem, hard drugs were associated primarily with musicians, bohemians, and dissolute doctors (because they had the power of prescription). Few people knew anyone who used heroin (or, for that matter, marijuana, which had also enjoyed a vogue before the war), and the head of the Federal Bureau of Narcotics, Harry J. Anslinger, approached the end of a long career of agitation for harsher drug laws earnestly believing that his work would soon be crowned with the ultimate triumph: the virtual eradication of the trade in both drugs. To the consternation of Anslinger and other experts, however, the menace resurfaced, much like one of those prehistoric creatures that in the horror movies of the day had a habit of coming to life after spending eons encased in ice. One fairly restrained historian of drug abuse—David Musto, of the Yale School of Medicine—has estimated that the country had forty thousand heroin users at the beginning of the sixties, and half a million at the end.

The new epidemic spread with particular ferocity among young blacks—the children of the great migration from the rural South to the urban North. In keeping with the pattern of other transplanted groups—the Irish, the Italians, the Eastern Europeans—it was this second generation, raised in the new environment by parents whose habits and culture had been shaped by the old, who proved to be the most badly disoriented. Amid racism far more extreme than the prejudice those earlier migrants had encountered, facing an economy that seemed to have little use for them, they were a ready market for the heroin traffickers.

Whether heroin can fairly be called the cause of the many ills that have been laid at its door is arguable, but it looked that way to the growing number of people who saw the drug take over the lives of friends and near relatives. With its resurgence came spectacular increases in all the crimes that promised easy money: shoplifting, purse snatching, burglary, and theft of every sort, especially from automobiles. Although most people on heroin recoiled from more physically taxing forms of criminality, there were enough exceptions to account for plenty of muggings and holdups as well. In major American cities, the spread of heroin played a terrible role in the process that turned neighborhoods into ghettos and led to the decade's worst legacy: the emergence of what would come to be called the underclass.

David knew little about narcotics when he set out on his expedition with the old man. By the time he returned home, he knew some things the reigning experts in the field didn't know. The neighborhood he visited that night—a tiny Italian-American enclave that centered around a six-block-long street called Pleasant Avenue— was not known as an important source of narcotics. Indeed, according to the latest police intelligence, the Mafia generally shunned the drug business, regarding it as too dangerous. Several years would pass before the police and federal narcotics agents came around to believing that East Harlem was a central distribution point for heroin and cocaine going to Harlem, the Bronx, New Jersey, and parts of the Midwest.

David had never set foot in the neighborhood, but, as he told the old man, he had heard of Pleasant Avenue in connection with gambling. The old man replied that he had been a numbers runner in his youth. "But now the numbers guys can't find room to stand on the sidewalk on Pleasant," he said. "It's all junk. Heroin. Everything above 116th Street is junk." He had begun working for Ernie Boy's superiors years earlier, when their main activities—and his—had been gambling and loansharking. "I'm not a saint," the old man told David. "Who doesn't want money? But not heroin, not needles in kids' arms."

David's car, a green Ford, wasn't a police vehicle, but it looked dangerously like one according to the old man. "This car is going to heat up," he said as he got in. "Whether it's a cop car or it isn't, it looks like a cop car. Anybody in the neighborhood sees me in this car, I've got trouble." The old man decided to lie on the floor of the backseat once they reached East Harlem. David would describe what he saw, and the old man would interpret it for him. This precaution satisfied them— but not Serpico, who had been invited to go along. He had still not forgiven David for identifying him as a cop, and now he protested that they were going to get the old man killed by accompanying him to East Harlem. After registering his disapproval, Serpico got out of the car, and David and the old man continued without him.

They drove up the FDR Drive to the Ninety-sixth Street exit. As they turned onto First Avenue, the old man got into the backseat, explaining that they were about to pass Metropolitan Hospital, where Ernie Boy's mother went for thyroid pills. "She sees me with you, it would be just like Ernie Boy saw us," he said. When they stopped for a light at 106th Street, the old man told David to drive another ten blocks, and then start paying close attention.

At 116th Street, David saw a glut of double- and triple-parked cars outside a restaurant called the Delightful. "That's Buckalo's place," the old man said. "Half the avenue hangs out in there. Heavy action."

"Don't the precinct cops up here give out parking tickets?" David asked.

"I know for sure you never worked East Harlem," he answered. "There's no parking tickets up here. A lot of these cars are hot, but the cops don't touch them. The cops are all taken care of." One of the local cops, according to the old man, was a regular at the Delightful. "He's in there selling guns to the kids moving packages." Seeing David's shocked expression, the old man added, "What's the big deal? You never heard of a cop selling guns?" The old man had been an eyewitness to such a transaction barely a week earlier. Sitting in the Delightful, he had seen Ernie Boy Abbamonte buy five pistols—two .38 specials (the kind of revolvers cops carried), two .32s, and a .25 automatic. When a drug dealer needed heavier weaponry, the old man said, he went to a barbecue shop on 116th Street and rented a machine gun.

They came to a luncheonette and candy store that the old man described as "Nunzi's place."

"What do you mean, it's his place?" David asked.

"He owns it. It's a regular luncheonette, and he runs his junk business in there." The old man added that Nunzi was a small-time operative in the employ of someone named Jinx. Here, too, David was startled to see double- and triple-parked cars—a sign that cops were being paid off, and as David said later, "that all these people knew each other, so they would know whom to go to if they wanted to get their cars out."

David was supposed to watch for 2272—a social club run by Ernie Boy. On their first pass up First Avenue, a Con Ed truck blocked his view, but the old man snuck a look out the window and excitedly pointed out a double-parked bronze Lincoln. "That's Armand's car!" he announced. A few blocks farther uptown, he called David's attention to a pharmacy and explained that if the police were watching someone on Pleasant Avenue—the parallel street to the east—he could go into a tenement, and by way of a series of secret panels and passageways, come out of this building on First. A lot of the buildings were interconnected in this way, the old man said. He knew about these passages because he had helped build them.

At 120th Street, the old man told David to make a right turn and drive down Pleasant Avenue—"the Avenue," he called it—where the "real heavy action" was. There he pointed out several "mills"—apartments and storefronts used for cutting, packaging, and stashing heroin—and introduced a new cast of characters: Jerry Z., Johnny Echoes, Funzi of 111th Street, Funzi of 118th Street, and Bath Beach Funzi.

"Wait a minute," David said. "I've got three different Funzis here."

"What's wrong with that?"

"Don't any of these guys have last names?" David said.

After two circuits up First and down Pleasant, they decided they would be pushing their luck to linger in the neighborhood any longer, and the old man told David to drive over to a safe spot by the East River. When they had parked, the old man got out and brushed off his clothes, muttering about the dirt and dust. "This floor is terrible," he said. "Don't you think it's time you bring the car into one of those places and put a vacuum cleaner in here?" David said he would need to make another tour of the neighborhood soon. In the meantime, he would be checking some of the license plate numbers he had noted down and collecting photographs for the old man to identify.

"Just to lock up Ernie Boy? You need all that?"

David explained that if he just locked up Ernie Boy there would be other Ernie Boys to take his place. He was after the people Ernie Boy worked for.

The old man shook his head sternly. David was deluding himself, he said. Armand and Jinx were too high up. "Just worry about Ernie Boy. That's all I'm asking for."

Early the next week, David went down to the Bureau of Criminal Identification to hand-check the plates. In later years, mobsters would lease rather than buy their cars, but this had yet to become standard practice, so David was able to trace several of the cars he had observed to people with significant arrest records for gambling or drugs.

The elevators at BCI were notoriously slow. Waiting for the down elevator, David encountered a detective named Poppin, whom he knew slightly. Poppin asked David what he was doing there, and David said he was hand-checking records. Poppin said he was doing the same.

"You're in narcotics," David said. "Did you ever hear of a guy named Armand?"

Poppin had spent seven years in narcotics, where he was known as a rough-and-tumble cop who would work the most dangerous neighborhoods and the diciest undercover situations without backup. He regarded David as an exotic character—as far removed from his own milieu as some Scotland Yard inspector in an English mystery novel. "David wasn't in the real world," he recalled, long afterward. "He wasn't a grunt like I was. He was not really a detective. He was at DOI, and what kind of cases did they work on? Crap!" So it came as a shock to Poppin that David, of all people, had got a line on someone the Special Investigating Unit (SIU)—a citywide team of narcotics detectives who worked exclusively on major cases—had been trying to identify for months.

"Armand—that's one of the hottest names on the wires," he said. "No one knows who he is."

"Well, I do," David said. "I've got his name, his address, and his plate number."

SIU was divided into teams of four to six detectives each. Poppin's team had been working on a case involving a suspected dealer named Pickles. The name *Armand* had surfaced in some of the wiretaps put into place during the Pickles investigation, and it had become apparent that he was a more important figure than Pickles. Although Poppin and his group had moved on to other matters, another team of SIU detectives had picked up the trail, and Poppin mentioned one detective in particular who ought to hear what David had. His name was Robert Leuci.

By now, David knew he was on to something big. "I was ecstatic," he recalled. "I was thinking, 'This is going to be a great investigation!' " He and the old man met again on Sunday, February 13, this time under an approach ramp to the Triborough Bridge, in the thick of a snowstorm that David would later describe as "the only thing I don't blame John Lindsay for." (A lot of New Yorkers did blame Lindsay, if not for the snow, then for the slow pace of the city's snow removal efforts, especially in Queens, which contributed to a growing feeling among residents of the outer boroughs that Lindsay was Manhattan's mayor, not theirs.) David had brought a yellow legal pad, a pen, and a list of questions. After an hour, he could distinguish Funzi of 111th Street, Funzi of 118th Street, and the Funzi who hung out on First Avenue (a.k.a. Bath Beach Funzi), who picked up for Sal. But the old man was growing impatient with David's questions.

"Are you sure you're a cop?" he asked. "How come you don't know Bath Beach Funzi? Everyone knows Bath Beach Funzi."

"Humor me," David said.

They sat together in his car for four hours while the snow fell. By the time they had finished talking, David had a primitive map of the area, pinpointing some of the important hangouts and stash houses, and he understood that there were two main drug operations, one run by Armand out of a grocery store on Pleasant Avenue (a grocery store with a secret drug storage room, which the old man had constructed), and the other by Jinx out of Nunzi's luncheonette on 116th Street. Armand and Jinx each had scores of employees: cutters and packagers, who were mostly older men and women and did the work on a cottage-industry basis in small, stifling apartments (the windows had to be kept closed to prevent drafts); second-level dealers who actually handled the drugs; larbos—flunkies who acted as chauffeurs or lookouts; and delivery boys, like Ernie Boy. When someone made a major buy, the keys to his car would be handed to an Ernie Boy, who would put the load in the car and drive it out to the purchaser's neighborhood. Then he would make his way back to Pleasant Avenue, return the keys to the buyer, and tell him where to find his car.

The old man found an opportunity to mention the memorable fate of Whitey Marsh, an associate of Armand's who, after being exposed as a police informer a few years earlier, had been found, headless and armless, his genitals stuffed into his mouth. David's parting words were a solemn promise to safeguard the old man's identity at all costs.

The next step was to tell his superiors what he had. In view of what he knew by now about John Walsh and his anticorruption operation, David argued that the old man's information was too sensitive to turn over to the police department. But Robert Ruskin, who had recently succeeded Arnold Fraiman as Commissioner of Investigation, insisted that DOI had neither the manpower nor the expertise to handle a narcotics case. To assuage David's concerns, however, Ruskin agreed to bypass Walsh and relay the case directly to Howard Leary, "commissioner to commissioner." Moreover, he would ask Leary to refer it to Captain Daniel Tange, the commander of the Special Investigating Unit. David was pleased by that idea, for SIU was where Poppin and his friend Leuci worked, and David had it on Poppin's authority that Captain Tange was a straight arrow.

The upshot of Ruskin's call to Leary was the arrival, a few days later, of a deputy inspector and two detectives from SIU. One of the detectives was Robert Leuci, who was stocky and had round cheeks, gentle features, a thick head of dark, wavy, stylishly coiffed hair, and a moustache that did not completely accomplish its intended purpose of making him look like a savvy detective—which he was—rather than a high school kid. Leuci seemed to consider David's information important. At any rate, he took a stream of notes while David talked, and he was in the process of copying David's maps and charts by hand when David offered to make photocopies.

The other detective, Gene D'Arpe, and the deputy inspector, James Lane, seemed less impressed, especially after David made an allusion to the untrustworthiness of the uniformed cops in East Harlem. (He didn't tell them about the gun-running cop, however.) Lane wanted to know if David could supply the date and time of the next big shipment. When David said he couldn't, he was told that tips like his were routine—that narcotics detectives had a saying for hazy information of this sort: "Where's the bania?" Which meant, Where's the drugs? "What you got," Lane said, "is general intelligence. I could get this kind of stuff in the squad room of any station house."

"Well, if this is such common knowledge," David said, pointing to Leuci, "why is he writing it all down as fast as he can?"

Despite his demeaning assessment of David's information, Lane demanded the old man's name—repeatedly. Just as repeatedly, David refused. "But if you want," he said, "you can write out a list of questions for me to ask him. That way, if he's full of shit, as you say he is, then he can't answer the questions." Some of the questions, David suggested, could be traps: inquiries about made-up characters or requests for information SIU already had.

Historically, New York City cops had made a distinction between "clean" money, involving gambling, blue law, and liquor violations, and "dirty" money, involving prostitution, drugs, robbery, burglary, and more serious crimes. In 1964, when Bob Leuci was a uniformed cop weighing a possible transfer to plainclothes, he sought advice from Inspector Michael Codd, a future police commissioner who was then the commander of the Tactical Patrol Force, to which Leuci was assigned at the time. "If you had a son working here, would you tell him to go into plainclothes?" Leuci later remembered asking Codd.

"Why are you asking that?" Codd replied.

"Because I understand it's a really dangerous place—there's a lot of corruption there," Leuci said.

"You're right—stay where you are," Codd counseled him.

Later that same year, though, Leuci had a chance to go to narcotics, and Codd assured him that "there's not a cop in the world who would take drug money."

That was far from an accurate statement even in 1964, when Codd made it, and by the time of David's meeting with the delegation from SIU, the Narcotics Division was one of the most corrupt parts of a heavily corrupt department. The NYPD was still basking in the glory of what the public (with a nudge from Hollywood) viewed as law enforcement's greatest triumph over the heroin trade: the French Connection case, in which a major Mafia family was said to have been all but wiped off the criminal map. To those in the know, however, the case had a different significance. The Tuminaro investigation, as it was called by narcotics detectives, had produced a motherlode of police intelligence. Some of it had been used to effect the arrest of a handful of members of the Tuminaro crime family, but other suspects had reputedly made private deals with the police for sums of money that, by the bribery standards of the day, were breathtaking. Until then, corruption in narcotics had meant payoffs of a few thousand dollars at most; now, stories were circulating of bribes in the tens of thousands.

SIU had grown out of the team of detectives put together for the Tuminaro investigation, and some of the veterans in the unit had become the beneficiaries of long-term arrangements with major drug figures in Little Italy and East Harlem. "One of my partners had worked on the periphery of the case," Leuci said later, "and when I would mention an Italian name to him he would say, 'We can't work that guy—he has a commitment.' And I'd mention another guy, and he'd say, 'Yeah, that guy has a commitment,' and I'd say, 'Who doesn't have a fucking commitment? And what is this fucking commitment bullshit anyway?' The French Connection case is what opened the door, and then the door just kept on opening wider and wider."

Eight years after the French Connection case, a consensus of authorities held that the Mafia had largely bailed out of the narcotics business. Pro- and antidrug factions, it was said, had fought a war ending in victory for the antis, who considered drug dealing too risky, and perhaps even a little unsavory. Although the detectives in SIU knew better, this was a convenient fiction, for it relieved them of the need to explain why so few of the people they arrested were Italian. It also lent credibility, by analogy, to the thesis that no cop would touch drug money.

The unit had been established to go after the higher-ups of the drug trade, but SIU detectives preferred certain higher-ups to others. The Italians, "commitments" aside, were extremely careful. The top people never handled drugs or money. "Everything they did was on consignment," Leuci explained. "They would give away drugs, in the sense of saying, 'I'll give you five kilos, and you'll owe me a hundred thousand dollars—you pay me a thousand a week,' or whatever." Blacks and Latin Americans made more tempting targets, because even the major dealers among them carried drugs and money.

SIU was largely composed of men who, as David later observed, were poor in their twenties and rich in their thirties—and in prison (or under indictment) in their forties. From a series of trials and departmental hearings in the mid-seventies, there emerged a portrait of a unit in which the relatively honest cops were those who merely gave handouts of confiscated drugs to their informants and pocketed much of the money they seized—a practice justified as a transfer of wealth from the undeserving to the deserving and a way of making sure, in an imperfect world, that drug dealers paid some price for their crimes. "The prevailing attitude," one former SIU detective recalled, "was that the money was ill gotten, and who were you taking it from? The drug dealer doesn't deserve it—I have a family and I deserve it. Those were the practices. It wasn't viewed as such a terrible thing." The less honest cops were those who would take a bribe to let a suspected dealer go (or to let him get off lightly) or who resold the drugs they impounded.

The detectives assigned to SIU tended to live far beyond their police salaries. Fancy vacations were a tradition in the unit—a way of celebrating major collars. (According to another tradition, such vacations were rarely docked against a detective's store of annual leave.) A number of SIU men had impressive houses well outside the usual police neighborhoods of Queens and Staten Island. Some of them wore long suede or leather coats. Some went in for expensive haircuts and manicures. One spent nearly $10,000 on cosmetic dental work. Several drove luxury cars. Anyone looking for evidence of something wrong would not have had to look very far. But in 1969 and 1970, no one was looking—except for David.

The commander of the Narcotics Division at the time was Assistant Chief Inspector Thomas C. Renaghan, a colorful and hard-nosed— but soft-bellied—Irish cop of the old school. Renaghan was on close terms with one of the city's leading gambling figures, Hugh Mulligan, who was later revealed to be making police payoffs on other gamblers' behalf as well as his own. During Renaghan's tenure, Mulligan was, in effect, doing job interviews for the Narcotics Division. If you were a cop who wanted to get into narcotics, you went to Mulligan, and if he considered you trustworthy, he put in a good word for you with Renaghan. These aspects of the Renaghan regime would come to light, however, only after his voluntary retirement in 1970. At the time, Renaghan was said to be a severe disciplinarian who had been sent to narcotics to help clean up the place following allegations of "financial irregularities" under his predecessor.

Narcotics was a highly remunerative, and not very demanding, assignment for a supervisor. "You didn't have to do anything except sit in your office and open your desk drawer," Leuci said. "I had bosses who wouldn't even talk to me if I didn't give them money. I'd say, 'Can I get next week off?' and they'd open their drawer. That's the way it was."

In 1972, when SIU was finally consumed by scandal, attention would be centered on the most sensational and tawdry aspects of the story, and the public would not have much outrage left over for such minor departures from approved procedure as the faking of affidavits, the use of illegal wiretaps, and the compensation of informants in the coin of drugs. But these all-but-universal practices were, in a sense, the defining characteristics of narcotics work in the NYPD, and they probably played as much of a role as the theft of money and drugs or the sale of information in explaining the way David was treated by the SIU delegation that came to hear his story. He wanted to be involved in a major drug investigation, and the top people in narcotics—even Deputy Inspector Lane, a comparative newcomer—knew right away that this was a relationship to be avoided, for it was an article of faith among them that catching major drug dealers and following the letter of the law were incompatible goals. Even if an investigation was conducted in what SIU considered to be an honest fashion, there would be procedural shortcuts that no outsider, especially not one associated with a "rat-type unit"—as DOI was viewed—could be permitted to see.

So David's visitors had been given a prepared script. Regardless of what he told them, they were supposed to tell him that they knew it all already. Lane and D'Arpe found the script easy to follow, but Leuci was torn. "I tried to tell him, 'This is worthless,' " Leuci explained later, "but as soon as he started talking, I was thinking, 'Holy shit! This is really good stuff!' It may not have been a hundred percent accurate, but David's informant had more information than anybody else had—that's for sure. Back then, there was very little real inside information about organized crime—about the Mafia connection with drugs. What little was known, people didn't put in files—they sold it. It was used as legal tender, you know. And here was this guy talking about names—nicknames—of very important people, and who and what they were, and how each person fit into the overall scheme of things. Armand—there wasn't a federal narcotics intelligence guy I spoke to later who didn't say, 'He's the guy!' And David had identified him. The truth is, David was describing what turned out years later to be the biggest drug cartel in New York. But no one knew it, not even David!"

Leuci figured he could trust David because Poppin had vouched for him. Poppin, in describing David, had used the essential, but ambiguous, phrase "good guy." "When somebody said to you, 'This guy's a good guy,' it covered a lot of bases," Leuci said. "It could mean the guy's a crook. Or it could mean that he didn't give a shit if you were. Generally, it meant a standup guy. The police department was like organized crime in its language. In organized crime, you trust someone immediately if he's vouched for by someone else you trust. So when someone I considered a good and dear friend—someone who knew me and knew the world I lived and worked in—when he told me that this guy was a good guy, that's all I had to know."

Leuci had been working on his own Pleasant Avenue case for months, and it had become a fixation with him. As he retraced his thinking more than two decades later, he had become fed up with being told whom to investigate or not investigate. David was offering him a chance to arrest a group of top-level Italian drug traffickers. Time would not be kind to Leuci's reputation for veracity, and in the Pleasant Avenue case the facts are open to less charitable interpretations—for example, that Leuci was out to make a spectacular score rather than a spectacular collar. Whatever his motives, though, David and the old man represented to him a significant breakthrough in a stalled investigation.

"We were knocking our heads against the wall," Leuci said. "We were going nowhere, and I said, 'My God, this guy can really do something for us!' My enthusiasm for David's information was really going through the roof. I was also taken with David himself. He was looking around at all of us in wonderment. I said, 'This guy's really funny—he's a believer.' He believed that there was a clear distinction between good guys and bad guys, and that we were all on the good-guy side, and we were fighting this great religious war."

So Leuci could not quite bring himself to give David the brush-off, and at his instigation another meeting was arranged, this time at SIU's offices on the third floor of the old 1st Precinct, near the Fulton Fish Market. "I'll never forget the day David came over," Leuci said. "I was late getting to the meeting, and Chief Renaghan saw me coming upstairs and called me into his office. He was this great old Irishman who was always chomping on a big cigar. I called him Uncle Tom, and he called me Little Guinea Fuck. He said, 'You little Guinea fuck, get in here! What in the fuck is that Jew doing upstairs?' "

Leuci explained that David had some good information.

"About East Harlem?" Renaghan asked.

"Yeah," Leuci said.

"Then I don't give a fuck how good his information is," Renaghan said. "He could have Vito Genovese on a platter. Get him the fuck out of here! If there's work to do, you do it! Stop trying to get help, especially from somebody like that!"

Shaken by the reprimand, Leuci continued upstairs, where he ran into Captain Tange, the head of SIU. Good-looking, clean-cut, religious, well spoken, and known as a martinet, Tange was one of the youngest captains in the history of the department, and there were those who appraised him as potential Chief of Detectives material. On his arrival at SIU, in 1967, he had delivered a tough speech, vowing to be merciless with any cop who was unproductive or corrupt— in his words, "if I catch you as much as stealing a piece of gum." For a few weeks, the unit had been plunged into a state of panic. Then Tange had quietly put out the word that he was more malleable than he had made out. He had purchased a house on four acres overlooking Long Island Sound, and he was depending on his men to pitch in with the mortgage money. "You have a new partner, and it's me," Tange had said to Leuci at the time.

Tange seemed to be as put out with Leuci as Renaghan had been. "Whose idea was this?" he demanded.

Again, Leuci explained the source of his interest in talking to David. "I'm telling you, he's got great stuff," Leuci said. "He's light-years ahead of where we are."

"Okay, let's see if we can get the informant," Tange said. "If we can get the informant, great, but I don't want this guy Durk around here. I already checked on him, and the guy's trouble. All he wants to do is come to work here, and don't tell me he wants to come to work here because he wants to work on narcotics. He wants to be a spy."

David arrived at SIU that day in blissful ignorance of the consternation he had caused. He was pleased to see that his welcoming party did not include Inspector Lane, who had given him such a hard time at DOI. Another encouraging sign, he thought, was a set of oak tag charts combining the old man's information with SIU's own intelligence. The charts were sitting on a table in the middle of the SIU squadroom, where—after David had been checked through the caged doorway that divided SIU (so top-secret were its activities) from the rest of the Narcotics Division—he was greeted by D'Arpe, a sergeant named Gabriel Stefania, and Leuci.

David had brought the old man's answers to a list of questions Leuci had composed at the end of their last meeting. They were good answers, according to Leuci. But that was all the more reason, he added, for SIU to question the old man directly. "You know nothing about narcotics," he pointed out.

"Okay, you'll have to educate me," David replied.

They argued this point for a while, and finally the SIU people presented a fallback proposal. If David wouldn't let them meet the old man face-to-face, what about a phone call? "You make the call, and let us talk to him," Leuci suggested. "We won't know the number."

But David, who considered himself bound to protect the old man's identity at all costs, figured they would find a way to trace the number. "Look, the purpose of the questions was to validate him," he pointed out. "So he answers the questions. Now he's validated."

When it became clear that the issue was nonnegotiable, David was sent to see Captain Tange. Having heard only good things about Tange, he assumed he would now have an opportunity to clear the air. Tange, however, had a message of his own to deliver. He had heard the story of David's chance encounter with a man from East Harlem who wanted to rescue his son from the drug business. He had heard it, he said, and he didn't believe it. There was no such thing, Tange asserted, as a law-abiding source. David must have something on the guy, and that being the case, there was no reason for David not to deliver him to SIU. "You're not going to put one over on us," Tange warned him. "You're not going to jerk us off. You're going to give us the name!"

David said he had no choice in the matter—he had made a commitment.

"You're just trying to worm your way into our office so you can get out of DOI, and be picked up here," Tange said.

"Well, you can think anything you want, but I am not giving you my informant," David retorted.

When every other argument had been exhausted, Tange pointed out that he was a captain and David a detective. This served to remind David not only of his place in the rank structure, but of the fact that, sooner or later, he would be transferred back to the police department, where his disloyalty would be remembered. Waving a finger at David, Tange told him, "If you ever do anything to embarrass this command, I'll have your back broken."

"Here I was giving them this stuff on a platter," David remembered, "and they were acting like I had handed them a bomb. First they tried the soft-paws approach—conning me into giving the guy up. With Tange, it was strictly threats—orders and threats."

At one point in the conversation, David found himself in the curious position of warning Tange and several of his underlings about security problems at BCI. He wanted to be sure that Tange's men, if they intended to check any of the old man's information out, would go down to BCI in person, as David had. If you called an inquiry in, David said to Tange, there was no way of knowing that some clerk wouldn't burn the case. Tange did not react well to the advice. "David was sitting in a room full of guys who were involved in all sorts of their own shit," Leuci said, "and here he was saying, kind of slyly, that maybe there might be people down there we couldn't trust. And we were all thinking, 'Who the fuck is this guy kidding?' Of course, he was absolutely right. Every one of us knew you could buy anything you wanted from BCI. But it was the kind of thing you didn't say. The only person who would say it was David!"

Tange concluded the interview by abruptly turning around to strike up a conversation with one of his men. When it became apparent to David that he had been dismissed, he started toward the door—where Leuci quietly intercepted him. In the presence of the other detectives, Leuci had treated him as badly as anybody. Now that no one was listening, he came on as a friend. He trusted David and valued his information, he said, and personally he would like nothing better than to work with David on the case. But David ought to understand that others in SIU felt differently. They were afraid that someone with David's background would raise a ruckus about extralegal practices—Leuci mentioned the example of "gypsy wires," or unauthorized wiretaps—in which members of the unit sometimes engaged. Leuci would try to persuade his superiors to give David the benefit of the doubt, but he wasn't hopeful. "Listen, Durk," he said, "I shouldn't even be talking to you, but I want to tell you something. Don't put your heart in this one."

As soon as Leuci had made this little speech, he regretted it. He had meant only to establish a bond with David, as a prelude to his efforts to extract the identity of David's informant. He had assumed that any friend of Poppin's—a purported "good guy" into the bargain—would know all about gypsy wires. But David was acting as if Leuci had made a major confession.

Years later, trying to recall how his life had begun to come unraveled, Leuci would home in on this brief conversation with David, and on the rash moment when he decided to give David his home phone number. At the time, though, he had plenty of confidence in his ability to steal David's informant, and he reasoned that once he had done so he would no longer need David. He was used to getting his way. He came across as affable and accommodating—the kid brother who just wanted to be part of the game. But he had a large store of charm, and he deployed it artfully. He studied people, figured out their hopes and expectations, and did his best to conform to them. Only the cops who had worked closely with him knew how well he had done for himself in his years at SIU.

Leuci came from a working-class Italian-American family. His father, a foreman in a pipe factory, was openly contemptuous of the quick money to be made in organized crime, which was the world of some of their not-too-distant relatives. The neighborhood where Leuci had grown up was half Italian and half Jewish; Leuci hung out with the Italian kids during the day, but at night he liked to visit the Jewish kids' houses, where he listened to their parents talk about politics and literature. He was a compulsive reader—Conrad and Hemingway were favorites of his—and he became the first member of his family to graduate from high school. He even spent a year at a college in Kansas, until homesickness got to him. He was going to be a cop, he told himself, and what did a cop need with a college education?

Leuci's plan of action with David was simple. They would spend some time together, David would come to regard him as an ally, and before long he would be allowed to meet the old man. Then Leuci would be in the driver's seat, because the old man would see how much more Leuci knew about the narcotics world than David did.

Leuci was working on an investigation in the West Seventies. He began visiting David after hours and having long, late-night conversations with him. In very little time, he realized that David was adamant about protecting his source's identity. Even so, the visits continued. "I'd sit in David's apartment listening to him talk and trying to figure out what the hell planet did this guy come from," Leuci recalled. "He would go on until all hours of the night. He was almost evangelical. He was talking about the police world—what it was, and what it should be. The theme of our conversations was, 'If you had a fantasy of what you'd like the police department to be like, and how you would like to do your job, what would it be?' He saw the best side of people. If you supported cops, if you gave them the opportunity to be honest, their best instincts would come out. When I listened to him, I heard this wonderful, naïve view of the world. It was like an opera!"

As he listened to David, Leuci was pondering certain practical as well as moral questions that loomed ahead. Corruption in SIU was out of control, even by the lax standards of the rest of the police department. The unit had just been through a minor shake-up, resulting from some unsubstantiated charges made the previous year by a federal narcotics agent who was himself later caught dealing drugs. There was no telling when someone else might make accusations, and have the facts to back them up. That someone might even be David Durk.

Another year and a half would go by before Leuci felt free to do more than hint at the true nature of the corruption at SIU. Well before then, though, Detective Poppin had given David a rough picture of how things were. Every so often, David would run into him in court or at BCI and press him for the inside dope on what was happening (or not happening) with the Pleasant Avenue case. "I kind of sympathized with him," Poppin said later, "because they were giving him a hard time and I suspected he was on to something." But Poppin thought it best not to become involved in what he judged to be a volatile situation, so after several worrisome encounters with David, he called Leuci and begged him to "get this guy off my fucking back!"

"Hey, wait a second," Leuci said, "you're the one who brought him to me!"

"Don't remind me," Poppin said. "Look, talk to him, will you? This guy trusts you, for some fucking reason."

One day, though, Poppin sought David out in a hallway of the Manhattan courthouse and began talking about his urgent—previously unmentioned—desire to get out of SIU. "The whole place is really a mess," Poppin told David, "and it's going to blow wide open."

When David asked him to elaborate, Poppin gave him the names of half a dozen SIU detectives who, to his knowledge, were making scores. He said he had heard detectives talk of accepting payoffs of as much as $50,000 to destroy the records of an unauthorized wiretap or undermine a case in court. On more than one occasion, a fellow detective had approached him with an offer of money, and though he insisted that he had always refused, the degree of his own personal culpability was almost immaterial, he added. SIU was so rotten, according to Poppin, that no one would be safe in the event of an inquiry. It was a miracle, he thought, that the unit had not been swept by scandal long ago. One minor but widespread impropriety was the practice of taking days off that were not docked against a cop's annual leave, so that the records showed him working when he wasn't. In SIU, as in other detective units, three-day work weeks were common. This meant that if an SIU team fell under investigation, it could be hard for anyone to show that he had not been present when a bribe had been paid.

"We had the best sick-leave record in the whole department, because no one ever got sick—officially," Poppin said. "The official record would show you were working with the team even if you were off. It would show you were at a given place at a given time, when you weren't. I figured if I stayed too long I would get in trouble, and history bore me out. Entire teams were arrested because of the actions of one guy. It was not difficult to get yourself jammed up."

Early in David's discussions with SIU, he began renewing his appeals for permission to work on the Pleasant Avenue case personally, along with a group of DOI investigators of his choosing. But Commissioner Ruskin wasn't buying. DOI, he reasoned, was a small, overworked unit with no experience in the narcotics area, and Renaghan and his people would be furious if Ruskin trespassed on their turf. David, Ruskin had decided, was simply dissatisfied with his regular duties and looking for a chance to launch a grand investigation of his own concoction. Undoubtedly, there was corruption in SIU; there was corruption everywhere. But Renaghan and Tange had assured Ruskin that David's case would be investigated, and they would never have the nerve to burn a case that had come to them from the police commissioner himself. What David was experiencing, Ruskin assured himself, was not a corruption problem so much as it was a personality conflict. Ruskin told David to have patience and show "a spirit of cooperation."

Cooperating with SIU was easier said than done, however. Tange had designated John Egan, one of his lieutenants, as David's official contact, and Egan was almost invariably out when David telephoned. On one of the rare occasions when David succeeded in getting through, Egan told him that a team of SIU detectives had made several trips to East Harlem without locating any of the cars that David had identified.

Another time, when David was told that Egan was out, he asked for Leuci, who came on the phone to say, "I'm not supposed to talk to you."

"Gee, that's odd," said David. "I'm a detective, and you're a detective. Why can't we talk to each other?"

"We've all been ordered not to talk to you without a boss present," Leuci said. "But I'm asking you, for the record, to tell us who the informant is."

"After what you just said, I should tell you who the informant is? Go fuck yourself!"

All the while, David was meeting the old man once or twice a week, usually in David's car, over carryout calzone or manicotti. "Where are the pictures?" the old man kept asking, and David kept coming up with excuses. He had promised to bring a set of mug shots for the old man to examine. But the only way to get them was through SIU, and David had made repeated requests, to no avail. Rather than admit his powerlessness, however, he told the old man that investigations of this kind took time. "It's being worked on," he said, "but there's a problem with current photos."

Things were not going well for the old man. Vinnie, the son he had hoped to keep out of the drug business, turned out to have been in it all along, first as an apprentice, then as a full-fledged member of Ernie Boy's team. This came out in the course of one of David's talks with the old man. During another, the old man reported that Vinnie was no longer moving packages—because he had been caught in the act of "borrowing" a kilo of heroin from his girlfriend's father, a major distributor. He had intended to make a windfall profit by selling the kilo directly to a black dealer in Brooklyn—the sort of high-risk transaction that was frowned on by the Pleasant Avenue types. Now he was living at home again, lying in bed, chain-smoking, and watching TV.

The old man had asked for the arrest of a single drug dealer, and that dealer was not only still at large but was prospering as never before. According to the word on the avenue, Ernie Boy Abbamonte was buying a house in Sands Point, near the estate of Frank Costello, the venerable Mafioso credited with the inspired idea of carving the nation into family territories. The old man found it galling that a "fucking punk like Ernie Boy" could afford to live in Sands Point, "down the road from Costello." It seemed to him that the police could arrest Ernie Boy whenever they wanted. He told David that a couple of detectives from the 25th Precinct had very nearly done so. After stopping Ernie Boy's car one day, they had found a large quantity of heroin, two handguns, and a shotgun, and they had brought him in. Instead of formally arresting him, however, they had urged him to get on the phone and arrange his own ransom. Within a few hours (as the old man relayed the story), friends of Ernie Boy's had delivered $50,000 in cash, and the detectives had agreed to set him free—with the three kilos, but without the guns. But Ernie Boy had balked at the terms. It was unreasonable, he had said, to ask him to walk the streets, unarmed, with three kilos of heroin. Won over by this argument, the detectives had let him have one of the guns as well.

David went back to Ruskin with this story, hoping, once again, to get a DOI investigation going. By now, however, Ruskin had heard as many complaints from SIU about David as he had heard from David about SIU. David was meddling—that was how Ruskin read the situation—and this latest tale sounded like a convenient excuse for further meddling. Ruskin had been Commissioner of Investigation for only a few months, and he was already thinking that David and problems related to David took up too much of a commissioner's time. Ruskin told him to leave Pleasant Avenue alone—to let SIU work the case in peace.

In desperation, David decided to go back to Jay Kriegel. In their previous discussions of corruption, David had been talking mainly

about the enforcement of laws that were not of fundamental concern either to the Lindsay administration or to New Yorkers in general. Now, it seemed to David, what he had to say was of a far higher
order of urgency. "This isn't gambling—this is narcotics," he told
Kriegel. "You've got to see this firsthand. I'll show you the goddamn
cars that the Narcotics Division can't find."

On the night of March 28, 1969, David Durk and Jay Kriegel drove
up to East Harlem in Kriegel's car, a snazzy MG convertible. It proved
to be a lucky night for such an expedition. David was able to point out
Armand's bronze Continental and several other vehicles that SIU
professed to have been unable to locate. Kriegel said later that he was
struck by what seemed to be burglar-alarm wiring spread across a
block of dilapidated storefronts that didn't look as if they could possibly contain merchandise requiring such fancy protection. David took
the occasion to tell Kriegel all about the old man, and about Tange's
threats, Leuci's hints, and other signs that something was badly
amiss with the Narcotics Division and SIU.

In a sense, this was hopeful information. Unlike many of the things
John Lindsay had attempted to do in his three years as mayor of New
York, straightening out the Narcotics Division would not require the
cooperation of the city council or the state legislature; it was wholly
within the mayor's power. Here was a problem that could be set right,
and by setting it right Lindsay might actually have an impact on the
drug traffic. On police-community relations, too, for, as the old man's
testimony suggested, suspicions of corruption were rife in neighborhoods of the city where drugs flourished, and nothing was more
likely to turn law-abiding citizens against the police. Kriegel, if he
had been disposed to regard David's evidence in this light, might have
thanked him for identifying a place where the Lindsay administration could make a difference and then eagerly relayed the tip to the
mayor. But making a difference had never been the Lindsay administration's only purpose, and at this particular period, other objectives
had moved powerfully to the fore.

Lindsay had been elected mayor at the height of America's post-war prosperity—the height, also, of postwar optimism and generosity, and of a certain trusting attitude toward government. Like Lyndon Johnson, whose landslide victory in 1964 was propelled by the same political tide, Lindsay entered office with a dizzying array of bold (and not always well-considered) plans. Over the next three years, the tone of politics, nationally and locally, changed, and the base of support for Lindsay's sort of activism was badly corroded. The Vietnam War played a big part in this process, of course, but so did a growing feeling among more fortunate Americans that the less fortunate were not properly grateful or well behaved. As Americans, especially city-dwellers, became more anxious about their possessions and their personal security, their anxiety gave rise to the politics of law and order.

The governor of New York State, Nelson Rockefeller, was one of the first important political figures to seize on this issue. In 1966—a gubernatorial election year—Rockefeller prodded the legislature into enacting a law that dictated five years of involuntary "rehabilitation" for anyone found to be a drug addict, even if he had not been convicted of a crime. Later, Rockefeller advocated the creation of "emergency camps" for addicts, and New York State, at his urging, adopted a set of severe mandatory prison sentences for those convicted of drug-related crimes. The Rockefeller drug laws, as they came to be known, had no discernible impact on drug use or crime. (They did seem to have the effect of reducing both arrest and conviction rates, as police officers, prosecutors, and judges became more hesitant to consign petty users and dealers to the law's mercy; they also clogged the courts with cases that, in former days, would have been plea-bargained. For those convicted, however, prison sentences got longer, and prison building was the area of greatest expansion in state government for many years to come.)

Rockefeller never did achieve his life's ambition of the presidency, but the man who preempted him in 1968, Richard Nixon, showed that drugs and crime could be very potent political issues at the national level. Nixon's proposals—including no-knock search warrants, tougher penalties, and a massive program of border seizures known as Operation Intercept—had no measurable impact on crime or drug use either, but they sounded tough, and sounding tough was the order of the day.

John Lindsay had tried to resist simplistic solutions to the drug problem. Early in his mayoralty, he had put the emphasis on treatment programs and on the economic revitalization of depressed neighborhoods. By 1969, however, the federal money behind New York's ambitious redevelopment plans was starting to run out, with little to show for the sums that had been spent. Although New York had avoided a single, massive burst of racial violence of the sort that had struck Newark, Detroit, Los Angeles, and Washington, D.C., there was no less desperation per capita in its slums than in other cities, and the wear and tear of vandalism, arson for profit, and real estate abandonment had left sections of New York looking scarcely better than if a riot had hit them. Meanwhile, crime had increased sharply, and the charge that Lindsay and liberals like him were soft on crime—that they had "handcuffed the police"—had become a heavy political liability. The first priority of every important member of the Lindsay team, accordingly, was to remake the mayor's image, with the goal not only of getting him reelected but of positioning him to run for president a couple of years down the road, a topic of endless, giddy speculation in the Lindsay circle—speculation all out of proportion, it turned out, to his viability as a national candidate.

As the 1969 mayoral election drew near, Lindsay began to resort to the common-denominator vocabulary of politicians discussing crime: more police, more arrests, tougher penalties. He called on Washington to send a thousand federal narcotics agents to New York. He called on the police department to redouble its efforts to lock up drug dealers and to "zero in on the leaders of organized crime who sit behind the scenes directing this insidious traffic." In practical terms, what this mainly came down to was a substantial expansion of the Narcotics Division, and, in particular, of the unit that specialized in going after major traffickers: SIU.

The Narcotics Division, whatever its faults, made arrests and seizures (statistically, SIU had a dazzling record of accomplishment), and these occasions were opportunities for the mayor to stand beside his police commanders and proudly show what he was doing to wage war on drugs. David was asking Lindsay to confess that the whole business was a sham—that SIU had become virtually an appendage to the criminal enterprise it was supposed to destroy. For Jay Kriegel, whose quick mind had helped make him one of Lindsay's closest advisors, it was the work of a millisecond to calculate the political fallout. As the police historian Thomas Reppetto later observed, "A mayor doesn't get a lot of credit for exposing a police scandal, unless he's brand new in office. The headline isn't going to say, 'Mayor Takes on Age-Old Problem.' It's going to say, 'Police Scandal.' "

David had a vision of a transformed police department—an institution that existed to support and encourage good cops and good police work. For him, an honest reckoning with corruption was the essential first step. But the people at City Hall saw the department and its needs in a very different light. Looming over all such questions was the painful memory of the quest for a civilian review board. With that one great, lost battle, the Lindsay administration's idealism had been just about spent where the police were concerned, and now the word was out: no more fights with the police department. Lindsay would give cops computers and better radios and a new headquarters—all the things the Rand Corporation had recommended; he would pose with them when they made arrests, and praise them to the skies. And that was to be pretty much the extent of his police program from here on out.

After driving back downtown together, David and Kriegel had a long talk while parked in front of a synagogue next to the Durks' building. Kriegel, according to David's subsequent testimony, said he was persuaded of the need for a major overhaul of the police department. Once the mayor had made it safely past the election, Kriegel indicated, he would at last be in a position to tackle the issue of police corruption, even if Leary and some of his top people had to go. But

Kriegel added that Lindsay could not afford to take on such a struggle now—not with the campaign just around the corner.

Although David still hoped to influence decisions at City Hall, his sense of affinity with the mayor and those around him had largely evaporated. Over time, Kriegel's conversation had become increasingly concerned with priorities, trade-offs, timing (David's, it seemed, was always wrong), and "blank checks"—as in, "We don't have a blank check on that one, you know." Kriegel had become an expert in toting up the political pluses and minuses of every policy option, but it seemed to David that the city itself had gotten lost in the equation.

CHAPTER

TEN

—————

The term *whistle-blower* implies the act of a moment—a simple deed, even if you have to screw up your courage to commit it. For David, blowing the whistle was a five-year pilgrimage in which, sometimes alone and sometimes accompanied by Serpico, he pressed the corruption issue on a series of "people with flags in their offices." Even the decision to give up on the Lindsay administration and go to the press meant only that one phase of his struggle had ended and another had begun.

In New York City, in the 1960s, the press and the police had a cozy thing going. Crime reporting meant manning the "shacks"—dingy pressrooms located next to the major police facilities throughout the city. From the shacks, reporters monitored the police radio, responded to promising emergencies (sometimes ahead of the cops), and cultivated warm relations with those bosses and detectives who were in a position to dispense hot information about the latest gruesome crime or glorious arrest. It was the rare reporter who would willingly jeopardize his contacts by challenging the police side of the story; you pretty much had to be a minister or a bank president if you had a complaint against the police and wanted the press to take it seriously.

This was the pattern not only with the tabloids and the TV and radio news shows, but also with the city's (and the nation's) most esteemed daily, *The New York Times*. While the *Times* would not permit itself to wallow in the details of an ax murder or a Mafia roundup as the *New York Post* or the *Daily News* would, stories from the police blotter accounted for much of its crime coverage, and the balance consisted mainly of faithful recitations of policy pronouncements coming out of City Hall or Police Headquarters. It was less juicy flackery, but flackery all the same.

"Except for a few scandals, we were Pollyannas when it came to the police," Martin Arnold, a longtime veteran of the *Times* local staff, has said. "Not only cops but lawyers and judges were treated with a kind of civics-book courtesy. Occasionally, there would be a big investigative piece about an abstract component of the system—the prisons, for example. But no one questioned anybody's honesty or competence. Every judge was some sort of legal scholar. We gave them a respect far beyond anything they deserved."

Arthur Gelb, who took over the job of *Times* city editor in 1967, had served a brief term in the shacks in the late forties. He remembered what police reporting had been like then, and he was disturbed to see how much it was still like that. Crime was way up; heroin addiction had become a national calamity; there had been riots and near riots in inner-city neighborhoods around the country; academics were starting to write about the police officer as an isolated and overwhelmed figure upon whom society had placed impossible responsibilities. And hardly a hint of all this could be found in the way the *Times* treated the police.

A tall, long-limbed man, Gelb invested a good deal of care in his dress and deportment, and his journalistic heart was torn between hard news and the arts. Stephen Crane, Lincoln Steffens, and John Reed (as well as Eugene O'Neill) had been youthful heroes of his, and his reverence for the great muckrakers had endured through a twenty-year apprenticeship at the *Times*. In a highly bureaucratic environment, his warmth and spontaneity stood out. "There was nothing of the apparatchik about him," one former reporter said, after

Gelb's retirement in 1990. When Gelb heard a story idea he liked, his enthusiasm was without limit, and he would rush around the newsroom looking for a young reporter to assign it to. Sometimes he would send a reporter off with a whispered, "And remember, *there's a great deal of interest in this story.*" He could be equally dramatic in his dissatisfaction with the finished work. With Gelb, a reporter always knew where he stood.

Gelb saw that the old approach to crime and the police would no longer do, and he began soliciting advice about how to handle these subjects differently. One of his advisors was the chief public relations man for the president's crime commission, a young former journalist named David Burnham. Usually, when a reporter becomes a PR man, it is safe to assume he cares more about salary, benefits, and job security than about what he does for a living. Burnham was an odd case. After stints as a reporter for United Press International and *Newsweek* and as a writer for the *CBS Evening News*, he felt unfulfilled. His employers had wanted the obvious; he had wanted to dig beneath the obvious. He took the job with the crime commission in the hope of learning as much as he could about how the criminal justice system worked, or, quite often, didn't.

A lot of energy and seriousness of purpose was packed into Burnham's slight, balding figure, and there was a scary glint in his eye when he became exercised about something. Burnham on the track of a good story reminded one admiring colleague of John Brown at Harpers Ferry. He had been summoned to the *Times,* ostensibly, to offer suggestions on the paper's crime coverage. The appointment was not a job interview as such. At one point in the conversation, Gelb went as far as to ask Burnham to propose some names of people the *Times* might consider hiring for the police beat. At long last, however, Gelb posed the question Burnham had been waiting for: "What about you?" Burnham joined the *Times* in the summer of 1967. He was hired, like other newcomers, on the understanding that his first six months would be a trial period—a chance to prove his worth.

In the nervous weeks that preceded his move from Washington, D.C., to New York, he sought counsel from many sources, and one of his crime commission colleagues—Alfred Blumstein, later the dean of the School of Urban and Public Affairs at Carnegie-Mellon University—said something that made a lasting impression. "You should focus your energies," Blumstein said, "on writing stories that show why the police or the district attorneys or the judges do not achieve their stated goals—what stops these agencies from working as they are supposed to."

Blumstein's advice, Burnham realized later, was a rationale for aggressive journalism ideally suited to the cautious surroundings of the *Times.* It conceded, up front, that the press's role was not to challenge the objectives of the institutions it covered but to measure those institutions against the objectives they set for themselves. Between their claims and their accomplishments, Burnham sensed, lay territory wide and rich enough for a reporter to spend a lifetime exploring.

It was virgin territory in the local pages of the *Times.* Burnham "totally changed the way the *Times* covered the criminal justice system—and not only the *Times,* but American journalism," Arnold recalled later. "He opened up a whole new era of skepticism." At the outset of his *Times* career, though, Burnham was in no danger of being perceived as a muckraker. He did the circuit of law enforcement conferences and composed sober, thoughtful articles; CRIME RESEARCH IS FOUND LAGGING and INNOVATION URGED IN SOLVING CRIME were two of his early efforts. Gelb took Burnham to task for the infrequency as well as the academic tone of his output. When Burnham's probationary period was up, he was told that he had neither passed nor failed. He would be given the rare privilege of another six months in limbo.

Late one night in the spring of 1967, David Durk was home with his family when his former partner at the 18th Precinct, Gregory Roth, appeared at the door. Roth was on duty, in uniform, and badly shaken. He wanted to talk about some things that had been happening on West Sixty-fifth Street. A mailman who lived in one of the tenements there had come home to find his apartment ransacked and his collection of family photographs missing. A woman with four children, whose husband was hospitalized with cancer, had complained of urine being poured into her apartment through a hole in the ceiling. Another tenant had found a dead dog left to decompose in a vacant apartment next to hers; the front door had been removed to help spread the odor. That very day, Roth had taken an arson report from a woman whose bed had been set on fire while she was at work.

The buildings in which these incidents occurred stood on a site being assembled by one of the city's largest and most respected real estate firms, Pease and Eliman, for the planned construction of a thirty-one-story luxury apartment tower and, next to it, a fourteen-story office building that would house the Jewish Guild for the Blind. Many of the tenants had already moved out. Those who remained had become the responsibility, from a real estate point of view, of a burly young man named John Chaisson, who had worked his way into his current profession—building management—by way of the demolition business. He lived in a suite at the nearby Mayflower Hotel and visited his properties, accompanied by a couple of henchmen and a Doberman pinscher, in a blue Cadillac convertible that had his initials on the license plate.

Roth had turned in reports that were as graphic as he could make them, but to no avail. He could only conclude that someone above him was being paid off. "I feel ashamed talking to these people," he told David. "Can you do anything about this? Who do you know? Because I'm getting nowhere with the police department."

David tried to get a DOI investigation going but was unable to persuade his superiors that DOI had jurisdiction. Then he had the inspiration of calling the *Times*. He reached John Kifner, a reporter on the metropolitan staff. A few nights later, David gave Kifner a tour of the area and showed him a copy of Chaisson's yellow sheet. Five times, Chaisson had been arrested for felonious assault. Five times, the charges had been dismissed.

The upshot was a powerful front-page story—TENANTS IN "DOOMED" WEST SIDE BUILDINGS CHARGE HARASSMENT. Kifner quoted Chaisson as saying that he had never "put my hand or my mouth on anybody." The people at Pease and Eliman, for their part, took the position that whatever might have transpired under Chaisson's management was not *their* fault, since they had not hired him; his employer was a dummy corporation set up by the sellers of the properties. "The street was the reason I got interested in this," William Lese, the Pease and Eliman vice president who had conceived the plan, explained to Kifner. "When you came out of Lincoln Center, there were these people sitting on their bongo drums, and intermixed with them, rent-controlled tenements where people thought they were getting a castle for sixty dollars a month. There was a lot of crime on that block, and I feel pretty good about cleaning up this trouble spot."

By the time Kifner's article appeared, Chaisson was out of a job. He had been fired as soon as Kifner began asking questions about him. "If there's anybody that's been grossly abused in this, it's been me," Chaisson declared. The article prompted several city agencies to announce investigations, and Chaisson soon found himself under indictment. It was the first story David had leaked, and it was a memorable, front-row experience with the power of the press. "It certainly got everybody moving," he recalled.

Then as now, David was a close student of the police news, and he could get fairly emotional when a story struck him as off the mark. In the fall of 1967, the *Times* ran an article about an experiment in the 20th Precinct, which supposedly proved that expanded foot patrol was a way to reduce crime. The reporter was Burnham, and David had been following his work with mounting displeasure. "I thought he was living in a bubble," David said later. The 20th Precinct experiment was part of a highly successful effort by the police in the Lindsay years to justify major increases in manpower. To David, it was clear that what the city needed was not *more* cops but more effective cops. It was equally clear to him—and so he told Burnham, after reaching him by phone—that the evidence in the 20th Precinct had been cooked. According to a lieutenant quoted in the story, crime had gone down by 20 percent. According to David, the pilot program had not been in effect nearly long enough to evaluate its results, and crime had gone up in the neighboring precincts as much as it had gone down in the 20th. Besides, there was no way the city could afford the same level of foot patrol everywhere else.

That story dealt with, David moved on to a broader critique of Burnham's work, and to a discussion of some police stories the *Times* had overlooked. As was his habit, David jumped around a lot, introducing a considerable cast of characters in a short space of time. Later in their relationship, Burnham would use the word *cosmic* to describe this mood of David's, and he would learn that it was possible to talk him down from the cosmic state. At the time, he just sat there, dumbfounded, trying to understand some small part of what David was saying. "He laid out quite a lot of stuff," Burnham remembered. "He seemed quite insane."

David looked back on their meeting as a "disaster" and blamed himself for trying to educate Burnham in too many aspects of the police world at once. He also blamed Burnham for failing to mention the key fact that, being on probation, he needed attention-getting stories in a hurry. In a subsequent conversation, Burnham clarified his status at the *Times*, and David gave him a usable tip about a police intelligence unit that was spending most of its energies on student radicals rather than serious criminals. This was more like it—more like what Gelb wanted and expected. But it was small potatoes.

In July 1968, Burnham landed on page one with a long front-page feature on police violence, which pointed out that virtually all the department's highest awards went to cops who had been in shootouts. On David's advice, he had asked the police department for data on the screening of recruits, and the numbers helped him show that the department had virtually never let someone go for using unnecessary force. (Or for any other reason: it was next to impossible for a probationary cop—unlike a probationary reporter—to be fired.)

In December, Burnham hit page one again. "Night after night, in obscure corners all over New York, policemen on foot and policemen in patrol cars disappear into their 'coops,' " he wrote. ". . . Cooping appears to have become a regular part of police operations and in some instances it is even accepted by the citizens. In one precinct in the Bedford-Stuyvesant area of Brooklyn, for example, one coop in a park became so well known that the residents referred to it as the 'annex.' "

Burnham had been introduced to cooping—the expression and the practice—by a retired cop to whom he had put his standard question about what kept the police from doing their duty. One of Gelb's deputies had told Burnham that cooping was beneath the *Times*'s notice, but he had persisted, doing most of the reporting on his own time and recruiting a copyboy to go out with him at night and take photographs of cooping cops. The lighting conditions dictated long exposures and the use of a heavy old box camera and tripod, making the whole operation anything but discreet. "When the camera clicked for the first time it sounded incredibly loud," Burnham said later. But the cops, to his relief, slept on.

The man who covered the police for the *Daily News*, William Federici, was livid when he saw the cooping piece. "That's no story!" Federici hollered at Burnham. "Everybody knows it!"

Another harsh critic of the story was David Durk, who lambasted Burnham for singling out cops as opposed to other figures in the criminal justice system. "The only reason cops are sleeping on the late tour is because they don't have a goddamn thing to do!" he complained. "They assign cops to these insane posts! And if you bring in a case after one A.M., you know you'll have to wake up the desk officer to get him to book the collar, and he's going to be enraged. He's going to say, 'Why weren't you in the coop?' " The photographs that ran with Burnham's article—photographs of radio cars occupied by sleeping cops—bothered David even more than the article. The department, he told Burnham, would blow up the pictures, find out who the cops were, and punish them. Burnham thought David was fantasizing. He pointed out that the *Times* had deliberately blurred the pictures to make the numbers on the cars unreadable.

As it turned out, David had predicted the police response fairly accurately. In a speech to his assembled commanders, Commissioner Howard Leary belittled the scope of the problem, but warned: "For your men to patrol ninety-five percent or even ninety-eight percent of the time is not good enough for me." (The use of these wildly high percentages, which implied that a cop was somehow not entitled to an ordinary coffee break, robbed the speech of any credibility it might have had inside the department.) Meanwhile, Walsh's deputy, Joseph McGovern, summoned Burnham to headquarters and grilled him about the dates, times, and places of his observations, and the names of his sources. "McGovern was quite scary—he was sort of a bully," Burnham recalled. He declined to provide any of the information McGovern wanted, but, even so, the department managed to identify—and discipline—most of the cops unlucky enough to have had their pictures printed in the *Times.*

"Are you happy now?" David asked him after events had borne out his fears.

Burnham viewed the department's reaction as a sad commentary—but a commentary on the workings of bureaucracy, not on the merits of his story. He was sorry for the cops who had been made scapegoats, but he wasn't going to spend a lot of time worrying about them. You couldn't make an omelette without breaking eggs. And while David had been right about the response of the department, the story had a larger effect he failed to anticipate. The Lindsay administration had called for a "fourth platoon"—a new police shift that was supposed to bring added coverage in the high-crime hours of the evening. The fourth platoon could not be instituted without a change in state law, and the PBA was fighting the necessary legislation, claiming that—in the words of the union's always-quotable president, John Cassesse—it "would give Lindsay the uncontrolled right to play field marshal with New York's law enforcement officers." At first, the legislature seemed inclined to back the union. After Burnham's story appeared, the political mood shifted, and the fourth platoon won approval—one of the rare occasions when the pols in Albany gave Lindsay something he had asked for.

To Burnham, however, the reaction in Albany was not as important as the reaction at the *Times.* Gelb thought the cooping piece was terrific, and when Gelb liked a story, he made his pleasure known. "Wonderful! Wonderful!" he would exclaim, or "Oh, this is terrific!"

With the cooping story, Burnham's probation was over. The *Times* had accepted him.

———————

Toward the end of 1968, or perhaps early in 1969—none of the participants is sure just when—David brought Frank Serpico to a dinner with Burnham at a steak house in Greenwich Village. David and Serpico had by now sized up the Bronx investigation for what it was: a carefully limited inquiry that would pose no threat to business as usual outside Serpico's own unit. They told Burnham the story of Serpico's career in plainclothes: Brooklyn, the Bronx, Foran, Behan, Walsh, Kriegel, Fraiman, and the rest. David talked about corruption elsewhere in the department. But it was all strictly off the record. The rationale for talking to Burnham, David and Serpico agreed, was insurance. If anything happened to them, Burnham would tell the world what they had been up to. Otherwise, he was forbidden to tell anybody, including his editors.

Even if the evening had been on the record, Burnham might not have blabbed about it, for he found the conversation exceedingly hard to follow. What he retained were "all these names flashing around"—Walsh, McGovern, and so on—"and a lot of precinct numbers and police initials." He "had an instinct that there was something there, but it was a puzzle, and I couldn't, of course, use it." When he got home that night, he typed up his notes of the dinner— such as they were—and filed them away.

During the spring and summer of 1969, David was hounding SIU about Pleasant Avenue, and hounding DOI about SIU's inaction. Here was evidence of a far worse form of police corruption than the gambling pads. While plainclothesmen were widely distrusted within the department, the Narcotics Division was held in high esteem, and the detectives assigned to SIU were the elite of the elite. Kriegel had indicated, after his trip to Pleasant Avenue, that only the small matter of John Lindsay's reelection stood in the way of a purge at police headquarters. In June Lindsay went down to a humiliating defeat in the Republican primary, and suddenly it seemed unlikely that

Kriegel's views, or Lindsay's, would matter much after the end of the year. But the mayor declared his intention to remain in the race—on two minor-party lines—and in late September the *News* released a straw poll that showed Lindsay, to general astonishment, running far ahead of the presumed favorite, the machine Democrat Mario Procaccino. David seized the moment to bring up the subject of corruption with Kriegel again. How soon, he wondered, might the mayor get around to appointing a new police commissioner?

"I never said we were going to get rid of Howard," Kriegel replied.

David, who thought he had heard Kriegel say exactly that, blew up. He called Kriegel a liar, and added, "All bets are off."

Kriegel responded that David was being "childish."

That night, David, who had been telling Kriegel about police corruption for more than three years, made up his mind that he would rely on Burnham and the *Times* from here on out. By election day, when Lindsay won a narrow victory, he and Burnham had begun plotting a major exposé, which would bring together some of what David knew about SIU and the Narcotics Division and the information that Serpico had supplied about plainclothes. For the time being, though, everything was still off the record, and would remain so while David made an exhaustive effort to go through channels. The idea, he explained to Burnham, was to make it clear to everyone that they had gone to the press only after pursuing every other possible course. "We're going to talk to everybody," he said. "City, state, and federal."

Burnham, almost alone among the many outsiders in whom David confided during these years, believed the problem was as bad as David said it was. To put together a major story on corruption, however—and Burnham was thinking in terms of a series of articles—he would need more time than a newspaper reporter was normally allowed to invest in a single assignment. To get that kind of time, he would have to get Arthur Gelb excited, and so, one day that fall, he brought David and Serpico to Gelb's office for a background briefing.

Serpico was not sure he trusted Burnham, and he was sure he *didn't* trust the *Times*. On the way to Gelb's office, Burnham was

explaining some of the difficulties he might encounter in documenting the story to his editors' satisfaction, and Serpico sourly predicted
that the *Times*, like everyone else, would find a reason to sidestep
the issue. Almost as soon as they arrived, David told Gelb that everything they said was for background only. He added that Serpico
didn't believe the *Times* would have the nerve to print such a story, in
any case.

"Who told you that?" Gelb demanded, looking at Serpico.

"He did," David said, pointing to Burnham.

"Thank you, David, for that show of trust," Gelb said.

If Serpico had doubts about the *Times*, Gelb had doubts, at first,
about Serpico. He was wearing an earring and looked (so Gelb
thought) like a buccaneer. "He had long hair and a beard, and that
was before reporters did," Gelb said later. David, in Gelb's recollection, was the "impresario," and Serpico the uneasy leading attrac-
tion. Serpico talked around the story at first, coming clean only when
Gelb interrupted to say, "Either you trust me or you don't." But the
meeting accomplished its purpose: Gelb was hooked. Maybe Durk
and Serpico were exaggerating, he told himself, but even if they were,
it was a hell of a story. After they left, Gelb instructed Burnham to cut
himself away from everything else he was doing and devote himself
full time to police corruption.

———————

David's situation at the Department of Investigation had deterio-
rated. He had fallen into the habit of dividing his professional life in
two: his days were given over to the cases his superiors had assigned
him, and his nights, weekends, and spare moments to the cases that
they had told him not to work on—or would have told him not to
work on, if he had asked. He longed for the day when he would be
paid to do what he considered his real work. His bosses, meanwhile,
longed for an investigator who would do what he was told without
grousing about it.

That summer, Burnham mentioned David's name to a former federal prosecutor, Henry Ruth, who was running a criminal-justice

research and planning program out of the Justice Department, in Washington. Ruth had grant money to dispense, and he was looking for people with ideas about how to spend it. He sought out David, who put forward two ideas. The first was to study the value of decoys and undercover agents. The second was to attempt to assess the feasibility of recruiting police officers on college campuses. Ruth went for the recruiting idea, and the grant came through in timely fashion. In August 1969 David was promoted to sergeant. (He was promoted not because anyone had decided that he had leadership potential, but because, according to the completely mechanical and "objective" process by which the department chose supervisors up to the level of captain, he had taken a written test and had come away with a high score.) He expected to remain at DOI, in keeping with a request that Commissioner Ruskin had sent, as a formality, to Commissioner Leary. But for reasons that no one ever shared with him, Leary's office turned the request down, and the newly named Sergeant Durk was reassigned to desk duty in the Washington Heights section of upper Manhattan. After only a few days there, however, he was given a leave of absence from the NYPD, and he started recruiting.

In the fall of 1969, David began making periodic sweeps of colleges (Harvard, Yale, and his alma mater, Amherst, among others), where, in small group sessions that he had set up in advance, he sought to convey his view of police work as the best job in the world—the perfect cure for the postgraduate blahs. A portion of the audience, inevitably, consisted of students who had come to gawk or jeer, as they might have come to a recruiting session for Dow Chemical, the manufacturer of napalm. David was delighted to have these people on hand, for they were meat for his argument. "If you believe that all is lost and the next step is the barricades, this job is not for you," he would say. "If you see social progress as a mass movement with you as the director, this job is not for you. But if individuals count, become a cop. If you want your values to prevail, you or your surrogate has got to be there. . . . You say you want to do good. I'm telling you how. . . . Maybe you plan to hide behind a mask and join some company. You think once you get to the top you can throw off your mask and say, '*Shazam*, it's me, good guy.' Sometimes you find that the mask fuses with your face."

Although the project had been conceived as a feasibility study, it snowballed, and Henry Ruth, for one, was astonished by the reaction. At a time when cops were persona non grata on many of the nation's college campuses, hundreds of students turned out to hear David, and many responded enthusiastically to his pitch. "He seduced them," recalled Burnham, who wrote about David's campus appearances for the *Times*. "It was a really neat idea: 'Why go into the Peace Corps? Stick around here.' "

One person who didn't think the idea was so neat was Elmer Cone, the NYPD's Chief of Personnel. Cone had a TV in his office, and when David went to see him—armed with the names of twenty aspiring cops from Yale—he found Cone and three deputies watching a baseball game. It was the World Series, and the Mets were in it, as virtually every New Yorker but David—a conspicuous nonfan of organized sports—was well aware. The TV remained on throughout his visit, but Cone and his men found time during slack periods and commercial interruptions to make a number of wry remarks about David's recruiting scheme, their basic thrust being that no college graduate in his right mind would want to become a cop, and that those who did were bound to be troublemakers.

Between the baseball game and the relaxed demeanor of his hosts, the atmosphere was almost barroomlike. Still, David made an effort to be deferential. Even after he had heard himself described as a "starry-eyed idealist"—a term that grated—he continued to address everyone by his right rank, and to speak in what for him was a fairly mild tone of voice. "I told them that if I had a choice, I would rather be called a *pragmatic* idealist," he recalled. "I was fairly well behaved in those days." It was only when someone suggested that David was a dilettante who didn't know what real police work was about—it was only then that he lost his cool, offering to bet that he had made more felony arrests than all the other men in the room put together.

He had gone into the meeting with the idea of somehow speeding up the recruiting process for his applicants. By the time he left, he had secured Cone's unqualified assurance that the NYPD would never hire any of them. Cone was as good as his word. But other cities, including Washington, D.C., and Los Angeles, were more receptive, hiring scores of people David had directly recruited and many other college graduates who came forward independently.

———

There was a period in the early eighties when, under the terms of an edict from Mayor Ed Koch, David made a point of not talking to reporters. With that exception, he has been talking to them—and prodding, interrogating, testing, and wearing them down—for three decades. His technique was still in an early stage of refinement when he began dealing with Burnham, but even then he could be a trial to a reporter's patience and a challenge to his sense of dignity.

Between October 1969 and April 1970, David and Burnham rarely let a day pass without talking to each other. David introduced him to merchants and cops, taught him the vocabulary of police corruption—words like *pad, nut,* and *score*—and generally threw himself into Burnham's work as wholeheartedly as Burnham did. They met at restaurants, at Burnham's house, at Burnham's mother's apartment, at David's apartment, and most often, at the *Times,* where David spent so many hours and seemed so thoroughly at ease that he was often mistaken for a reporter. When Burnham was out, David sat at his desk, made phone calls, and chatted with reporters and editors. If David was on the phone, the *Times* took messages for him.

The Burnham-Durk relationship became a topic of some interest around the newsroom, and sometime that winter, David was called in to see Abe Rosenthal, who had recently been promoted to the post of managing editor. Unlike his courtly predecessor, Clifton Daniel, Rosenthal saw it as part of his job to closely question his reporters whenever they were working on a big story. In this instance, he felt that it behooved him to interrogate the source as well as the reporter. "But Durk wasn't just a source," Rosenthal recalled. "He was in the middle of all this."

It was a long and emotional session. "He said that what I was alleging was monumental, and I had to convince him," David said later. Rosenthal, for his part, formed an impression of David as "kind of a mysterious fellow, and quite brave to risk himself the way he did," and he was reassuring when David mentioned some concerns that Gelb and Burnham had expressed about the use of anonymous sources. As long as *he* was convinced, Rosenthal said, the *Times* would find a way to run the story.

For Gelb, however—and the handful of other people at the *Times* who had an idea of what Burnham was up to—the question of sources remained a major worry. By January 1970 Burnham had spent three months on a project that Gelb had envisioned as the work of a few weeks. He had found plenty of people who were willing to talk about their brushes with corruption, but hardly any who were willing to be identified. Gelb was after Burnham to get people's names on the record, and David felt some of the pressure as well—he felt it, and resented it.

Gelb took the position that since it was in the public interest for the story to be published, concerned citizens ought to be willing to come forward. It was a line of argument that David was familiar with, for his superiors at DOI had often said the same thing after he had come to them with information gleaned from people who didn't care to be witnesses or undercover operatives. "The *Times* kept asking me to be specific," he recalled. "For instance, they wanted me to name a liquor store guy who was not only paying off the police but had paid a twenty-five-thousand-dollar bribe to the state liquor authority for permission to move half a block. I said, 'If you mention a place like that—if you even give a hint about its location—that guy would be destroyed.' "

Yet it was David who finally came up with the idea that, more than anything, served to calm Gelb's anxieties. What if (he proposed to Burnham) he brought in a delegation of cops to give Burnham's superiors an unofficial seminar on corruption? The article would still have to cite people without giving their names, but Gelb would be able to say that *he* knew who some of the sources were and had questioned them directly. Burnham was enthusiastic, especially when David added that he might be able to get an inspector to come along.

After twenty-seven years as a cop, Paul Delise was looking forward to retirement. "I've got six kids—you know what I mean?" was his first response to David's invitation. A few days later, he chewed it over with Serpico. "Listen, Dave wants me to go down and talk to some friends of his at *The New York Times* about what's going on," Delise said.

Serpico said he knew about the *Times* meeting—that he would be there. "Are you going to go down?" he asked.

Delise restated the fears he had expressed to David but wound up saying he would go if Durk and Serpico wanted him to. "You guys do what you have to do, and I'll back you up a hundred percent," he said. He had discussed it with his wife. "I just will not be able to face myself if I don't help them two guys in what they are doing," he had told her, adding that he might have to find another line of work if the police brass ever got wind of what he was doing.

The *Times* briefing, which took place on the night of Washington's birthday, 1970, had a cloak-and-dagger quality. There were six police officers in all: David, Serpico, Delise, and three (a captain, a lieutenant, and a detective) who have yet to come out of the closet, twenty-five years later. David greeted them, one by one, as they got off the elevator on the third floor, and guided them to a conference room by a roundabout route that spared them the ordeal of passing through the newsroom proper. They sat down at a table with a tape recorder in the middle (this was to help the *Times* defend itself in the event of a lawsuit), and David introduced them as "Patrolman X," "Inspector Y," and so forth. Only David was there as himself, but Gelb had ordered beer and sandwiches, and as the evening progressed, people began to address each other by their true names.

Looking back on that night, the participants agreed that Delise was the key figure. Delise did not have a beard or wear an earring. There was nothing antiestablishment about him. His sincerity and modesty were unmistakable. He was fifty—about Gelb's age—and like Gelb, he had spent most of his life in loyal service to a single institution. His experiences with corruption ranged over three decades and many assignments. And he was an inspector. He was a whistle-blower that the *Times* could be comfortable with.

As a mounted cop in Harlem in the fifties, Delise had made a practice of watching for drug transactions while he pretended to have his mind on directing traffic. One Sunday morning he had arrested a drug dealer outside a poolroom on 116th Street. The dealer had pointed out that he had a couple of hundred dollars on him and more money at home, and that since he was already on parole, he couldn't afford another arrest at the moment. Delise had refused to take the hint. Being on horseback, however, he had flagged down a sector car to transport his prisoner to the station, and on arriving there had discovered that the sector car cops had done some negotiating in his absence.

"Hey, listen, Sarge," one of them told Delise (who had recently been promoted), "this guy is making a good offer. He's got a couple of thousand dollars at home. I'll tell you what—we'll go get it, and we won't take a penny. It's yours."

"You son of a bitch," Delise replied, "how can you suggest something like that?"

"We're all doing it," the cop told him. "We kick these guys in the ass, we take their works from them, we put 'em on a subway train, and whatever they have in their pockets is what we take."

From mounted, Delise had gone to the Narcotics Division, where he was surprised to find that his men were not pleased to have him accompany them on busts. After his promotion to lieutenant, Delise had occasion to bring charges against four narcotics detectives for giving drugs to informants. Once, while inventorying an arrested dealer's possessions, Delise announced, "There's three thousand dollars here, by my count," and the dealer replied, "No, there's only two thousand," and they kept going back and forth like that until Delise belatedly realized that the dealer was trying to give him a thousand-dollar bribe.

Delise made good collars in narcotics, but his bosses didn't seem to appreciate him. The explanation was finally provided by a friendly sergeant, who said, "Paul, you know why they hate your guts in the front office? It's because you're not collecting for them. Comes Christmastime, all of these cabarets and what-not are just waiting for you out there. All you have to do is go in and say, 'I'm Lieutenant So-and-so from Narcotics,' and they'll give you an envelope. They'll even give you for last year, 'cause you weren't around last year. Then you take half for yourself, you go into the front office, and you see the inspector, and he takes half, and he brings the other half into the boss—and you'll be off the shit list."

Delise thanked the sergeant for the information, but added, "Lookit, if this is what you want to do, go ahead. It's not my cup of tea."

Gelb was touched by Delise's stories—touched and, then, fired up. It was, he told himself, a first: the first time a high-ranking police officer had talked to the press, openly, about corruption.

—————————

For years David had been trying to generate some outrage on the subject of police corruption. Now that he had finally succeeded, he felt oddly equivocal. Sometimes, it seemed to him that his new friends at the *Times* were a little *too* outraged. It was partly a class thing: he didn't like the sight of men in suits and ties expressing horror and indignation at the sins of men in blue uniforms. With Burnham, David had many arguments about what he called "the free cup of coffee"—his metaphor for the small favors that merchants did cops. Burnham considered free coffee and free meals a small issue in themselves, but a significant first step in the process that led cops to regard graft as acceptable. "That's where it begins—it's the training ground—it's where a cop learns the ropes!" he would say, attempting to justify his efforts (which David ridiculed) to document the scope of such behavior. David described Burnham's reasoning, with scorn, as "the slippery slope theory—you take a free cup of coffee, and it'll start you right down the road to selling heroin!" In the aftermath of

the Bronx plainclothes investigation, John Walsh had made his protégé, McGovern, responsible for coordinating all the department's
efforts to maintain internal integrity, and under McGovern there had
been a wave of disciplinary actions against cops caught in minor violations. To treat free meals as serious corruption, David contended,
was to buy into the Walsh-McGovern philosophy.

"Well, I understand the distinction," Burnham replied.

When Gelb and Rosenthal made what David considered self-
righteous statements about police graft, he brought up the *Times's*
own dealings with the police. Trucks were not ordinarily permitted
on the West Side Highway—a restriction that posed a large inconvenience to anyone trying to deliver a piece of merchandise quickly to
locations in Upper Manhattan, the Bronx, or Westchester County;
and yet, David would point out, *Times* delivery trucks frequently used
the West Side Highway. What did the *Times* drivers know that other
drivers didn't? Parking was not permitted on West Forty-third Street
between Seventh and Eighth Avenues; but *Times* trucks often parked
and double-parked there, in front of the loading bays from which
they got their papers, and *Times* typesetters and printers put their private cars on the street as well. And though there was usually a large
complement of police officers in the vicinity, they saved their summonses for outsiders; they never seemed to bother anyone employed
by the *Times.* Between the cops and the *Times's* security guards—
some of them ex-cops—the *Times* was in effective command of a public street, David argued. (Gelb found this sort of tit-for-tat irritating.
He had made inquiries of the responsible authorities in the *Times*
circulation department, and they had assured him that paying off
the police was not a current *Times* practice. As far as Gelb was concerned, that settled the question.)

In David's mind, the scandal—as he had so often said to Serpico—
was only partly about police corruption. Just as significant was the
widespread knowledge of it on the part of people who could have
done something. It was by no means clear to him, though, that the
Times would see things in that light. He knew that Burnham, despite
their occasional quarrels, fundamentally agreed with him. His big

worry was that when push came to shove, Burnham's editors would strip the story of the parts that threatened to be most embarrassing to Walsh, Leary, Kriegel, Fraiman, and John Lindsay himself, leaving an article devoted to the crimes of ordinary cops.

It was not a groundless fear. During one of his visits to Kriegel's office, he had been invited to eavesdrop on a conversation in which Kriegel—or so it had seemed—virtually dictated the contents of a *Times* editorial to its ostensible author. Indeed, at the ownership and management level, the *Times* had a crush on John Lindsay. The editorial page, under the leadership of John B. Oakes, was so taken with him that when, at a low moment, Lindsay vowed not to run for public office after leaving the mayoralty, the *Times* promptly published an editorial expressing the hope and the expectation that he would reconsider.

Between the editorial page and the news pages there stood a theoretically inviolable wall. But Gelb and Rosenthal had also proved far from immune to Lindsay's appeal. Gelb, having met Lindsay as a congressman planning to run for mayor, had arranged a luncheon get-together with Rosenthal—the metropolitan editor at the time. On election night 1965, according to the recollection of John Corry, one of the reporters who covered New York City politics in those days, Rosenthal and Gelb hugged each other, and one of them (Corry did not say which) exclaimed, "We've won!"

"Bad form for objective newsmen," Corry wrote in his memoirs, "but understandable at the time. Abe and Arthur were young, and so was John Lindsay, and they were arriving together as new princes of the city."

As metropolitan editor and, later, deputy managing editor, Rosenthal greatly increased the space that the *Times* gave to local news, and people in and out of the *Times* were struck by the number of column-inches that got devoted to the dashing mayor. During the subway strike that greeted Lindsay at the dawn of his mayoralty, Rosenthal played tennis with the mayor one day and, to the surprise of some *Times* colleagues, returned to work in a police car. That summer, with the threat of riots in the air, Lindsay invited Rosenthal and a group of other editors in to talk about the danger of spreading inflammatory rumors. Rosenthal continued to see Lindsay on a fairly steady basis, in social as well as journalistic settings, for the rest of Lindsay's term in office. He considered their relationship merely businesslike, but it represented a conspicuous break in a long tradition of noncontact between *Times* editors and newsmakers, and some of Rosenthal's subordinates thought that he and Gelb were too easily flattered by the attentions of the mayor, and too quick to take phone calls of advice or criticism from Lindsay and his aides. Usually, this was something that reporters muttered to each other when Rosenthal and Gelb were well out of earshot. On one memorable occasion, however, a veteran member of the metropolitan staff, Emanuel Perlmutter, refused an assignment by declaring to Rosenthal's face that he would not be a flack for the mayor's office.

By 1969 the relationship was no longer so chummy—certainly not in the mayor's mind, for the *Times* had been a cause of considerable grief to him. Martin Tolchin, the paper's chief City Hall reporter, had written at length about the high pay and vague duties of some of Lindsay's outside consultants. Richard Severo, another metropolitan reporter, had raised big questions about the success rate of some Lindsay-backed drug rehabilitation programs. There had also been a series (the work of five reporters) on corruption in the Human Resources Administration. Faced with the choice between a good story and the temptation to protect the mayor, the *Times* had pursued a number of very good stories. (Perhaps the choice was easier now that Lindsay was a little older and less popular.) But the police corruption story was potentially far more damning, and David was not alone in wondering how eagerly the *Times* would go after it. Burnham wondered about that, too.

David Durk had never been an easy person to live with, but it was only after he took up the public work of recruiting cops, and the private work of exposing corruption, that Arlene's patience and ingenuity in the role of wife and mother were fully tested. Lacking an office, David turned the apartment into a sort of police substation. "When I think back to my childhood," Joan Durk recalled, "I think of a steady stream of people. There was a kind of open-house quality to our life. Always people coming in and out—cops, informants, newspaper reporters, lawyers."

When David was out, the phone was often ringing. The recruiting project had been the subject of magazine articles and TV news pieces, and complete strangers (as well as friends and neighbors) had taken to calling up with police problems that they wanted David to look into. One person might be calling to report a column of foul-looking smoke coming from a nearby chimney; another, the mysterious disappearance of his housekeeper; a third, the fact that somebody was attaching wires to her head and draining her life juices. They all had one thing in common, according to Joan: "They never seemed to realize that they had reached a *home.*"

It often fell to Arlene to answer the phone, and she dreaded the experience. "You never knew *who* was going to be on the other end of the line," she remembered. "That can be very disruptive if you're trying to raise a family—if you're trying to run a normal home. Once I got a call in the middle of the night from someone at the *Daily News,* who asked me if I knew that Frank Serpico had been arrested in Brooklyn—which turned out to be totally untrue. I remember saying, 'Do you *know* what time it is?' He thought I was asking him a question. He said, 'Yes, it's three thirty-two.' "

It was not the sort of household in which the whole family sat down for breakfast and dinner together. Every engagement involving David was tentative—subject to last-minute cancellation if, say, someone called up with a tip on a homicide. At social events, the conversation often turned to the subject of law enforcement, and sometimes the tone of the conversation was edgy, for it was a time when many people did not care for cops. At a Christmas party given by some friends of the Durks', they met a pair of identical-twin psychiatrists with matching haircuts that resembled Brillo pads. One of them began talking about an index of authoritarian personality known as the F Scale, and the factors that might explain someone's decision to become a police officer. Latent homosexuality, for example.

"I've read that stuff," David replied. It was the sort of stuff he had usually read. "The F Scale was validated on middle-class subjects, so you might apply it to me if you want to. But to apply it to the typical cop? You probably picture him leaving the station house with his nightstick raised high, looking for somebody to club over the head. The typical cop is worried about his mortgage and his pension. The last thing he wants to do is get into a fight."

Although David still carried his gun and shield, he was technically on leave from the department, and sometimes he spoke of finding another line of work. In her heart, Arlene hoped that he would, although, knowing how much he loved the job, she found it hard to say so. "If you're married to a policeman," she has said, "there's always that apprehension when he's at work. There's always that relief when you hear the key turning in the lock." David, with his propensity for afterhours law enforcement—and his interest in corruption—gave her more than the usual cause for concern. When they were going somewhere by car, Arlene instinctively watched his gaze, hoping that it would stay on the road and not drift off to the side, where he had a habit of spotting people who were committing or contemplating illegal acts. But she usually kept this to herself, lest her fear communicate itself to the children. "It was always important to me that the kids should not think anything unusual was happening—that they should feel safe and secure. Even when there were bodyguards in the house later on, there was not that sense of living on the edge of danger. No one ever said, 'Look, kids, something terrible might happen,' so they really didn't take it too seriously."

Since she was married to a cop, she tried to enjoy it. On the wall of the Durks' living room was the target on which David had taken his qualifying test at the police pistol range. (He had been first in his class in marksmanship.) An acquaintance of Arlene's—a wealthy woman with an art collection that included a black-painted coal shovel—made approving noises when she saw the target, with its dense pattern of hits streaked over the center. "How was that done?" she asked.

"With a gun," Arlene replied, matter-of-factly.

In her efforts to maintain a semblance of normal domestic life, Arlene adopted what might be called a strategy of containment. Rather than contest the basic premise of the household—that things had to revolve around David and his schedule—she set boundaries. She conceded David the living room, but declared the dining room and bedrooms off-limits to police work. She permitted him to bring informants home with him but demanded advance notice whenever the guest was someone who should not be in contact with the children. "At those times, you stayed in the back of the house," Joan recalled. But Julie Durk, who was still a preschooler, could not always resist the temptation to peek.

Arlene placed a high priority on having a child-friendly apartment. Joan was ten and had a lot of friends, who tended to congregate at the Durks'. Sleepover dates were common. Sometimes, coming home late, David would have to tiptoe around the sleeping forms of little girls.

As a husband and father, he was affectionate but often distracted. One day, finding Joan with a classmate, he asked her, "Can you introduce me to your friend?"

"No, Daddy," Joan replied, "I can't introduce you, because you've known her since we were in first grade."

His main contributions to domestic comfort were the occasional meal—David loved to cook—and the occasional trip to the Adventure Playground. Arlene appreciated these gestures but was careful not to count on them. Least of all did she count on his coming home at a predictable hour. Whenever he arrived, though, she would listen to the news of the day—the latest revelations about SIU or his recruiting trips or what was happening at the *Times*—with sympathy, for, as she recalled, "I shared his frustration that other people were content to have their offices and their titles, and not put themselves on the line the way he did." But sometimes she listened with less than meticulous attention to detail. "I wouldn't say I tuned any of it *out,* but I didn't necessarily follow every little nuance."

"Someone once said to me, 'How could David have put you through all these things?' " Arlene recalled. "It struck me as a very bizarre comment, because I don't think he's ever intending to put anyone through anything. He has to do what he thinks is right. David is David."

The spring of 1970 arrived, and David was still lining up appointments for himself and Serpico.

"This is just another one of your fucking friends who won't do anything," Serpico would say when David mentioned another public official they could go to.

David would respond that it scarcely mattered whether any of these people acted or not, because their inaction would only lend added force to the eventual indictment. "We win either way," he liked to say.

One of the officials they visited during these months was the head of a federal "strike force" against organized crime, who listened attentively to what David and Serpico had to say about corruption, acknowledged the seriousness of the problem, and explained that he could not afford to do anything at the moment that might deny him the cooperation of John Walsh and the police department. He gave David his home phone number and asked him to call back in a year.

Another person they went to see was Robert Morgenthau, a former U.S. attorney for the Southern District of New York, who was just about to take office as the Lindsay administration's man in charge of narcotics policy. Morgenthau asked David if he had any "hard evidence" that the top people in the police department had failed to act against corruption. After thinking it over, David replied that he and Serpico could try to make tape recordings of John Walsh and others. But first they would need a tape recorder, and an understanding that if they were caught, they could say they were acting at Morgenthau's behest.

Morgenthau asked for two days to ponder these requirements, and reported back that he was unable to meet either of them. David would have to come up with his own tape recorder. If he got caught, Morgenthau would disavow all responsibility.

"You've got to be kidding," David said. "What is this, *Mission: Impossible?*"

(Morgenthau later explained that he had actually been a private citizen—without access to surveillance equipment—at the time of the meeting with David and Serpico, and that they had tied his hands by forbidding him to tell the mayor or the police commissioner.)

Burnham, like Serpico, was getting impatient with these expeditions. He had finished his reporting, and he pleaded with David and Serpico for the only thing he still needed: permission to make their saga a part of his exposé.

Both men, in fact, longed to have their story told, yet they worried about what it would mean for their careers. Serpico, by now, was assigned to Manhattan North, under Delise, and his thinking was going in two directions at once. On the one hand, he clung to the hope of being made a detective and feared that he could kiss that hope good-bye if he were cited in a newspaper article impugning the leadership of John Walsh and Howard Leary. On the other hand, as he frequently told David, he had had his fill of being a cop and was likely to leave at any moment.

"Well, if you're going to quit, make it count," David would say when Serpico talked this way. "Because you can take all these people with you."

In early April, fed up with waiting, Burnham sat down, wrote his articles, and turned them in. To his dismay, there was no reaction from his editors, not even from the normally voluble Gelb. He had written the biggest story of his career, and no one at the *Times* had a thing to say about it.

Dark fantasies swept over him. What if a highly placed person at the *Times* had spoken to a highly placed person at the mayor's office? What if the *Times* had been assured that Lindsay had already begun a confidential probe of police corruption and that any publicity would compromise the results? If something like that had happened, would someone have bothered to tell Burnham? In his more sober moments, he was sure that the paper—at any rate, Gelb—was committed to the story. Still, the pressure was getting to him.

Like J. Edgar Hoover in his sphere, John Walsh, in his, was reputed to have sharp ears and long arms. Burnham became seized by the fear that Walsh's agents would break into the *Times* newsroom and search his desk. As a precaution, he asked for a special, unmarked locker for his notes.

"This is going to sound like a B movie," David told Burnham one day, "but if anything happens to me there is certain information I want you to have." He handed Burnham a sealed envelope containing a sheaf of corruption-related materials and asked him to put it in a safe deposit box. At the time, Burnham did not think that David was being overly melodramatic.

Toward the middle of April, Burnham did what he calls "the single most manipulative thing I've ever done in my life." At a cocktail party, he ran into Tom Morgan, the mayor's press secretary. Burnham had already downed a couple of drinks, and "I just decided that it was time for the story to run," he said later. "I had to jar it loose. I had to overwhelm the *Times,* and I had to overwhelm Durk and Serpico." After the usual exchange of pleasantries and inquiries, he said to Morgan: "Tom, you know I'm working on this big piece about corruption—police corruption. It's very exciting, and I know how pleased you and Mayor Lindsay will be when it comes out." As soon as the words *police corruption* were out of Burnham's mouth, Morgan's eyes widened, and Burnham knew his comment would not be forgotten.

In a matter of days, the mayor's office issued a press release stating—without explanation—that Lindsay had established a committee to "review all city procedures" for investigating corruption. It was to be an in-house review. Three of the five committee members were prominent figures in the Lindsay administration: Corporation Counsel J. Lee Rankin, Commissioner of Investigations Robert Ruskin, and Police Commissioner Howard Leary. The other two were Frank Hogan and Burton Roberts, the Manhattan and Bronx DAs.

Burnham never told Gelb or David of his role in the chain of events leading to the creation of what became known as the Rankin

Committee. He told Gelb immediately about the announcement itself, however, and as he had hoped, Gelb declared that the corruption pieces would run right away—this was the news peg the *Times* had been looking for. Burnham then called David to inform him that events had forced his hand. It was a Thursday afternoon. The plan was to run a brief story about the mayor's corruption panel in Friday's paper, and to commence Burnham's series on Saturday. While the editors busied themselves with the usual deadline stories for Friday, Burnham made a few changes and updates, including the insertion of a paragraph reporting that the mayor had acted "after the Lindsay administration learned the *Times* was conducting a survey of police corruption." No one at the *Times* ever asked him how he knew this.

For weeks Burnham had been troubled by the seeming inattention of his editors to a story he considered tremendously important. Now they made up for it with a vengeance. He had written a three-part series, the first part devoted to the extent of police corruption, the second to its history, the third to possible remedies. Gelb declared that the structure was anticlimactic: the three parts would be boiled down to one, and if good material had to be discarded, well, there would be plenty of opportunity for follow-up in the weeks ahead. Burnham had hardly begun to absorb this painful news when Gelb began rattling off ideas about what to cut, what to add, and how to make the language as strong as possible within the bounds of accuracy and libel law. This was Gelb's way with any article he really cared about, but the experience was always a little unsettling for the reporter. Suddenly, Burnham's series—the product of a long and intensely personal reporting process—became raw material on an assembly line. Burnham, Gelb, and Mitchel Levitas, an assistant metropolitan editor, retired to an office to rough out the new structure in bursts of talk punctuated by occasional intervals of silence, after which Gelb would put his fingertips together, gaze up at the ceiling, and dictate a neat, distilling phrase. When they had finished their work, Martin Arnold, who was known as a wordsmith (and as a quick worker), was asked to turn their decisions into a readable draft.

The next morning, Gelb's secretary typed up the paste-and-cut job of the night before, and Gelb sent word to the mayor's office that a story about to appear in the *Times* contained allegations against high city officials. As a courtesy, the *Times* would deliver a copy to City Hall, in order to let the people named in it see what was said about them and, if they so wished, respond. This mission was given to Burnham, and as he headed downtown, story in hand, he was filled with apprehension—about the article itself and about the prospect of facing so many important and (as he imagined) angry people. "I had this horror that they were going to call me into a room and start shouting at me," he said later.

On his arrival, he caught a glimpse of several of them sitting outside Morgan's office. He gave Morgan the story, then retired to the pressroom, while a conclave that included Lindsay, Morgan, Kriegel, Leary, Walsh, McGovern, Foran, and Ruskin deliberated. (Peter Maas, in *Serpico*, described it as a "dour gathering," with Kriegel "hunched over by a window . . . chewing on a fingernail.") Sometime later, Morgan appeared in the pressroom, bearing an official mayoral response. The allegations reported in the *Times* were "extremely serious," and the mayor urged "police and citizens alike to report specific knowledge of police misconduct." On the other hand, Commissioner Leary had informed the mayor that many of the instances of corruption specifically described in the article "were reported to the department in 1967" and had resulted in "a number of indictments."

While the mayor and his aides were responding to the story, Gelb and his deputies continued to fiddle with it, and there were some final, furious revisions that afternoon and early evening before Gelb invited David, Burnham, and Arnold to join him in his office. Gelb's original enthusiasm for the story had not faded. He spoke exuberantly about what a big move it was for the *Times* to take on an institution as powerful as the police department. He broke open a bottle of Scotch, followed by a second bottle. Around eight-thirty, the first edition arrived, and everybody hugged everybody.

The story began as a modest, two-column-wide box in the upper left-hand corner of the front page:

GRAFT PAID TO POLICE HERE
SAID TO RUN INTO MILLIONS

————

SURVEY LINKS PAYOFFS TO GAMBLING AND
NARCOTICS—SOME ON FORCE ACCUSE
OFFICIALS OF FAILURE TO ACT

The inconspicuous place and the low-key headline were no accident: the editors had labored long and hard to avoid even the appearance of crusading journalism. "The challenge was to translate the zeal and bright-burning flame of Serpico and Durk into an approach that wouldn't sear the very page it was printed on," Mitchel Levitas recalled. "We had to bear in mind the self-image of the *Times*." But the article minced no words about the extent of the problem, and it spared none of the officials who had tolerated it. The *Times*, for all of David's suspicions, had come through.

When Burnham left work that night, he had a copy of the paper in his hand, and he was more than a little drunk. The subway car he boarded at Times Square was unbearably hot—or at least the alcohol streaming through Burnham's blood vessels made it seem so. During the ride home he got up and stumbled out into the space between cars for a blast of cooler air.

When he reached home, he found his wife already asleep, and since there was no one to share his excitement with, he fell asleep, too. At about two in the morning, though, he awakened to the sound of a motor running in the street. Peering out the window, he saw a police car idling in front of the house. He couldn't quite have said what he was afraid of, but he was certainly afraid. He stayed at the window for the next twenty minutes, until the car went away.

The story came in for criticism at the *Times*. There were those— reporters and editors—who called it "improperly sourced," a view emphatically shared by the mayor and those around him. On Saturday, Gelb and Rosenthal were guests at Gracie Mansion, and Lindsay subjected them to a harangue about taking the word of a couple of disgruntled cops. (Lindsay seemed to be taking the word of his police commissioner, who, according to Maas, had described Burnham's article as "a lot of general crap"—the product of the overwrought imaginations of a "psycho cop" and his "college pal." After several days of reflection, Leary denounced the *Times*—this time publicly—for relying on the testimony of "prostitutes, homosexuals, and malcontents.") There had been, by now, a number of *Times* stories that gave Lindsay displeasure. Later, he would say that he might have been president if the *Times* had gone easier on him. Gelb, for his part, would look back on the corruption story as the best one of his career.

A few days after it ran, David flew to California for another round of recruiting sessions. At four in the morning, he was asleep in a Los Angeles motel when he heard a knock at the door. It was Martin Arnold, who explained that he had been assigned to write a profile of David. When David protested that he needed his sleep, Arnold replied that the job had to be completed in a hurry; the *Times,* he said jocularly, needed to have an obituary ready, in case David got knocked off.

Arlene, Joan, and Julie were at home in New York, and David was anxious about threatening phone calls in his absence. His worries mounted when he tried to call home and learned that the phone was out of service.

"That was the week that I was sure the phone was tapped," Arlene recalled. "There was enormous static on our line, and I called the phone company, and a whole series of people came to correct the problem. Someone would come one day, and without my calling again someone else would come the next. All of them had ID, but every time someone came, the phone got weirder and weirder. There were times when, if you were in the bedroom, you could hear conversations in the living room—and the phone was on its cradle. People told us that just by the mere fact of calling us, *their* phones went out of order. And then the phone went completely dead, and David out in California had no idea what had happened. It was sort of surrealistic."

One caller who managed to get through was a man with—it seemed to Arlene—a chilling voice. "He said he wanted to speak to David. I said David wasn't home, and I asked who it was. He said,

'John Walsh.' It was a very strange call—it was a little like getting a call from God. I asked him for his number, so David could call him back. He was quite taken aback. He said, 'He *knows* my number.' "

———

There is no reason to suppose that the police were any more corrupt on April 25, 1970, than on April 24. Nor had the mayor, the City Council, or the various district and U.S. attorneys suddenly been invested with new powers. Only one thing had changed: *The New York Times* had published an article. But that was enough to accomplish what years of pleading and hectoring by David and Serpico had failed to accomplish: it made police corruption a matter of immediate concern to the elected leaders of the city.

The issue quickly overwhelmed Lindsay's preemptive strike against it: his in-house committee of inquiry. Within days, Lindsay was being denounced right and left for trying to rig the results. His critics pointed out that three of the five committee members held public office at the pleasure of the mayor, while one of them—Howard Leary—was the man most obviously responsible for the problem he was supposed to be investigating.

On May 1, an ad hoc band of congressmen, led by Ed Koch, denounced the Rankin Committee and Leary's inclusion in it. Two weeks later, the committee sent a letter to the mayor discreetly proposing its own liquidation, on the grounds that "an independent investigative body, appointed by you from the private sector," would be better equipped to handle "an undertaking of far greater magnitude than that originally envisioned. . . ." A week after that, Lindsay created the Knapp Commission.

PART
THREE

CHAPTER

ELEVEN

———◦———

Ascandal is a pivotal event in the life of any organization—a moment, like war or revolution, when the normal flow of history is interrupted, rules evaporate, and new possibilities arise. The corruption scandal of the early 1970s sent cops to prison, and drove cops to suicide. (Others, counting themselves lucky, were merely transferred to some police gulag or other.) It pushed a generation of police commanders into retirement, and propelled another generation to power. In the history of New York City, there have been few prettier illustrations of the capacity of a newspaper article to refocus minds and redirect careers.

At first, the police brass did their manful bests to appear as scandalized as anybody. In early June of 1970, David received an urgent summons to the offices of Internal Affairs, where, with three tape recorders running simultaneously, he was ordered to recount every instance of corruption of which he knew. "Let's start with captains and up," he wryly suggested. "*I'm* running this investigation," replied an unamused inspector.

Neither David's name nor Serpico's had appeared in Burnham's article. (They would not surface until a few months later.) But the story had spoken of two honest cops who had gone to a series of high officials of the department and the city government, and those same officials knew perfectly well who the two cops were. They knew, and they saw to it that David and Serpico knew they knew. The elevators at headquarters developed a habit of emptying whenever David entered them. "David Durk, you are funny," Deputy Commissioner Benjamin Ward—later the city's first black police commissioner—said when their paths crossed one day. "Everyone in this building is praying that you don't come and visit them in their office. You could destroy a man's career. All you have to do is go up and shake his hand in front of everyone—and he's through! No one will ever talk to him again. But I want you to know I'm bigger than you, and I can knock you on your ass. I'm the only person in this building that's not afraid of you."

"I like you, too," David replied.

For four months after the appearance of Burnham's article, the police department remained frozen in place. Howard Leary was still police commissioner, John Walsh was still first deputy, and David was still on leave, for, rather than find out what Leary and Walsh would do with him if they got the chance, he had accepted an invitation from the Justice Department to continue his recruiting project for a second year.

Then in September, with Burnham and others in the press keeping up the pressure, Leary quietly resigned and, carrying on a grand tradition of New York officials felled by scandal, sailed off to Europe for a holiday, later to resurface as head of security for the Abraham & Strauss department store chain. To Barry Gottehrer, who wondered why someone would give up the post of police commissioner to become "a gumshoe at a second-rate department store," Leary spelled out his thinking thusly: "Barry, the art of politics is, you've got to remember that you're always standing at the bottom of a cliff, and up on top there is a rock teetering. To be successful, you have to learn two things. You always have to keep one of your eyes on that rock, so you realize immediately when it stops teetering and starts coming rolling down. The second thing is, once it starts rolling, you either get out of there, or it crushes you."

It was a frenzied time in David's life. Now that corruption had been officially discovered, reporters, prosecutors, legislators, and elected and appointed officeholders of every imaginable kind swarmed in, looking for a piece of the territory to call their own; and when David wasn't off recruiting, he was often sharing his expertise with one of these second-wave pioneers. He was also keeping up his ties to his network of sources and developing new ones. (The fact that he was no longer on any police agency's payroll wasn't going to stop him from making cases.) He had become a minister without portfolio—a one-man police department for those who were dissatisfied with the official thirty-thousand-man department.

And he was talking to the Knapp Commission—the body created, in effect, to finish the work that he had started. That summer, while the commission went into lawyerly hibernation (to reemerge in the fall with staff, offices, and a plan of action), David had a series of wide-ranging and easygoing conversations, mostly at the Yale Club, with Whitman Knapp, the Wall Street lawyer (and former prosecutor) who had been chosen to be its chairman. A mild, amiable, sixty-one-year-old Yankee lawyer with a high-pitched voice and a toothy grin, Knapp approached his task with the endearing directness of Mr. Magoo crossing a busy street against the light, and David took an immediate liking to him.

But as time passed, and David began dealing with others on the commission staff, an element of distrust crept into the relationship. The responsibility for debriefing him fell largely to a staff attorney named Nicholas Scoppetta. By the time they started conferring, the commission was no longer in a leisurely mood. The city council had allocated $325,000 for the investigation—and the money was fast running out. The heat was on, therefore, to come up with fresh evidence of corruption that could be used to justify additional funding. Like the people at Internal Affairs, Scoppetta pressed David for specifics. Who? What? Where? When? David feared that Scoppetta and others at the Knapp Commission would misuse such information by setting traps designed to catch cops in acts of small-time corruption. (They were considering a plan, for example, to put out undercovers with unlicensed hot dog stands and have them offer cops bribes.) Scoppetta, in turn, wondered if David really knew as much about corruption as he professed to know. One lengthy conversation that stuck in his memory—and craw—had to do with nightsticks: the cheap and ineffective ones issued by the department, and the good ones that cops were forced to spend their own money to buy. David was trying to get Scoppetta to see that such things made cops cynical and prone to break rules. Scoppetta did not have time to talk about nightsticks. He was after hard cases, and, deciding that David had none to offer, he dismissed him from his thoughts—very nearly dismissing, in the process, just about the hardest case that the Knapp Commission would unearth.

For more than a year, David had been trying to get the old man's tips about the Pleasant Avenue drug trade investigated and, in a parallel struggle, to get Bob Leuci to confirm David's suspicions about the Narcotics Division and its celebrated Special Investigating Unit. "Durk is the world's greatest nudge," Lawrence Goldman, an assistant DA who played a minor part in the eventual turning of Leuci, said later. "He nudged Frank Serpico to death, and he nudged Bob Leuci to death to get him to come forward."

On the morning of October 5, David Durk and Frank Serpico testified before a Brooklyn grand jury that was considering a perjury charge against Captain Philip Foran, the former DOI chief investigator who had encouraged Serpico to contemplate a future at the bottom of the East River. The jurors applauded David at the end of his testimony, and he walked out of the room in a buoyant mood. (A premature buoyant mood, it turned out. The Brooklyn DA's office waited six weeks before calling Foran to testify, and with David's and Serpico's testimony no longer fresh in the grand jury's memory, Foran declared that he had never been shown any $300. They had come to him, he insisted, to discuss a *possible,* not an actual, payoff, and Serpico had refused to cooperate with an investigation, for fear of being "marked lousy or something like that." One of the prosecutors told David afterward that Foran had "charmed" his way out of an indictment. He was later convicted on departmental charges, and fined thirty days' pay—and then, in a gesture of support from his peers, was elected president of the Captains' Endowment Association.)

After completing his testimony that day, David was on his way to the Brooklyn DA's office when he ran into Leuci, who had recently been transferred there. "You fuck!" David exclaimed, seizing Leuci's arm. "You're going to talk!"

Leuci thought it over for a moment, and, in a matter-of-fact voice, replied: "Okay, I'll talk." And for the rest of that day, he talked, first to David and then to a series of prosecutors in Brooklyn and Manhattan.

David saw Leuci as precious cargo—a detective who was prepared, in return for certain guarantees, to talk honestly about corruption in the Narcotics Division and to work undercover to expose it. But at the Manhattan DA's office, the assistant DA responsible for police corruption cases—Kenneth Conboy, the chief of the rackets bureau—was neither very grateful nor, it seemed to David, very sensitive to the fragility of the gift. Conboy was a trim, severely handsome man who never appeared in public less than perfectly coiffed. His expensive attaché case usually lay near the corner of his desk, perfectly aligned with the edges, and the handkerchief in his breast pocket was folded, David thought, as precisely as a work of origami. Conboy believed that it was important for the DA's office to assert its authority at the outset of any undercover investigation. The office had the power to make deals with criminals, but only after they had come clean. If Leuci had knowledge of corruption, it was his duty as a police officer to divulge it. Only then would Conboy, not Leuci or Durk, decide the terms of any deal—and whether there would be one.

"Is Mr. Leuci prepared to implicate his own partners in the corruption?" Conboy asked.

"No, he isn't," David replied, for that was Leuci's main precondition. He was willing to go undercover, but only with a guarantee that he would not be asked to implicate his former partners—the people he had been "in bed with"—in past criminal acts. "I thought he made a very good moral point," David said later. "He didn't want to take immunity and sink them for things they had all been doing together."

After half an hour alone with Leuci, Conboy informed David that Leuci hadn't given him anything specific, which, indeed, he hadn't. In the face of Conboy's unbending attitude, Leuci had clammed up. Then, according to David, Conboy began to talk about the difference between anecdotal evidence and the sort of information you needed to bring an indictment.

"I'm not asking for an indictment!" David protested. "I'm asking for an investigation! I've come to the right place, haven't I?"

"Look, David, he's your witness," Conboy replied. "You can do anything you want with him, but you can't commit this office."

Leuci had been in a state of acute ambivalence all along. "On the one hand, I'm thinking, 'How do I save myself?' " he explained years later. "On the other hand, I'm saying to myself, 'Who is this fucking maniac, and what am I doing with him?' Because I knew it was going to get far more complicated than David Durk believed. What he was asking me to do, without his knowing it, was to eat my gun, so to speak." Leuci was ready to call it a day, but David insisted on one more stop: the offices of the Knapp Commission.

Surely, he told himself, the Knapp Commission would not turn away a narcotics detective who was disposed to talk about corruption. Scoppetta, as it happened, wasn't in the office, and when one of his fellow attorneys, Paul Rooney, interviewed Leuci, the same pattern repeated itself, with Rooney coming on strong, much as Conboy had. Rooney was tall and had reddish hair and a dry manner. He was wearing red suspenders and a straw hat. His attitude, David recalled, was "Okay, tell me your story." Listening to Rooney, Leuci had the urge (so he told David afterward) to snatch his hat and step on it. Like Conboy, Rooney concluded that Leuci was not prepared to be specific.

"What David does is he turns people's hearts, and once he has their hearts, their minds follow," Robert Levinson has said, describing David's unusual approach to the cultivation of sources. An FBI agent who began working with David in the late sixties, Levinson had a number of opportunities over the years to see how, when David delivered an uneasy witness to prosecutors or fellow investigators, the bond he had established would sometimes rupture. "You have fellows coming in supposedly to do the follow-up, and they're going for the jugular," Levinson explained. "They want—boom! boom! boom!—the facts. They don't want to sit down and spend some time with these people—treat them with the kind of care and attention that is needed to persuade them to go ahead and cooperate with all their heart."

Over the next few months, though, David kept bringing up Leuci with Whitman Knapp, and Knapp, in turn, would bring him up with the commission's chief counsel, Michael Armstrong, and with Scoppetta. Finally, Scoppetta decided to call Leuci in for another round of questioning. He was spurred to do so not only by pressure from David, but also by the Wurms files, a set of documents, compiled by a federal narcotics agent named Ike Wurms, alleging rampant criminality among the city's narcotics detectives. Narcotics was Scoppetta's turf at the Knapp Commission, and the Wurms files, which had come into the commission's custody toward the end of 1970, left him flabbergasted. Reading reports that spoke of crimes ranging from bribery to murder and that implicated more than seventy cops (including Bob Leuci, under his street name of Babyface), Scoppetta began to think that SIU might be as bad as David had made out, and that Leuci might be worth another shot.

———————

On a Sunday morning in early February of 1971, David got a call from Leuci. He was at wit's end. "I hadn't slept for three days," Leuci recalled long afterward. "I was like a bag of worms. I was panicked, and I went to see Durk. I trusted him—I always trusted David." Leuci had spent two long nights with Scoppetta, bobbing and weaving around the topic of corruption in SIU and Leuci's willingness to participate in an undercover operation along the lines that he and David had sketched out in October.

Rank-and-file cops would not be the main targets, Scoppetta had agreed. But Leuci was distrustful—the Knapp Commission, after all, was in business to catch cops. Scoppetta had spoken of wiping the slate clean, but Leuci was afraid that the slate could never be wiped clean—that even if he didn't wind up in prison, he would lose his job, and he and his family would be pariahs.

David, in his talks with Leuci, had appealed to his idealism and his love of police work; the undercover operation they had discussed would be an act of loyalty to the NYPD—to his fellow cops. Or so David had said. But how could Leuci be sure anyone else would see it that way? Perhaps the slate *could* be wiped clean, as far as criminal prosecution went, but what was to stop the department from finding some charge or other to level against him (it wouldn't be difficult, he implied), and firing him?

Leuci hadn't yet made any deals, and he was in no mood to. He told himself that he hadn't admitted anything yet, and that the Knapp people didn't have anything on him. He didn't think they did, anyway. But what if they did? Or what if they went looking for something? Was it realistic for him to think that they would let him back out now, to go on his merry way? Each alternative seemed worse than the next, and he blamed David for getting him into all this. Leuci rushed around the apartment like a madman, at one point slamming his head down on a butcherblock table and opening a bloody wound near his hairline. "I was getting him a cup of tea, and I heard this bang," David recalled.

In his calmer moments, Leuci's biggest concern was how the police department would react if he went along with Scoppetta and the Knapp people. How, in particular, would the new police commissioner, Patrick V. Murphy, react? Scoppetta had made certain promises, but Scoppetta was in no position to promise what mattered most to Leuci—an assurance that he would still have a job when it was all over.

David suggested that they put the question to Murphy. He would have to be consulted in any case, David reasoned, since the plan was to have Leuci reassigned to SIU—something that couldn't happen without the police commissioner's okay. David would call up his old Justice Department boss, Henry Ruth, who was now working for the City of New York as the head of the mayor's Criminal Justice Coordinating Counsel. Ruth was close to the new commissioner; indeed, he had recommended Murphy for the job, and Lindsay and Murphy had first met at Ruth's apartment, in Brooklyn.

Since nothing less than an immediate show of support from the commissioner seemed likely to have an effect on Leuci, David called up Ruth and told him to come over right away.

Ruth was at home, spending a relaxed day with his in-laws, and he wondered if it was really the case, as David made out, that the biggest revelation of police corruption to date hung in the balance. When he arrived at David's apartment, he saw that David hadn't overstated things. A former organized-crime prosecutor for the Justice Department, Ruth quickly sized up Leuci as "an incredible witness—I had never talked to anyone who had the depth of knowledge of police corruption that he had." He also perceived that Leuci was in "a totally negative mood—he was nowhere when we started." Ruth read Leuci as someone who couldn't be won over with the standard prosecutorial ploys and promises—"the traditional interrogation con job," as Ruth put it later. "He had very little faith that anyone would protect him," Ruth said. "After all, he was a cop, so he knew all the games. He had played them himself."

Ruth was an old hand at dealing with troubled witnesses, and his presence had a soothing effect. The three men—Leuci, David, and Ruth—went at it for five or six hours, and gradually Leuci came around to thinking that the consequences of cooperating with the government might not be as dire as he had feared—that life would go on, and maybe it would even be a better life, in some ways, than before. He became willing to talk about specific solutions to his concerns. The proposed undercover operation would focus on fresh situations rather than old ones, so Leuci wouldn't be put in the position of incriminating his former partners for offenses that he, too, had been guilty of. Commissioner Murphy would confer his blessings; he would be made to understand that Leuci was cooperating for the good of the department, not in order to help outsiders bring shame on the department. (Ruth promised to talk to Murphy about that.) Eventually, Leuci agreed to go forward, and from David's apartment he proceeded to Scoppetta's, where the official negotiations resumed.

That night, or the following one (the principals were unsure which when they tried to reconstruct the sequence of events later), David was one of three men who questioned Leuci in Scoppetta's dimly lit living room, the other two being Scoppetta himself and George Carros, a BNDD agent on loan to the Knapp Commission. Ruth had urged Scoppetta to bring David into the discussions. But Scoppetta was not happy about David's participation, and during a break he cornered David in the kitchen. "This is not the same as it was," he said. "Let me go back to talking to him alone." Reluctantly, David departed.

As soon as he did, Scoppetta launched into a speech about the high-security nature of the investigation being planned. Leuci should never have gone to David's apartment, Scoppetta told him. That, however, was water over the dam; the important thing was, David had to be kept in the dark from here on out. He talked to the press. He couldn't be trusted to keep such an operation under wraps; hadn't he already confided in Henry Ruth?

Michael Armstrong, who played an intermittent role in the talks with Leuci, said later that he, too, considered David unreliable, because "all he had to do was get the idea that someone wasn't doing things his way, and he would go to *Time* magazine." Armstrong, who had little if any knowledge of David's previous dealings with Leuci, went on to say, "Leuci was none of his goddamn business. He had nothing to do with Leuci turning for us."

Henry Ruth, looking back on the same episode, speculated that security was not the real reason—or the sole reason—for the decision to cut David out of the Leuci operation. It was probably a matter, Ruth theorized, of two different ways of treating witnesses. "The main difference between David and traditional interrogation is control," Ruth explained. "Prosecutors and cops want to have total control over their witnesses, and the more incriminating evidence they get, the more control they have. With David, it's a process. He's willing to lose control in the first interviews, but gradually he gains trust. And he doesn't betray that trust—he'll stay with a witness forever, whereas traditional law enforcement might keep promises for the moment, but once the case is over, the shepherding usually stops. When they see someone like David who doesn't come at it from control, they distrust him."

Leuci, like Ruth, had wanted David to be in on the planning of the operation. But now, in the face of Scoppetta's and Armstrong's hostility, he changed his tune. Scoppetta had largely accommodated Leuci in his desire to be spared the ordeal of making cases against his former partners. The investigation would (as David had proposed) center on fresh situations, not old ones, and its primary targets would be superior officers, lawyers, judges, and bail bondsmen—not ordinary cops. Although Leuci had agreed to go after a cop who happened to fall into the net, he told himself that it would not be difficult for him to protect anybody he wanted to protect. And Scoppetta had committed himself to a federal, rather than a local, investigation. With the Knapp Commission's approval, he would ask the Justice Department for a temporary position as a special federal prosecutor for the express purpose of working with Leuci.

Leuci liked the sound of that. It would be a federal investigation, and no one from the NYPD would have anything to do with it— except for the commissioner, whose role would be limited to ordering Leuci's transfer back into SIU.

Leuci was now engaged in some very quick and subtle recalculation. A few months earlier, he had regarded David as a potential savior. But David did not have the clout that Scoppetta, as a special prosecutor reporting directly to the Justice Department, would have. Besides, David was still fixated on Captain Tange, Pleasant Avenue, and SIU's possible ties to major heroin traffickers. An inquiry that delved into those matters would inevitably raise questions about Leuci's former SIU teammates, and under pressure, they might raise questions about him.

"I was concerned that a big investigation centering on the Narcotics Division would ultimately affect everyone in it," Leuci recalled. "What I was trying to do was to move the attention away from myself and into other areas. Certainly, in retrospect, that is not the most honorable characteristic."

Fortunately for him, Scoppetta was already inclined to believe that the Pleasant Avenue story was less than David had made it out to be—that there was some more innocent explanation for the events that he had construed as a sellout. Leuci fed into this predisposition. David's original information, he told Scoppetta, had amounted to no more than general intelligence, just as David had been told all along. It was true that the case had been—as Leuci put it—"shitcanned," but only because "we were afraid of David Durk—we think the guy's a psycho." If Leuci had implied anything else, he had been conning David—playing with him, in order to learn how much David and the Knapp Commission knew about Leuci and SIU.

Like Scoppetta and Armstrong, Leuci now adopted the view that it would be dangerous to let David, or any New York City cop, take part in the operation. It had to be strictly a federal affair. (Later, in an apologetic phone call, Leuci told David that it had become necessary to do and say things that might hurt him. "He said he was in a jam— that his very life was at stake—and he had no choice," David recalled.)

"Without David Durk, there never would have been a Bob Leuci," Leuci said, long afterward. "But with David Durk, there was a real danger that Bob Leuci would not continue."

Leuci had told Scoppetta a lot about SIU and its problems, but he had kept his testimony safely oblique, and off the record. Only now did Scoppetta ask him for a formal rundown of his own crimes. Leuci replied by telling a story about an SIU investigation of a major heroin ring. Failing to come up with enough evidence for an indictment, the detectives working on the case had decided to turn a profit on their lack of success, by contacting the target and offering to back off. Leuci, who had a mobster cousin, had acted as the go-between, nego- tiating a $10,000 bribe on his and the other detectives' behalf. He also told Scoppetta about two other, similar situations in which he had been involved.

"Three things—is that all you've done all these years?" Scoppetta asked him.

"Nick, that's it," Leuci replied.

It was hard to imagine that Scoppetta would accept such an answer. In Leuci's brief criminal memoir, there was simply no explanation of how he knew so much about the temptations that other cops, at other times, had succumbed to—or why he was so obviously consumed with guilt. Later, Leuci was asked for a character assessment of Captain Tange. "He'll take money," Leuci replied, but he was never required to explain how he knew this. He had confessed to three crimes, taking care to make them crimes that he couldn't be successfully prosecuted for. Was it possible that he could make a clean break with his past, and never even be required to talk straightforwardly about his and his ex-partners' offenses? Leuci had hardly dared hope for such an uncomplicated way out of the fix he was in. Now he was beginning to.

For it was becoming clear to him that his interests and the government's coincided. He would end up as a prosecution witness, and if he had a lengthy criminal history—if he had been "turned" in the traditional sense—he would be easy meat for the defense. In any case, the three admissions were duly recorded, and in the months to come, when one or another of Leuci's handlers suggested that he was hiding something, he told them where to get off. "As soon as they began to ask me anything specific about my past involvement," he recalled later, "I would say to them, 'If you fuck with me like that, we're finished!' Because I knew what that would mean. It would mean implicating my partners, and I had nothing to gain by that—nothing. So I would say, 'This is what I can do for you. I can make cases against lawyers. I can make cases against judges. I think I can make cases against organized-crime guys. I can make cases against really venal, corrupt cops—guys who I feel would have been criminals, had they not been cops.' And someone would say to me, 'How about telling us some of the things that *you* did?' And I would say, 'If you keep on pressing me about that, I'm fucking gone! You can subpoena me before a grand jury if you want, but then I become a different person—I'm an adversary. Then maybe my life is ruined, but you're not going to make any fucking cases.' "

At one point, Leuci asked Scoppetta if he understood how dangerous the proposed investigation was likely to be.

Scoppetta said that he did.

"What if I guarantee you that whatever happens to me is going to happen to you?" Leuci said.

"What are you talking about?" Scoppetta asked.

"I'm telling you that if I get killed, I guarantee that you get killed," said Leuci, who had been playing up his family ties to organized crime. "If something happens to one of my children, the same thing is going to happen to one of your children. If someting happens to my wife, something's going to happen to your wife. Are you still prepared to go ahead with the investigation?"

Scoppetta assured Leuci that he was.

In the official and semiofficial annals of the Leuci operation, however, there would be no reference to such disagreeable passages as this. Scoppetta and his colleagues later cooperated with an August 1972 *Life* magazine article that explained Leuci's decision to come forward in terms of his intense emotional kinship with Scoppetta and portrayed their relationship as one of unsullied, mutual respect, built on a common heritage as poor Italian-Americans, reared in the slums.

Leuci's first act as an undercover agent was to purchase, from a friendly detective at headquarters, the location of every authorized wiretap in New York City. With this proof of his talents, Scoppetta flew to Washington and conferred with top officials of the Justice Department. With the approval of Attorney General John Mitchell, Leuci officially went undercover, and Scoppetta was given an office unto himself (in the same building as the Knapp Commission) and the title of Special Assistant United States Attorney.

Leuci's undercover career lasted a year and a half, and left him with what *Life* called a "racing stripe" across his rib cage—the result of the repeated removal of strips of adhesive tape that had held a microphone to his chest. In the end, Leuci was forced to turn against a number of his former SIU colleagues, after it came out that Leuci himself was guilty of far more than he had officially acknowledged; and as he gradually admitted his own crimes—hundreds of incidents in which he had, among other things, accepted bribes, sold information, or stolen money or drugs from suspects—he implicated others as well. A number of the nonpolice defendants ultimately got off by using Leuci's past to tarnish his credibility. As for Leuci himself, he was allowed to serve out his twenty years and then prodded into retirement.

But the Leuci operation, for all its failings, completely validated David's original suspicions about SIU and the Narcotics Division. "What everyone assumed at the time to be typical Durk paranoia turned out to be absolutely correct," Lawrence Goldman has observed. As a result of Leuci's work, fifty-two cops, out of a unit that had never had more than eighty members, were transferred, dismissed, or indicted, and several more (including Captain Tange) avoided indictments by cooperating with federal prosecutors. Two committed suicide (in the traditional police manner, by shooting themselves in the head) before their cases came to trial. One, a sergeant, drank himself to death. The corruption that Serpico had reported involved gambling, and a lot of people already knew that the enforcement of the gambling laws was largely a sham. "The attitude," Goldman recalled, "was, 'Sure, cops are corrupt, but it's gambling, and no one really gives a shit about gambling.' " Leuci's information bumped the scandal into the major leagues.

For David, however, it was a painful sort of vindication, since the prosecutors disregarded much of his advice about how to use Leuci, and then flatly excluded him. Leuci himself was ordered to have nothing further to do with David, and when, from time to time, he violated his instructions, calling David on the phone in order to seek his advice or sympathy, Scoppetta and others chastised David for trying to interfere. At one point, federal marshals were sent to his apartment to bring him downtown, where he was warned that he risked being indicted for tampering with a federal witness.

⸻

Passing Leuci along to the feds was a painful act of self-sacrifice for the Knapp Commission. (Leuci would not surface again until after the commission's work was over.) Around the same time, however, the Knapp people came up with another prize catch, William Phillips, whose fourteen-year police career had been one of "virtually unrelieved corruption," in the words of the commission's final report.

The commission had retained the services of an electronic-eavesdropping specialist, a bizarre little man named Teddy Ratnoff, who coveted acceptance in both the law enforcement community and the underworld. Ratnoff was doing bugging work, simultaneously, for Xaviera Hollander, the East Side madam who later christened herself the Happy Hooker. In March 1971, he got wind of her efforts to purchase a comprehensive police-protection package from a well-connected patrolman. Ratnoff suggested that he might be able to help her out in the negotiations. Then he went to the Knapp Commission, and offered to be present—wearing a wire—when the deal went down.

Before any cash could change hands, however, Patrolman Phillips became suspicious and subjected Ratnoff to a frisk, revealing the transmitter. An exceedingly brutal as well as corrupt cop (he had spoken of having "killed three fucks" for unidentified offenses), Phillips was still trying to figure out a suitable fate for Ratnoff when the Knapp Commission backup team came rushing to his rescue.

Phillips had been so adept and aggressive about making money that other cops in his precinct had sometimes paid the assignment officer for the privilege of working with him. Now he was convinced to put his talents to work for the commission, recruiting fellow cops—a captain, a lieutenant, a PBA delegate, and a former narcotics detective—to alter their testimony against people they had arrested and to shake down (or simply hold up) gamblers, pimps, loan sharks, and illegal liquor dealers. (A year later, Phillips was indicted for murder—the double murder of a pimp and a prostitute. After a hung jury in his first trial, he was convicted and sent to Sing Sing for a life term.)

In the fall of 1971, the Knapp Commission went public with its evidence, and the city was captivated. At the commission's first round of hearings, in October, Phillips was the star witness, with a supporting cast that featured Patrolman Waverly Logan, who told how he and other members of a largely black unit called PEP (Preventive Enforcement Patrol)—a much-ballyhooed effort by the department to respond to the special needs of ghetto residents—had made as much as $3,000 a month in payoffs from drug dealers; and Edward Droge, Jr., a Brooklyn patrolman, caught in the act of taking a $100 bribe in a drug case, who testified that out of roughly seventy-five cops with whom he had worked in the Bedford-Stuyvesant area, all but two were on the take. With their testimony, and audio and film recordings of cops aggressively soliciting graft, the hearings dispelled the rotten-apple theory of police corruption with a vengeance.

For a while it looked as if David Durk and Frank Serpico would not be part of the Knapp Commission's hearings. That, at any rate, was Knapp and Armstrong's original intention. The Durk-Serpico crusade, Armstrong explained later, was now an old story—"penny-ante stuff, in relation to the contemporary corruption we had succeeded in coming up with." Moreover, if *they* testified, the commission would have to give equal time to everyone they mentioned in an unflattering light, and the inquiry would become caught up in the question of whether the mayor, who was laying plans to run for president the following year, had ignored evidence of corruption. This "muddy exercise," Armstrong said, "would have detracted from our purpose, which was to focus on the police department."

Here perhaps was the essence of David's quarrel with the Knapp people. The commission, they told themselves, had been set up to investigate police corruption—misdeeds committed by cops. Perhaps Kriegel and Fraiman et al had not acted as forthrightly as they should have, Scoppetta would later observe (a viewpoint that was widespread among his colleagues), but it was not the commission's job to investigate lapses of that sort. "Our job was to make cases. Certainly, we didn't view our job as embarrassing public officials."

For David, embarrassing public officials was vital. It seemed cruelly wrong to him to punish cops for taking (as many had) small sums of money and not to bring a measure of shame to the better-paid and more powerful officials who had conveniently overlooked the problem, even if they had done so out of no worse motive than the desire to keep their careers on a smooth, upward path. As David declared when he finally got his chance to testify, "If you suggest, or allow others to suggest, that the responsibility belongs only to the police, then for patrolmen on the beat and in the radio cars, this commission will be just another part of the swindle."

To the commissioners and their staff attorneys and investigators, David seemed a little crazy on this subject, and from their point of view, the kind of investigation he was demanding might well have been crazy. The Knapp Commission, like other "independent" investigative panels, had been staffed with people drawn from the private sector. That didn't mean they were unconnected. Knapp was a former Manhattan DA; his chief counsel, Armstrong, had worked at the U.S. attorney's office. (They also shared Yale as an alma mater with the mayor.) They were not planning to pack up and leave New York City after they completed their work. They would move back to, or on to, well-paid jobs in the city's legal establishment. The work of exposing police corruption would be a feather in their caps. If they were to carry their mission further and seriously examine the culpability of Arnold Fraiman (now a judge), Jay Kriegel (Lindsay's most trusted aide), and John Lindsay himself, they would gain a reputation for indelicacy and unreliability, and needlessly offend some very influential people.

There is no reason, however, to doubt the sincerity of the Knapp Commission's own explanation for not going after the higher-ups. It would indeed have been a muddy exercise, and one of the muddiest things about it would have been figuring out where to stop. Fraiman and Kriegel (and perhaps Lindsay) had received explicit information about corruption and had failed to act on it. Plenty of other public officials, in the course of performing their duties, had seen and heard things that *ought* to have made them suspicious. What about the many prosecutors, for example, who had read the arrest reports and affidavits coming out of SIU?

Milton Mollen was a criminal-court judge at the time. Years later, after he had overseen a vigorous investigation in the early 1990s of a resurgence of police corruption, Mollen recalled that he and his fellow jurists had often talked among themselves about the frequency of "dropsy cases," in which a defendant supposedly threw drugs or other contraband to the ground in the full view of a pursuing police officer. "It wasn't in accord with common sense," Mollen said. Yet, though suspicion was rife, he and his judicial brethren made no attempt to call their suspicions to the notice of anyone who might have acted on them. When they professed their surprise, as some of them later did, about the extent of the corruption, they were playing (David thought) a game of "cultivated ignorance" or "deniability."

As a potential witness, David posed a threat not only to the particular people whom he might name but, implicitly, to the entire leadership of the city's criminal justice system, since that leadership had placidly coexisted with the problem for years. As in postwar Europe, there was a desire to forget—to assume that everybody had been part of the Resistance.

If the matter had been left up to Knapp and Armstrong, David would not have been called. In a partisan world, however, there were others in government who shared his desire to see the Lindsay administration brought before the bar of justice. One day, David found himself appearing on Barry Gray's radio talk show with Matthew Troy, a Democratic city councilman from Queens, and he seized the occasion to tell Troy what was happening with the Knapp Commission. Troy thereupon shot off a telegram to Whitman Knapp demanding that David and Serpico be invited to appear (and adding that a failure to do so would "give credence to a strong rumor" that the commission was "in business solely to protect the administration from being connected with the corruption probe"). To reestablish the commission's credibility, Knapp announced that David and Serpico would be asked to testify after all.

Now came a new, and no less contentious, phase of David's dealings with the commission, the issue being just what was he going to testify *about*. David was negotiating with Armstrong, a savvy, square-jawed, ambitious, good-looking prosecutor—a quarterback in lawyers'-league football—who was an artful and persistent questioner of evasive witnesses. They argued relentlessly. David wanted to talk about some of the inquiries that the Department of Investigation had curtailed—one involving the buying of judgeships, for example.

But Armstrong declared that subject irrelevant, and he was not swayed by David's argument that before cops could be expected to abide by the law they would have to see it being applied to judges as well. Armstrong, on the other hand, wanted David to testify about the uniformed pad in the 18th Precinct and his successful campaign to undermine it by getting five other cops in his sector to stop taking money. If he told *that* story, David explained, he would be one more witness against rank-and-file cops who had no real choice in the matter—unlike their bosses. And what was to stop Internal Affairs from going back through personnel records and figuring out which cops he was referring to? "I am not going to destroy someone's life," he recalled telling Armstrong, "just because I happened to have been there to see him take a free meal or whatever. You know damn well these things are systemic!" David also made the point (according to Armstrong's recollection) that his reputation with other cops, and his effectiveness as a police officer, would be undermined if he talked about such things.

"You're just like everybody else!" Armstrong retorted. "When it doesn't serve your agenda, you're not willing to testify—you're not willing to make the kind of sacrifice that you don't hesitate to ask of others. You expect guys to get out there, and be heroes. You condemn Jay Kriegel and everyone else because, according to you, they weren't willing to upset *their* good relations with the police, and here you are, telling me that you won't upset *your* good relations with the police. Shit, Dave, you're just like everybody else!"

In the small hours of the morning before David took the stand, there came a time when Armstrong asked him a trial question about free meals. "If you try to divert my testimony with a question like that," David replied, "I'm going to testify that the last free meal I had was on the Knapp Commission, and there were eight lawyers and investigators, and they were all ordering steak and lobster!"

———⊶⊷———

"Do not recall" and "left my mind" were the phrases that stood out in the testimony of John Walsh—a John Walsh who, having been forced into retirement after a thirty-year career, was a pale memory of the once-feared first deputy commissioner. In asking Serpico to serve as his personal undercover agent, Walsh explained to the commission, he had intended to contact him at a later date, but he had expected Inspector Behan to set up the meeting; with Behan's failure to do so, "the incident left my mind."

At the outset of the hearings, Whitman Knapp promised to withhold judgment until the inquiry was over. He couldn't quite bring himself to withhold judgment on Walsh. "The ball was dropped in April," he pointed out. "From April to October, nothing was done."

"I assumed everything was going all right," Walsh replied, apparently forgetting that moments earlier he had blamed his inaction on a lapse of memory.

"Why the hell did you wait six months before checking with Behan?" Knapp demanded. Walsh fell silent.

Arnold Fraiman conceded that he had done nothing about Serpico's charges, and, in hindsight, that it might have been constructive to have mentioned them to *somebody*. "If I did make an error in judgment," he said, "it was not the only one I made during three years as commissioner." Howard Leary, who had originally dismissed the *Times* story as a slander purveyed by "prostitutes, homosexuals, and malcontents," now had a strikingly different complaint: somebody should have come to *him*. By their failure to do so, Fraiman and Kriegel had needlessly "allowed a horrible thing to develop" and had done "a terrible thing personally to Durk and Serpico," two "courageous men."

Jay Kriegel testified that David and Serpico had complained to him about "the pace of the investigation," not about the department's failure to act at all. In any case, he said, they had thoroughly "handcuffed" him by forbidding him to confide in Leary or Walsh. It remained far from clear, however, what would have stopped Kriegel from generally informing the police commissioner, the Bronx district attorney, or any one of a number of other officials with suitable investigative resources that the department had a serious corruption problem and the mayor wanted it cleared up.

Kriegel said later that for him the stunning moment in the hearings was the testimony of Walsh and the discovery that this dreaded figure was, like the Wizard of Oz, an empty shell. Others were more struck by what the hearings revealed (partly through Kriegel's own testimony) about the mayor and the people around him, and their remarkable ability to coldly calculate the political pluses and minuses of a situation that seemed to call for immediate action. There was some dispute about how much Kriegel had actually told Lindsay about the scope of the corruption problem, the dispute being between two accounts Kriegel gave the commission—before and after his memory had been refreshed by the mayor. There was no dispute about Lindsay's response, which was one strangely at odds with his image as politician of principle. Instead of reacting to the information itself, he had given Kriegel a tongue-lashing for receiving it behind Howard Leary's back.

Kriegel testified that he had advised the mayor to "spend more time with the police commissioner" on the corruption question. And Lindsay, when reporters sought his comment, declared that he had followed Kriegel's advice, by repeatedly urging Leary and other police commanders to take "vigorous and firm" action against corruption. What more, he seemed to say, could anyone expect of a mayor?

Although Lindsay had been spared the indignity of a sworn appearance before his own commission, the damage was severe, just the same. He had been reelected, in 1969, without the support of either major party—an extraordinary feat, and, for the city, a "golden moment," as Jack Newfield and Paul DeBrul observed in their book *The Permanent Government*. But, "instead of using the gift of liberation to make difficult decisions," Newfield and DeBrul wrote, "Lindsay's staff, and then Lindsay himself, became seized with the ambition to run him for president in 1972." He became a Democrat, and began cutting deals and spending city money (and money that the city had borrowed, unwisely) with an eye on short-term political gain. He decided to launch his campaign in Florida, in the belief that its large population of New York retirees would give Lindsay an advantage. But many of those retirees heckled and jeered when they encountered Lindsay on the campaign trail, and he finished fifth in the primary. "I think the handwriting is on the wall," Meade Esposito, the Democratic boss of Brooklyn, commented a few weeks later. "Little Sheba better come home." And he came home, a much-humbled figure, to serve out his last two years as mayor and then fade from view.

As bad as the hearings were for Lindsay's reputation, they would have been worse if Bob Leuci had testified. Because Leuci was off working for the feds, his evidence had to remain secret, and thus the Knapp Commission never squarely addressed the degree of corruption in the area of narcotics. A veil was therefore also thrown over the connection between the Lindsay administration's failure to respond to David's pleas and the spread of heroin in the same years—a period when, as Adam Walinsky, a lawyer and ex-aide to Robert F. Kennedy, wrote in *The Village Voice* in March 1973, there were "no laws against the selling of heroin," merely "a system whereby, for the appropriate license fees to the appropriate authorities, certain people obtained a protected monopoly franchise to sell heroin, at least to certain classes of people."

———

The two faces that New Yorkers saw most often during the hearings were those of Whitman Knapp and Michael Armstrong. They had done their work well, and it was the sort of work—exposing corruption, quizzing malefactors—that in past scandals had brought lasting public acclaim to the likes of Judge Samuel Seabury and Thomas E. Dewey. This time, however, the public seemed to sense that what Knapp and Armstrong and their associates had done, however industriously, was the easy part. The heroes of the hour were David Durk and Frank Serpico. (Perhaps the anticipation of that possibility was another—unconscious—factor in Knapp and Armstrong's initial decision not to have them testify.) Just as the high-ranking officials who testified seemed to encompass all the shades of chicanery and opportunism that people in power are capable of, these two, as a pair, seemed to embody all the city's native virtues.

The story of their long crusade was politics that cut to the bone. "To the sordid record of police corruption unveiled by the Knapp Commission has now been added an even more depressing saga of official indifference born of the apparent belief that graft was so ingrained it was better left unchallenged," *The New York Times* editorialized.

Serpico, testifying before "a forest of microphones and at least eleven television cameras" (according to David Burnham's account in the *Times*), gave simple and well-formed answers in a soft voice. He spoke of "an atmosphere in which the honest officer fears the dishonest officer, and not the other way around," pleaded with the commission to give the police some moral guidance, and called for a permanent outside body to keep the department honest in the future. He had trimmed his hair and put on a suit and tie for the occasion, and it was difficult for anyone watching him in the great hall of the Chamber of Commerce building to find the wild-eyed character who had so frightened Arnold Fraiman.

For David, appearing before the Knapp Commission was a cathartic release, the climax of a five-year struggle, and his words were all the more forceful for the fatigue, anxiety, resentment, and passion of his delivery. "At the very beginning, the most important fact to understand," he said, reading from a statement on which he had labored for days, "is that I had and have no special knowledge of police corruption. . . . The facts were there waiting to be exposed. This commission, to its enormous credit, has exposed them. . . . The fact is that almost wherever we turned in the police department, wherever we turned in the city administration, and almost wherever we went in the rest of the city, we were met not with cooperation, not with appreciation, not with an eagerness to seek out the truth, but with suspicion and hostility and laziness and inattention. . . ." For most

New Yorkers, police corruption was a nasty but abstract problem. For David, it was what stood between cops and their pride. The average cop, he testified, longed to be honest but was convinced that "he lives in the middle of a corrupt society." The police department had become "a home for the drug dealers and thieves," in which "men who could have been good officers, men of decent impulse . . . were told in a hundred ways every day, 'Go along, forget about the law, don't make waves and shut up. . . .'

"Some people say that the cops live in the midst of inhumanity, amidst all the violence and cheating, violence and hate, and I guess to some extent it is true," he told the Knapp Commission. "But being a cop also means to be engaged with life. . . . Being a cop is a vocation, or it is nothing at all, and that's what I saw being destroyed by the corruption of the New York City police department, destroyed for me and for thousands of others like me."

A long ovation followed David's statement, and Chairman Knapp, visibly nonplussed, decided to call a recess so that people could collect themselves. If there had been a machine for measuring such things, it would have shown a sharp citywide drop in cynicism after David's testimony, which was played and replayed on TV and radio, and printed and reprinted in newspapers and magazines. His father, for whom "You can't fight City Hall" was almost a philosophy of life, came by the Durks' apartment that evening. "He looked like he was going to burst, he was so proud," Arlene Durk recalled. "Someone *had* fought City Hall, and he had won—and it was his son." Strangers, encountering David on the street, rushed up to him to shake his hand. Some of his former colleagues in the 18th Precinct also looked on him as a hero. (To Frank Schiele—who, like David, had often been assigned to guard department-store display windows on the midnight-to-eight-A.M. tour—the scandal was a blessing, for it had liberated rank-and-file cops from the "shadowy deals" of their superiors.) Congratulatory cards, letters, and telegrams poured in, and though many of the authors were seeking to call his attention to scandals in their own bureaucracies, the underlying message of most of the communiques was "Right on!" Arlene, who had yet to decide that a listed phone number brought more grief than pleasure, found the phone calls exhilarating. "It gave you the sense," she said, "that there were all those people out there who wanted to see good things happen."

CHAPTER

TWELVE

I f the NYPD were a board game, it would have a square marked "Hollywood offers to buy your story—you tell the bosses to get lost!" That was where David seemed to have landed as a result of the anticorruption crusade and the recruiting project. The movie—the dream of a flamboyant producer named John Foreman—was to be a vehicle for Paul Newman, with whom Foreman had a partnership at the time. Early in 1971, Foreman invited his would-be subject and star to an introductory dinner. Newman, trying to make conversation, recalled that he had wheedled his way out of a number of speeding tickets over the years, sometimes by giving an autograph to the cop who had stopped him so that the cop could bestow the trophy on his wife or girlfriend. David berated Newman for acting like a "poltroon." Newman said afterward that David had been "hard cheese." Joanne Woodward—Mrs. Newman—laughed, and said it was a pleasure to encounter someone with the chutzpah to stand up to her husband.

David had become a celebrity. Johnny Carson had him as a guest on *The Tonight Show*. There were awards, speaking engagements, and consulting offers from police departments around the country. He accepted an offer to teach what became a popular course at Yale—

"The Police and Social Change." A group of Reform Democrats approached him about running for public office, and the same week, he was summoned to the White House, where Egil "Bud" Krogh, Jr.— later to achieve modest renown as one of the "plumbers" of Watergate—vaulted over his desk, vigorously shook David's hand, and offered to "package" him as the Nixon administration's emissary to the campuses.

"My biggest mistake was not getting out of the department after Knapp," David said later. If it was a mistake, however, it was one in which he invested plenty of thought. He knew that some of his fellow cops regarded him as an opportunist who had enhanced his reputation by tarring theirs. To quit and write a book, run for office, or seize any of the other options of the moment would be to confirm them in that view. ("The dilettante charge would have stuck," he explained later.) They expected him to leave, and because they expected it, he couldn't bring himself to.

Besides, he thought of the corruption scandal as the triggering event of a full-blown police revolution—one he hoped to be part of. And so, to the surprise of a number of people, friends and enemies alike, he decided to go back to being a cop.

———————

Patrick Murphy, who became the new police commissioner of New York City in October 1970—the man on whom David's hopes for a place of honor in the post-Knapp police department rested—had deep roots in the NYPD. He had spent eighteen years there himself, and the ranks had also included, at one time or another, his father, two of his brothers, an uncle, and a nephew, to say nothing of all the blue-suited Murphys to whom he was more distantly related. Physically an uncommanding figure—short, with thin, gray-white hair, and a mild voice—he had a strong aversion (rare in the police field) to slang or coarse talk. A fast guess would have pegged him as the brother who had chosen the priesthood over the police. But he had a reputation for bold leadership, and in his first six months as commissioner he booted out virtually all of Howard Leary's top people (in

some cases, reaching several rungs down in rank for their replace-
ments), "flopped" (demoted) hundreds of plainclothesmen, and
announced that commanders would henceforth be held accountable
for corruption in their units, even if there was no evidence of their
complicity—an announcement soon accompanied by a flurry of
transfers and demotions that served to make the policy credible.

Murphy would never have had the chance to display all this boldness, however, if he had not first demonstrated an impressive capacity
for caution. In 1950, as a young patrolman, he put in for plainclothes
duty, only to recoil in horror at the corruption he found there. Murphy
applied for a personal audience with the police commissioner in order
to spell out what he had seen. The commissioner, Murphy recalled,
promised him, "You'll be hearing from me"—but he never did hear.

Murphy's reaction was to transfer out of plainclothes in a matter
of days, deftly explaining to his superiors (lest they think him over-
sensitive) that he needed an assignment in which he could more easily study for the sergeant's exam. Next he abandoned uniformed
patrol, where payoffs were also ubiquitous. It was as if he had lifted a
rock, had seen the worms and insects crawling underneath, and had
hurriedly put it back, vowing never to look in a place like that again.
He spent the balance of his NYPD career in such islands of probity as
Emergency Services and the police academy, efficiently rising to lieutenant and captain, and then, when the path to the top became steep
and crowded, left the NYPD for the chief of police's job in Syracuse,
New York—the launching pad for what was to be a remarkable,
meteoric career as the white knight brought in to lead a series of
troubled police departments.

If the nitty-gritty of police work was a dim memory for Murphy, the
politics, the hidebound traditions, and the bureaucratic cant of the
NYPD was all very fresh, and distasteful, to him. He was one New York
City cop who dared to speak the unspeakable—that the most cos-
mopolitan of American cities had one of the most insular, cobweb-
ridden police departments. "In many ways, Los Angeles and Chicago
have been ahead of us for decades," Murphy declared in an interview
with Tom Buckley, a reporter for *The New York Times Magazine*.

Murphy intended to be remembered—to have an impact. "There are plenty of guys right now saying, 'We can outlast these SOB's,' " he told Buckley. "We've got to try to prove they're wrong. My problem is, how do I get control of this monster of a department with all its pockets of power, its traditions, its mythology, its cynicism? How do I move the men who move the men down the line? It's a long-term project. For Leary it was enough to survive. This was the best job he had ever had and he didn't want to lose it. I don't feel that way."

Under Murphy, the NYPD stopped measuring cops by raw arrest figures and began looking at the resolution of their cases in court. (The old system allowed a crooked cop to undermine his own arrests with purposefully weak testimony and still look good in the eyes of his superiors.) A departmental ban on moonlighting was lifted, giving cops a legitimate route to some additional income. The Detective Division—long known as a domain in which connections counted for almost everything—was encouraged to start selecting and promoting on the basis of merit. These were simple, commonsensical, and in the NYPD context, radical reforms.

Murphy was shrewd enough, moreover, to perceive that the scandal which had made him commissioner gave him unusual leverage. He made a point of defending his men against some of the charges leveled against them in the Knapp Commission hearings (especially by William Phillips and the other rogue cops, who, as Murphy complained, had a vested interest in slurring their former compatriots, so as to make their own conduct seem less exceptional). But, at the same time, he consulted regularly with Knapp and Armstrong and made adroit use of the commission's inquiry to push through initiatives that might have been impossible to implement otherwise, such as the "field associates" program, in which selected recruits, besides performing the usual duties of cops, acted as undercover agents ferreting out misconduct in their commands. (How much misconduct they actually ferreted out is another matter; they may have been used more as a bluff than as a serious source of intelligence.) When intimations of fresh corruption surfaced, Murphy was not shy about transferring, censuring, humiliating, or demoting the officials he considered responsible. A few months after his arrival, Knapp Commission investigators observed eight uniformed cops in the Village taking packages of meat from a packing plant and depositing them in the trunks of their automobiles. Murphy suspended the cops and had charges brought against them. He also made a point of transferring the captain who commanded the precinct, as well as eight of his sergeants, and related charges were brought against two lieutenants, three sergeants, and nine other patrolmen.

A similarly thorough housecleaning followed the discovery that a group of plainclothesmen was on the payroll of a Harlem "bottle club." This time, Murphy ordered disciplinary proceedings against an inspector, a deputy inspector, and a captain, in addition to the sergeants and plainclothesmen directly implicated; later he transferred the two-star chief in command of Manhattan North for expressing reluctance to mete out the discipline that Murphy had decreed.

If Murphy's coming spelled trouble for bosses who were corrupt or lax about corruption, it spelled opportunity for some unusually dedicated and independent-minded commanders whose careers had been going nowhere in the Leary-Walsh era. For years to come, many of the most able people in the NYPD would look back on Murphy's tenure as a time when ability had counted in their favor. Yet, like many reform-minded leaders, Murphy expected subordinates to implement his policies unquestioningly. People had been addressing him as "commissioner" or "chief" for the better part of a decade, and his perspective on the police world was emphatically a boss's perspective. Those who expressed contrary views were often found wanting in imagination and put on the career shelf. Murphy had not tried to buck the system in his own long rise through the ranks, and now that he *was* the system, he expected others to be similarly compliant. And he had little use for whistle-blowers—not even the two he owed his job to.

—————

One of the personnel issues facing Murphy when he assumed office was what to do with Frank Serpico. For many months, the Bronx DA,

Burton Roberts, and others had used the lure of a detective's shield (the only reward Serpico wanted) to control him—to keep him testifying against his fellow cops. But although Serpico was now working with a Brooklyn narcotics unit (among colleagues who made their distaste for him evident on a daily basis), his rank was still patrolman.

In his memoirs, Murphy would profess to have been a "fan" of Serpico's, but he was careful to keep his feelings to himself when they might really have mattered. Murphy decided against an immediate promotion for Serpico. He had consulted his chiefs, he later explained, and had found no support for the idea. (Serpico suffered from the dual liability of being, in some boss's eyes, a "rat," and, in others', not a good enough rat. Assistant Chief Sydney Cooper—the new head of Internal Affairs—regarded him as "a reluctant dragon" whose testimony tended to "disintegrate on the stand.") The notion that the department had, in this affair, an overriding obligation to Serpico—or to history—apparently never crossed Murphy's mind. And so Serpico was left to "twist in the wind," as he has aptly put it, until the spring of 1971; and he might have gone right on twisting if he had not been shot in the head that February during a drug raid.

Even then, as Murphy wrote later, he "allowed the Serpico question to be kicked around for a while" in the hope of mobilizing the long-sought consensus. What finally drove him to action was not the thought of the still-unpromoted Serpico lying in the hospital, with recurring headaches—bullet fragments were still lodged in his brain—but, rather, the publicity he had gotten as a result. The shooting had landed Serpico, or, to be precise, an X ray of his skull, on the cover of *New York* magazine, promoting an article by Robert Daley that characterized him as a "hated, hunted man within his own department." That story and others like it, Murphy explained in a remarkably bald-faced memo, had put him "on the spot" to give Serpico a detective's gold shield, and so, at last, he issued the necessary orders. But by then Serpico was not in a frame of mind conducive to gratitude. He was no longer sure that the prize had been worth the chase—especially when he considered the disability pension (three quarters of his salary, tax free) which was now his for the asking.

Toward the matter of what to do with David Durk, Murphy exhibited a similar diffidence. They had met fleetingly in Washington, during a brief period when Murphy had been at the Justice Department and David had been busy with his recruiting project. After Murphy's arrival in New York, there had been a more formal meeting, brokered by Henry Ruth, in the commissioner's office. David hoped it would lead to an offer of a job as a deputy commissioner or special investigator—some position reflecting a recognition of his efforts. But, like Serpico, he heard nothing: there was no job offer, or any indication that his police future was even a question weighing on Murphy's mind.

Actually, Murphy thought about David quite a lot, as Robert Daley discovered when, in the spring of 1971, he went to work as a deputy police commissioner in charge of the department's dealings with the press. Daley had gained his entrée into the police world by writing a profile of David for *Life* a year earlier, and it was David who had introduced him to Serpico, thus paving the way for the *New York* article that brought Daley to Murphy's notice. Daley resolved to use his newfound influence to win David a job in the Murphy administration. But he got nowhere. Murphy didn't seem to notice the qualities that Daley admired in David—his courage, his infectious love of police work. "Pat required one hundred percent loyalty when he was running an organization," Henry Ruth recalled. "I think he thought of David as someone who went to a lot of parties on the East Side."

Murphy's boss was John Lindsay; Lindsay's closest advisor was Jay Kriegel; and the top ranks of the city's law-enforcement establishment were crowded with other officials who had heard and ignored David's pleas. The new police commissioner could not convey approval of David, then, without conveying implicit disapproval of a number of people whose favorable opinion was important to a commissioner's well-being.

Besides, David had leaked embarrassing information in the past, and who was to say he would not do so again? "No more *New York Times*, okay" were almost the first words out of Murphy's mouth in his initial meeting with David. Later, according to Daley, Murphy repeatedly discussed David at staff meetings, usually in the form of questions about what made him tick, what he would do next, and how to counter, divert, or preempt him. "It was amazing that a simple sergeant could so upset the timing and the thinking of the massive bureaucracy that was the New York City police department," Daley wrote in *Target Blue*, a memoir of his year with the NYPD.

While David's dream of a high-level job went unaddressed, so did his hope of getting the other thing he most wanted from Murphy: a reopening of the Pleasant Avenue investigation. There was no action on that front until May 1971, when, to Murphy's dismay, David made veiled references to the case on a Sunday-morning TV interview show. "I gave the Special Investigating Unit specific, concrete intelligence about a multikilo-a-week operation," he said. "No arrests were ever made, no action was ever taken by the police department. I understand that the case was closed."

The next day, Murphy ordered the Narcotics Division to launch a fresh investigation of David's charges, and as a backup measure, he asked Assistant Chief Inspector Arthur Grubert, the new head of intelligence, to look into the matter. Grubert was one of the honest, dedicated officials who prospered under Murphy. A steady, no-nonsense type—tall, thin, fit-looking, with grayish hair—he had begun to dismantle the security-state apparatus of the John Walsh regime. The NYPD, he decided, really didn't have the resources—or the need—to keep close tabs on Communists, Yippies, and student protest groups at Columbia University. Organized crime and the narcotics world, it seemed to Grubert, should be his primary focus.

Narcotics quickly reported back that David's allegations had no merit. Grubert, however, pressed on. He asked the narcotics people for the records of their original Pleasant Avenue investigation, and they were unable to supply any. That struck him as suspicious. His suspicions mounted after two of his own deputies presented him with the transcript of a wiretapped phone conversation which, they said, showed David's informant—his "old man"—to be a drug dealer. (One of those deputies, Richard Condon, who had been a protégé of John

Walsh's, would serve a brief transitional term as police commissioner in the late 1980s.) Grubert insisted on listening to the tape himself, and when he did it became clear to him that the words had been mistranscribed; the original conversation proved no such thing.

Around the same time, the old man bought a stolen police revolver from a woman (a waitress at the Delightful) who was in cahoots with a gun-running cop in the 25th Precinct. He brought the gun (a snubnose .38 that had been reported stolen from a police locker) to David's apartment, arriving with it in the middle of Joan Durk's tenth birthday party. David turned it over to a captain in intelligence, suggesting that it be placed, for confidentiality's sake, in Grubert's safe. But the captain, dismissing his concerns, ordered him to follow the standard police practice of carving his initials and shield number into the frame and depositing the gun at the property clerk's office.

That same night, David got a call from the old man, who reported in a frightened voice that the woman who had sold him the gun wanted it back. "Where's the gun, fucko?" she had said, implying that *she* knew the answer. Frantically searching for a plausible reply, he had told her he had given it to a cousin in Astoria. Now he would have to produce it quickly, he told David, or his life would be in jeopardy.

Grubert, learning of these events from David, was appalled by what they implied—that someone at headquarters had blabbed to someone at the 25th Precinct. Grubert declared that he would personally fetch the gun from the property clerk's office and find a gunsmith to remove David's initials and shield number, so the weapon could be returned to the old man in something like its original state. The time was nearly midnight, and the first gunsmith Grubert contacted did not have the right kind of blueing—a rust preventive that would cover up the damage. It was four in the morning when Grubert finally delivered the gun to David. He explained that he had wound up going to Yonkers, where he had had found a gunsmith who, while unable to match the original blueing, had reblued the weapon in its entirety, adding rust patches to make it look less shiny-new.

Shaken by the whole business, Grubert wanted to talk to David alone. As they walked down Central Park West early that morning, he gave David his home phone number and apologized for having previously disputed him on the subject of headquarters security. "Don't ever call me in the office," Grubert told him. "I don't trust anybody anymore."

"Grubert couldn't believe that they were so stupid, and so brazen," David recalled. "He kept using that word, 'brazen.' " The conversation moved on to other topics, including Grubert's son, who intended to go into law enforcement, either as a New York City cop, like his father, or as an FBI agent. Grubert vowed to do everything in his power to get his son to choose the FBI.

Grubert was setting up a narcotics intelligence unit, and in early July he accompanied David and Paul Delise to the parking lot of a restaurant in Queens for a clandestine meeting with the old man. For Grubert's benefit, the old man confirmed the stories he had previously told David, and added a few fresh details, including two new drug locations: a place called the Hole—a cutting room concealed behind a hidden panel in a candy store—and a bakery on First Avenue that doubled as a drug warehouse. Delise, who had worked on gambling investigations in the area, knew the bakery. "We've been across the street on a rooftop watching it," he told Grubert, "and it's got activity that's just not called for in that neighborhood for a legit business. Half the customers are coming out of Cadillacs and Thunderbirds. There's money and a hustle in that place. There's got to be."

As it happened, a team of detectives under Grubert was already running a narcotics investigation in the Bronx involving some of the same suspects the old man had identified. Fitting his information and their other findings together, Grubert's people decided that the Bronx locations they had been watching were subsidiary, and the investigation shifted its focus to East Harlem. At the beginning of 1972, a team of undercover agents moved into an apartment on Pleasant Avenue, where they could observe a barber shop that was a drop for heroin shipments, two public telephones that were used to take orders, and the Pleasant Tavern—the base of operations of Gennaro Zanfardino, whom the old man referred to as Jerry Z. A year later, after shooting miles of videotape, Grubert's unit and a team of FBI agents conducted a citywide roundup in which they arrested sixty-five people with ties to the Pleasant Avenue drug network. First Deputy Commissioner William H. T. Smith acknowledged that it was David who had first singled out Pleasant Avenue as a focal point of the city's narcotics business. Grubert, too, paid tribute to David's contributions. "Dave whetted my appetite," he said, "and any information he gave me proved out to be true."

After the arrests, David and the old man arranged to meet on the New Jersey waterfront to celebrate. The son he had hoped to keep out of the drug trade was now beyond rescue, and the two of them hardly communicated. Nevertheless, the old man had excitedly read the accounts of the roundup in all the major newspapers. He couldn't get over the fact that Ernie Boy was referred to as Oreste Abbamonte. "Where did they get Oreste from?" he said to David. "His mother doesn't call him Oreste." He had read about himself in those same papers (they had interviewed David about the origins of the case), and he relished his new, anonymous stature. At a family get-together a few nights earlier, a niece of his had spoken of the roundup, saying that if she ever met the "old man," she would give him a kiss. "My heart was bursting," the old man told David. "I wanted to announce it to everyone—'I'm the old man.' "

<hr>

David played no official part in the Pleasant Avenue investigation, but as a result of its progress his stock went up not only with Grubert but with Deputy Chief Sydney Cooper, the commanding officer of Internal Affairs, who had been asked by Murphy to see that every allegation of David's was fully investigated. A big, bald man, with the pale complexion of the workaholic, Cooper was, like David, a Jew, and by his own account he had paid a high price, professionally, for being unconnected and incorruptible. Because he had not been, as he later put it, "a money man," he had been obliged to live in a tenement and to depend on public transportation well after many of his contemporaries had acquired houses and cars. The material sacrifice hadn't been the worst of it, for in the pre-Knapp NYPD, the essential qualification for just about any job was a proven willingness to take money—that being the best evidence that a cop was not a potential rat. Twenty years had passed before Cooper was assigned to his "first white precinct," as he put it.

Another thing Cooper and David had in common was an over-abundance of formal education: Cooper had completed law school as well as college. But his background was one without social advantages. He had grown up on a chicken farm in southern New Jersey, going to work, at eighteen, as a civilian police aide in the Brownsville section of Brooklyn. His higher education had been a spare-time thing—a manifestation of general, irrepressible diligence. Cooper had consistently scored at or near the top on promotional tests, only to receive assignments that no one else wanted. He thought of himself as someone who had slogged his way into the top ranks on merit alone. He thought of David as a "young political manipulator" who had cultivated friends in the mayor's office and had slid from one cushy assignment to another, never leaving Manhattan.

Still, David was a hard worker—Cooper had to give him that. Most detectives, in Cooper's experience, were nine-to-fivers; David, once engaged on a case, would keep at it all night or all weekend, if need be, and that was Cooper's way, too. And (as Cooper was not the first to notice) David had a remarkable talent for finding out things. In moments of paternal affection, Cooper hinted that with "proper channeling" David had a chance of becoming a first-rate Internal Affairs man.

Murphy would undoubtedly have been pleased with that result, too, for Internal Affairs was a place where David's obsessiveness could be channeled into a recognized police purpose. But David had no interest in Internal Affairs or in working for Sydney Cooper, whom he regarded as a tyrant. Cooper had waited most of his adult life for a position of power, and now that he had it he seemed determined to mete out, in the few years remaining to him before retirement, as much punishment as he had experienced in the previous thirty. His manner with accused police officers resembled that of the prison-camp commandant played by Otto Preminger in *Stalag 17*.

A cop would be told to come in for questioning in the morning, instructed to wait in an antechamber the whole day, and sent home with orders to return the next morning, when the process would begin anew; the time to launch the actual interrogation, Cooper figured, was when the cop's nerves were completely shot. The side of Cooper that he showed his subordinates was only a little warmer.

Encouraged by Cooper to become his protégé, David responded with barbed questions. Why did Internal Affairs so consistently go after rank-and-file cops and let their supervisors escape unscathed? Where did it say that a cop suspected of a crime was not entitled to the same civil liberties as the rest of the populace? Why had a cop never been told, "We're sorry, you were wrongly accused?"

To Cooper, this was mushy thinking. Cooper knew he was regarded as a bully. He knew it, and he reveled in the role. At the Patrolmen's Benevolent Association summer camp in the Catskills, Cooper's appearance inevitably set off a shower of boos, and he would smile and raise both fists in the air, like a boxer entering the ring to fight the hometown favorite. It may not have been literally true that, as was widely reported, Cooper had once hung an accused cop out a window by his ankles, but Cooper seemed to enjoy being the subject of such legends. "That was my role," he recalled. "I had to be the boogeyman, and David did not want to be associated with the boogeyman. What the hell he thought he was going to be, I don't know. Did he think he was going to be loved?"

So it was a source of considerable distress to David that when his leave of absence ended, he found himself assigned to an anomalous position—not clearly permanent, not clearly temporary—under Cooper. For months, he had been pleading with Daley, among others, to put in a good word for him with the commissioner, and this was the apparent result. But, just as David began to lose hope, Murphy's opinion of him began to improve.

What changed his attitude was the burst of attention and favorable publicity David had received as a result of his Knapp Commission testimony. Murphy himself was blandness personified. *The New York Times Magazine*, operating on the theory that a bold new police commissioner ought to rate an article, had sent three different reporters to interview him before one returned with something publishable. Murphy, like many people, craved the quality that he lacked. He longed for media appeal, and when the Knapp Commission hearings were over, he was startled to find David's concluding statement reprinted on the op-ed page of the *Times*. Then, reading it, he was pleased to learn that David had said only good things about him, while speaking passionately of his own determination to remain on the force.

Sensing an opportunity, Daley delicately suggested that Murphy's own pale image might be brightened by association with David. Murphy was laying plans to turn the 24th Precinct, on the Upper West Side, into a "model precinct," and, at Daley's urging, he agreed to give David a highly visible role there as a sort of training sergeant. Murphy announced the experiment at the police academy, in a speech to graduating recruits. After he spoke, David was asked to say a few words about what he hoped to accomplish, and with Murphy looking anxiously on, he made a brief, eloquent statement about reducing crime and tension and increasing integrity and productivity. The people of the model precinct would get an inspiring example of evenhanded policing, he promised. They would see cars ticketed for illegal parking—and landlords ticketed for illegal polluting. The announcement ceremonies were a great success. John Lindsay even put in an appearance, and he took the opportunity to let David know that bygones were bygones. "I've always admired you from afar," Lindsay whispered to him.

Murphy had often been disappointed in the coverage given to his interviews and public appearances. This time, the story was played big, and a considerable to-do was made of the picture of the commissioner and the hero sergeant standing side by side. "Having David there was an act of genius," Murphy told Daley. He drafted a memo pointing out that David had credibility with the public; Murphy's own credibility would be enhanced, he wrote, if Daley would come up with further opportunities for the two of them to occupy the spotlight together.

That May, David became a "special aide" to the commissioner. The job was not an onerous one. Basically, it carried only one responsibility: he was to appear with Murphy whenever and wherever Murphy desired him to. All he had to do was speak positively of the commissioner and his reforms in public, and be pleasant, deferential company in their other interludes together. And if he performed well, there was reason to believe (Daley counseled him) that he might soon be rewarded with a more meaningful position. David was now in a position to "write my own ticket," as he said later. But, as he also said, "We all have our thresholds."

From one point of view, Murphy and David were natural allies. Murphy, like David, believed that the responsibility for keeping a police unit honest lay with its bosses. "Command accountability" was his management credo. He identified himself as an enemy of cynicism and bureaucratic thinking. And yet, they could hardly have been more different. Although Murphy was a great champion of new ideas, they were ideas that struck David as abstract and incorporeal—reforms that could be implemented with the flourish of a pen and summed up in a press release. Some of those press releases, it was true, had a grand ring to them. The model precinct, for example, was promoted as an island of utopian experimentation, where the best possible recruits would be assigned to work with experienced cops who would infuse them with "idealism, integrity, and desire for service," as Murphy declared. The precinct would be broken up into posts small enough to allow a cop to just about see from one end to the other, and each post would have a "neighborhood police team" of perhaps two dozen cops: a kind of miniature police force that would get to know the precinct's inhabitants and respond quickly and creatively to the problems troubling them. (The concept was a lot like that of today's Community Policing.) Young cops, after a period of initiation in the model precinct, would be dispersed around the city to plant the same values and habits in other commands.

In practice, however—and the model precinct was instituted rather suddenly—the concept consisted largely of sending cops to community meetings, where they listened wearily to the grievances of local activists and senior citizens and then made sweeping promises they had little intention—or means—of fulfilling. On reporting to his new assignment as sergeant in charge of the neighborhood police teams, David found that the regular sergeants and lieutenants had no use for such an interloper, and neither they nor he had been told what his duties were. (He and the model precinct parted company, by mutual consent, after a few days.) Nothing else about the program had been planned with much greater care.

Daley was the model precinct's greatest champion, and as it "subsided back into the mass of the police department," he pleaded with Murphy to do something. But Murphy's thoughts, Daley concluded, had moved on to other problems—other new programs. "He was a man who scattered acorns around the base of the tree, and apparently he cared little more about what happened to them than an oak did," Daley wrote.

Murphy saw the police department as an administrative structure, to be jiggered and rejiggered. In his year and a half as police commissioner, he had increased the number of supervisors in the field, dished out memorable punishments to cops caught taking money or overlooking illegal enterprises (and to their supervisors), and decided to suspend the enforcement of most of the gambling and blue laws. But, as important as these steps were, the leitmotiv of all of them was restraint. The implication was that police officers, like children, had to be kept out of places where they might get in trouble.

David saw the department as the sum of its people. The average cop, he believed, was of two minds about corruption. Although he might tell himself that much of it was a deserved fringe benefit for a profession that was underrewarded, he was also made uncomfortable by it. It seemed to David that if Murphy's list of don'ts had been accompanied by a list of dos—fresh strategies, initiatives, equipment, powers, and encouragement—to help cops prevent crimes and catch criminals, the rank and file might have concluded that they were better off, on balance, than before. Most cops, David was convinced, would gladly give up the pad for a sense of pride. The problem was, they had been forced to give up the pad, but they hadn't gotten the pride.

And when they examined the new rules that governed them, they couldn't help making comparisons with practices they saw at Police Headquarters, where a very different standard of propriety seemed to apply. Murphy and his new team of commanders were proud of having "killed Santa Claus," as one assistant chief put it; cops, that is, were no longer allowed to rack up extra income at Christmastime by dunning merchants and others for cash, and precinct Christmas parties had been banned, as had the mere presence of liquor in any police facility. But Murphy had a bar in his own office (he also had a refrigerator and a fireplace), and a few days before Christmas of 1971, the top brass themselves had held a party at which, beers and whiskeys in hand, they congratulated each other on having dealt a death blow to holiday revelry in the precincts.

In the press, Murphy was celebrated as a daring innovator, and the praise was, on one level, completely deserved, for corruption had subsided dramatically. Yet, at the same time, cops—including honest ones—made sneering remarks about his manhood and belittled him in station-house graffiti as a "Little Tin God" and a "Little Boy Scout."

Having engineered the scandal that had produced Murphy's appointment, David had a proprietary feeling about the results. Murphy was, in a sense, his creation, and he had been watching Murphy's progress with mounting anguish. Now that they had been thrown together, he poured out his anguish to Murphy. If Murphy wanted to rally cops to his side, David said—if he hoped to lead by inspiration instead of fear—he would have to demonstrate that a single standard of honesty applied to all; he would have to make it clear that small offenses would be forgiven; he would have to meet with cops face-to-face and acknowledge that the bosses, himself included, bore a share of the responsibility for the problem. He would have to "bleed in front of the troops," as David put it.

Daley thought that the differences between David and Murphy were largely due to a sort of language barrier. Murphy was a believer in calm, measured, concise speech. His top aides—men of much higher rank than David—had learned not to tax his patience or lay too many problems on him. His favorite was Albert Seedman, the chief of detectives, who when asked, "Any problems, Al?" routinely shot back, "No, boss." Murphy's method of terminating a conversation with a long-winded supplicant was to look at his watch and remark, with a smile, "Well, I'm running a little late." It was a technique that caused people of all ranks and descriptions to nervously conclude their remarks and be gone. But it had no effect on David. He went right on talking.

While Murphy had trouble following some of what David said, the "bleeding in front of the troops" idea was perfectly clear to him. Clear—and out of the question.

"I wanted to show him that he could get away with being a good guy," David recalled. "But he wouldn't even acknowledge that he understood what I was talking about."

To "bleed in front of the troops" would be—to Murphy's way of thinking—an act of weakness. Like Sydney Cooper, Murphy figured that being hated, or strongly disliked, by cops went with the territory. "If I had wanted to win a popularity contest, I would not have taken the job," he wrote in his memoirs. In any case, it was not the commissioner's job to deal with ordinary cops; he had sergeants and lieutenants for that.

David realized that he was not doing his career any good by pestering Murphy, but he went on pestering him nonetheless. "You think about things that no one else notices," Murphy said, when David tried to make an issue of the mayor's box at Yankee Stadium. "What do you think goes through a cop's mind," David had said, "when he's assigned to protect the mayor's box, and there's no mayor there—no city business being transacted—just a lot of Whitey Wide-ties with gorgeous girls, and the cops are supposed to see to it that these people aren't hassled." (Murphy, although David didn't know it, himself had a gold pass to Yankee Stadium, which his children often borrowed.)

After two weeks as Murphy's aide, David flew into his office one morning with a *Times* article about a city ethics board ruling, which held that officials of commissioner rank or above could accept free meals and other favors as long as they did not do so on a regular basis. David was outraged. Cops had no such escape clause, he said. For them, any gratuity was a criminal offense. This was an inconsistency that Murphy had to address if he valued his credibility, David insisted. Murphy didn't see the need. When David pressed the point, Murphy took a rubber stamp from his drawer, and stamped the front page of the *Times* CONFIDENTIAL. "Davey, my boy," he said, "the *Daily News* didn't carry this story. No other paper carried this story. Cops do not read the *Times*. We do not have to respond to it."

David lasted three weeks in the job. Murphy's displeasure crystalized when, in the Channel Seven makeup room before their joint appearance on *The Dick Cavett Show*, David got off on his double-standard rap again, and noted that Murphy himself had been guilty of behavior that, not to put too fine a point on it, smacked of corruption. The commissioner, David said, had several detective-chauffeurs who sometimes ran personal errands for him. And another thing: David had accompanied him to a number of functions where food and drink had been supplied but had yet to see him pay for any of it. The next morning, Murphy remarked that David looked tired. How would he like to become an exchange cop in San Francisco?

CHAPTER

THIRTEEN

———⟫●⟪———

T he new team at Police Headquarters, like the old team, had little use for a cop who passed unofficial secrets to outside agencies.
And David's sins went further than that, for most of his whistle-
blowing had been against people who were not demonstrably corrupt
themselves but had merely received information about corruption
and sat on it. This was an innovation in whistle-blowing, and it
caused widespread alarm. "His name struck fear into every boss's
heart," Jack Ferguson, who was then a lieutenant in charge of an
intelligence unit within the Organized Crime Control Bureau, remembered. "When he called, everybody got shook."

David had told the *Times* and the Knapp Commission not only what
certain highly placed officials had done or failed to do but what they
had said in their own defense—Kriegel's line about City Hall's reluctance to "upset the cops," for example. "He created the impression—
perhaps unintended—that he would take a shard of a remark made
five years ago and throw it back in your face," a former prosecutor
recalled. "This was very unwise."

To compound matters, it had come out during the hearings that
David had tape-recorded a phone call with Jay Kriegel. It was only a
single recording (made after Arthur Gelb had questioned his account

of the back-and-forth between them), and David testified that he later felt so bad about what he had done that he destroyed the tape; nevertheless, it was a fact that powerful people remembered. At the Manhattan DA's office, Lawrence Goldman, who had worked on cases with David and viewed him as a friend, was warned to steer clear of him. "There was this wariness whenever his name was mentioned," Goldman remembered. "I was told, 'Watch out, he might be taping you!' "

And so, in June 1972, when Commissioner Murphy put out the word that Sergeant Durk was available to any commander who cared to assume responsibility for him, there was a fairly resounding silence, and then considerable astonishment when a newcomer to the top ranks—William P. McCarthy, the Deputy Commissioner for Organized Crime Control—stepped forward and said, "If he's free, I want him."

McCarthy, who would soon be promoted to first deputy commissioner (John Walsh's old job), was tall and thin, with fair skin and bushy eyebrows—a handsome man with a professorially gentle manner that concealed a streak of hotheadedness. He had been a bomber pilot in World War II. He was a history buff who had sometimes been known, while interviewing subordinates who were up for promotion, to ask them what they knew about the Peloponnesian Wars. As the commander of the Traffic Division in the early 1960s, McCarthy had encouraged his men to ticket vehicles without fear or favor. Rewarded with a transfer to the civil defense unit, he had decided to retire, at the age of forty-seven, to Florida and a life of golf, reading, and teaching criminal justice. He had been drawing a pension for seven years when Commissioner Murphy, having exhausted the active-duty ranks in his head-hunting, invited him back.

Alone among the new leaders of the department, McCarthy figured that he owed David Durk and Frank Serpico a debt of gratitude. "This tempest that they had set off had made it possible for me to get back there with the kind of power that I always wanted but never had," he said, shortly before his death, in 1990. "By bringing David in, I was flying a flag. I was saying, 'I'm not like other palefaces—I don't speak with forked tongue.' "

Warned that David had a reputation for driving his bosses crazy, McCarthy remembered that he, too, had been a troublemaker—"a pain in the ass all the time I was in the department."

He was one of the few bosses whose definition of corruption, like David's, encompassed more than the act of taking money. Perjury, he knew, was common practice in the Detective and Narcotics divisions. If a prosecutor, reviewing an application for a warrant, told a cop that his affidavit was missing a crucial piece of evidence, the cop would simply make the necessary insertions ("he would go around the corner and add a few lines," as McCarthy put it) and submit the affidavit anew—and prosecutors rarely questioned the serendipity of these rewrites. A decade earlier, McCarthy had set up what came to be called the Tactical Patrol Force—a roving unit of cops who were shifted around the city in response to crime patterns. One day, two of McCarthy's men admitted in court that they had found a couple of marijuana cigarettes on the ground, rather than, as the law required, in the possession of the defendant. Another boss, who happened to be in the courtroom at the time, was outraged. He didn't care if they were telling the truth; the point was, they had blown the case. "If they were in my unit, I would fire them," he told McCarthy. In one of McCarthy's first acts as a deputy commissioner, he informed his subordinates (there were 2,700 of them) that he didn't want them doing anything they couldn't testify to under oath.

After McCarthy's death in 1990, the *Times* ran a very brief obituary describing him simply as a "retired police official" who had "directed efforts to combat narcotics traffic and organized crime." The obituary did not point out that under McCarthy, for almost the first time, these efforts actually amounted to something. McCarthy made it plain that he wasn't interested in the petty arrests that had long been the Narcotics Division's forte. The number of narcotics arrests actually declined by 50 percent in the first year that he was in charge, but when McCarthy was apprised of this worrisome trend by a deputy, he replied, "I don't care."

Until McCarthy came along, a narcotics cop who wanted to make an undercover buy of over fifty dollars had to submit a written request and get it approved by a series of bosses—a process that only aggravated the chronic police tendency to focus on low-level dealers. McCarthy had his detectives making buys for $25,000 and more, and then flipping the people they arrested in order to go after still-bigger operators.

Figuring that maybe 90 percent of the men under him had been taking money, McCarthy determined to do everything he could to win them over to a new way of operating. He met with rank-and-file cops and promised not to go digging into the past for minor offenses. He assured his detectives that in the future they would be free to pursue every legitimate lead and would not be punished for an honest mistake. "I wanted people working for me to know that in a sense I was working for them," McCarthy recalled. "I knew what it was to deal with bosses. If they made a mistake, I took the blame. I made lots of mistakes in my life."

In the Intelligence Division, McCarthy had a large staff of detectives whose job was to know what was happening in organized crime. In his first conversation with David, he was struck by the fact that David knew things the Intelligence Division didn't seem to know. "David lived in a slightly different universe from the average policeman," McCarthy said later. "He was not the easiest guy to get along with; he didn't fit into the discipline mode of a quasi-military organization. But he was a hell of a guy at developing information, and he had a lot of good in him, so I decided to let him loose."

McCarthy gave David an office next to his own and made him a one-man detective squad. He investigated, among other things, a pedophile cop who was selling guns on the side; mob control of gay bars; the buying and selling of liquor licenses by important figures in the Bronx Democratic leadership; and the theft of a congressional election. (David got a confession from an election board employee, who had rigged voting machines so that votes for the ostensible losing candidate, Allard Lowenstein, were counted in favor of the victor, John Rooney.)

Because he had McCarthy's ear, he possessed an enviable power to cut through bureaucratic rigamarole: to launch investigations on speculative evidence, to use unorthodox methods, to purchase tape recorders and other equipment, to have easy access to "buy money," and to explore leads of a chancy nature. The usual method of wiretapping, for example, required cops to be stationed in basements, sometimes "with water up to their ankles," as he put it. David had specially leased phone lines that eliminated this necessity. "How in the world did you get that?" his friend Jack Ferguson asked him. "Nobody but the FBI has that."

McCarthy was a boss after David's heart—one who understood the need for the occasional wild-goose chase and had no objection to being rousted out of bed in the middle of a night to hear some piece of late-breaking news from the investigative front (not much of an objection, at any rate: "You know, I had a different life before I met you," McCarthy commented, in the course of one of those oddly timed phone calls). During David's years at DOI, it had often happened that after being asked to look for wrongdoing in a low place, he had found it in a high place instead, and the investigation had been aborted. These experiences had left him with a rich legacy of frustration. Now he found himself working for a man who believed, just as he did, that the natural direction for any investigation to go was up— toward targets of ever greater power and status. Thus, a case that began in the spring of 1972 with an attempt to buy a case of "size-38 dresses"—that is, revolvers—from a man who called himself Bernard the Beast quickly evolved into an attempt to get evidence against crooked prosecutors and investigators in the office of the Queens district attorney, Thomas Mackell.

The Mackell investigation exploded in David's face that summer when an informant of his was nabbed, wearing a tape recorder, by Mackell's people and Mackell himself subsequently denounced David and the police department for playing a game of entrapment. The Manhattan district attorney, Frank Hogan, whose office had approved the operation, issued a public apology for what Hogan called "an excess of zeal" on everyone's part. But McCarthy stood by David, and when one of Mackell's people asked him if he would testify before a grand jury about the matter, McCarthy said he would "be there with bells and whistles to explain why we suspected your office." (A year later, with Governor Nelson Rockefeller preparing to remove him from office for his alleged role in stymieing the investigation of a get-rich-quick scheme involving some of his own subordinates, Mackell resigned.)

David had been commandeering detectives from various units on a case-by-case basis. The Mackell brouhaha—in which it appeared that a borrowed detective had alerted Mackell's office—persuaded McCarthy that David needed a squad of his own handpicked investigators. And McCarthy gave the new squad a mission dear to his heart: to investigate Mafia influence in the garment business. The Genovese and Gambino families and their front organizations had long been a law unto themselves in the garment center. The investigative strategy that McCarthy and David adopted was to go into the trucking business and wait for organized crime to come calling. Like the attempt to investigate the Queens DA's office, setting up a sting operation in the garment district was a stretch: nothing of the kind had been done before. But the Justice Department had created interagency organized-crime strike forces all over the country, and the Southern District strike force, which covered Manhattan, already had an informant with excellent mob connections.

Herman Goldfarb, the informant, was one of those strange fish who swim in the waters where crime meets legitimate business. At the age of fourteen, he had been employed as a pinball-machine revenue collector by a cousin of his known as "the king of the one-armed bandits." At twenty-one he had been a captain in the U.S. Army—an ordnance officer who (in Goldfarb's own telling) had built hospitals, bridges, and other facilities for the advancing Allied forces in France. In his thirties, he had made a bundle of money selling insurance to unions and small businesses in Brooklyn. Short and stocky, he drove a late-model Cadillac Eldorado and dressed like a character out of *Guys and Dolls;* when David first beheld him, he was wearing a sharkskin suit that was a couple of sizes too large for him, although he was fairly large himself. He had, by his own precise reckoning, an IQ of 159, and could read 2,205 words a minute. He could recite Tennyson, in a strong Brooklyn accent.

The scene of David's introduction to Goldfarb was the Federal Bureau of Investigation's New York offices, at Sixty-ninth Street and Third Avenue, where (in a room graced by a forbidding portrait of J. Edgar Hoover) federal prosecutors, FBI agents, and representatives of the police department met to weigh the possible launching of an undercover operation in the garment district—and Goldfarb's possible participation as prime undercover agent. David, who was trying to size Goldfarb up, took him aside during a break in the discussion and asked him what he expected in the way of compensation. To David's surprise, Goldfarb said he wasn't looking to make any money, because he already had plenty. The main thing he wanted, he said, was a reinvestigation of his conviction, in 1960, on a forgery charge arising out of a business swindle. Goldfarb swore he was innocent, but when one of the prosecutors told him that a pardon would be easy to arrange, he grandly responded that he wasn't interested in a "whitewash." What he wanted was a reinvestigation: "Let the chips fall where they may."

The precise nature of Goldfarb's past business activities was a blur to everyone in the room. As to his qualifications for his present assignment, however, there was soon general agreement. The stated objective of Operation Cleveland, as the enterprise came to be called, was to gather evidence against a truckers' group (the Master Truckmens Association), against the local truckers' union, and against one Matthew "Matty the Horse" Ianniello—all of whom had to be paid off by anyone trying to run a trucking business in the garment district. In less than a year, the goal had been achieved, and the operation was beginning to reach into other realms of blue- and white-collar crime.

Goldfarb was an undercover genius. A big talker himself, he had a remarkable ability to get people—mobsters, union bosses, fellow truckers—to spell out their criminal intentions. He had been instructed to make his payoffs to a middleman—one Spike Bernstein—rather than to Ianniello; at Goldfarb's suggestion, David arranged for Bernstein to be briefly detained by the police, so Goldfarb would have an excuse for going to Ianniello directly. By making profuse apologies and explaining that he hadn't wanted to be late with his payment, Goldfarb managed to defuse Ianniello's anger. Ianniello wound up accepting delivery of an envelope containing a hundred dollars and acknowledging (on tape) that Bernstein was his collector.

Although Goldfarb was ostensibly in the trucking business (with $60,000 in police seed money, he had purchased a company, Gerro Trucking, with actual clients and routes—and a single truck), the persona he adopted was that of a semilegit businessman with a lot of different schemes going, and before long people were coming to him, hoping to share in the action. "He talks so fast you're not sure what's happening, but you're making money so you don't care," one of the prosecutors explained later.

Through Ianniello, Goldfarb arranged a meeting with Anthony "Tony Pro" Provenzano, a prominent local Teamsters Union official, who went on to become the law enforcement community's favorite suspect in the murder of Jimmy Hoffa. Goldfarb and Provenzano negotiated a deal to have $2,300,000 in union pension funds invested in a mortgage on a midtown hotel, with Provenzano taking a 13 percent kickback. (A federal jury eventually found Provenzano guilty in the scheme, and he was sentenced to a four-year term. In a separate case, he received a life sentence for murder; he died in prison.)

In March 1974, Operation Cleveland suffered a blow: Les Wolff, a cop who under the pseudonym Les Dana had assumed the role of Goldfarb's partner, was indicted on bribery charges dating back to his days as an SIU detective—a member of the same team as Bob Leuci. The indictment had been secured by the U.S. attorney's office for the Eastern District of New York. The evidence against Wolff was slender (the case was never prosecuted), but federal prosecutors in Brooklyn, correctly believing that Leuci was still concealing some of his past offenses and suspecting him of involvement in the theft of the "French Connection" heroin—a matter that had the city's law-enforcement world in a tizzy at the time—were hoping to enlist Wolff's help in building a bigger case. (Wolff refused to give an inch, even when Leuci, to save his own neck, implicated him in a number of more serious crimes. By then Leuci's own credibility had been so badly damaged that, with his testimony as the essence of the new case against Wolff, a jury acquitted him.)

It fell to David to personally place Wolff under arrest, and take his gun and badge from him. Then came an emergency damage-containment session. The first order of business was to keep Wolff's photograph out of the newspapers, so no one would know that Les Wolff and Les Dana were the same person. The Eastern District prosecutors agreed to delay the announcement indefinitely; meanwhile, Goldfarb would tell his customers and business associates that Les Dana had left New York abruptly, in order to be with his parents, who had been in a car accident. With that cover story agreed on, the strike force partners turned to the question of a replacement: another law-enforcement officer who would participate in (and eventually testify about) Goldfarb's deals.

It was decided that a woman would create the fewest ripples: an attractive young woman who could be introduced as Goldfarb's secretary. David went to Captain Gertrude Schimmel, the unofficial doyenne of policewomen. "I need a real pelt," he told her. "Someone who will fulfill the fantasies of Matty Ianniello and Tony Provenzano."

Schimmel laughed and said she had a candidate: Joanne Myers, a five-foot-ten-inch policewoman who had long blond hair and a dazzling set of false eyelashes and drove a white convertible Maserati. Officer Myers, one of the first generation of women to go on patrol in New York City, had recently distinguished herself by nabbing a couple of burglars at a Brooklyn supermarket. ("It's a goil!" one of them had exclaimed.)

David arranged to conduct the job interview in his car, across the street from Carnegie Hall, where he and members of his squad were conducting a surveillance at the time. He thought it important to assure Officer Myers at the outset that she would not be asked to sleep with anybody for the City of New York. "The farthest I expect you to go is that if someone pats you on the behind, you can let them if you want," he said. Myers said she was prepared to go that far, and was hired on the spot; then, like a traded baseball player who is sent in to pinch-hit immediately upon reporting to the new team, she agreed to take part in a drug bust that happened to be going down that night.

Although Goldfarb had to fend off a lot of questions about Les Dana's disappearance, Officer Myers proved to be well cast in her new role, and before long the offices of Gerro Trucking were again a place where people felt moved to talk about a wide range of business deals, legal and illegal. Operation Cleveland had by now produced information that went far beyond the original mandate: tips about, for instance, a leading New York State judge who was described (by a union boss) as being in the pocket of organized crime; a mob-controlled schoolbus company; judgeships that were allegedly being bought and sold through the Brooklyn Democratic Party, under its long-time leader, Meade Esposito; and kickbacks being made to the boss of the state Republican Party, Joseph Margiotta, by appointees to public jobs. (Margiotta was imprisoned for extortion and bribery nine years later.)

These leads set David's digestive juices to work. For him, the great disappointment of the Knapp Commission investigation had been its failure to look at law enforcement corruption involving anyone but cops. In the course of its inquiries, the commission had come across a number of allegations against lawyers and judges. For the most part, they had never been pursued. The daily summaries of Goldfarb's conversations glistened with intelligence about public officials who were said to be under organized crime's influence, to have taken bribes, or to be disposed toward doing so. Catching mobsters had turned out to be surprisingly easy, and David longed to take Operation Cleveland in a new direction—to turn it into a vehicle for a wide-ranging investigation of, as he put it, "the nexus between organized crime and political corruption."

This was a reverie, however, in which some key people did not join. The chief of the strike force, who, as a formal matter, called the shots, was Edward M. "Mike" Shaw, a six-foot-six-inch Boston Brahmin—a graduate of Exeter and Harvard—who came to interagency meetings with his lunch in a paper bag and sat through much of the discussions eating tunafish on white bread and sipping milk through a straw. David did not care for Shaw. He was especially annoyed by Shaw's habit of saying, when confronted with a new lead, "Let's pass on this," and reminding all present that their mandate was to look at the garment district, not at crime and corruption wherever they might be found.

That was how Shaw reacted, for example, when Goldfarb reported a conversation with Harry Davidoff, the notorious boss of the Teamsters local that controlled trucking in and out of Kennedy Airport, concerning a possible partnership: they would set up a new trucking firm, to be called Tempo Trucking, whose core business, it seemed, would be the staging of hijacks.

Prosecutors had been investigating Davidoff for years, and there had been any number of predictions (never fulfilled) of his imminent indictment. To David, the chance to have an undercover agent go into business with Davidoff was irresistible. But Shaw resisted, citing, among other objections, the fact that the crimes that the proposed new venture would go after would mainly be taking place in Brooklyn and Queens—the jurisdiction of the Eastern rather than Southern District. To get the Eastern District involved, Shaw explained, would mean sharing the secret of the operation with a wider circle of people, and that, in turn, would add to the risk of exposure and perhaps put Goldfarb's life in jeopardy. William McCarthy, who had sat in on the strike force meeting at which the Davidoff venture was discussed, was livid about Shaw's rejection of it. "They'd rather kill the case than let Eastern District get it," McCarthy said, as he and David drove back to Police Headquarters afterward.

———⟶•⟵———

The world of law enforcement is a carefully stratifed society—sort of like an Arab fiefdom—in which only lawyers, judges, and prosecutors have full citizenship, and everyone else is at their beck and call. By dropping out of law school and becoming a cop, David had chosen—though he had not realized it at the time—to be forever under

the thumb of the profession he had shunned. During one of his stints
as a patrolman in Harlem, he helped arrest a man who had shot up a
bar during a dispute with a fellow patron. While David and the other
cops were waiting to testify in court, the judge and the opposing
counsels negotiated a deal in which the defendant pleaded guilty to
the amazing charge of "attempted possession of a gun." ("Nobody
consulted me—nobody consulted any of us," David recalled.) While
at DOI, he built a case against a staff psychiatrist at Bellevue Hospital
who was in the habit of taking bribes from murderers, holdup men,
and other palpably dangerous patients and then getting them transferred to ordinary civil hospitals, from which they could easily
escape. David brought his evidence to the Manhattan DA's office,
expecting an indictment and an arrest. But, instead, the psychiatrist
was allowed to quietly resign and retire to private life (and to continue teaching forensic psychiatry at a local university). The prosecutor handling the case explained to David that the man had a wife
and children to support, and private-school tuition to pay, so there
was no need to send him to prison—the loss of his job would be punishment enough. (More than twenty years later, David would
recount the episode with an anger scarcely less intense than if it had
just happened. "Cops are married, cops have kids," he recalled telling
the prosecutor. "If a cop had taken a bribe to let one of these people
go free, you wouldn't have any qualms about sending him to prison,
would you? Why is it that when someone is a lawyer or a doctor, the
first words are 'The embarrassment is enough.' ")

David had developed certain primal feelings about lawyers and
their rules of behavior—especially what he called "the law of colle-
giality," which came into play when the target of an investigation
was someone with a suit and tie and the means to mount a high-
priced legal defense. As Shaw and his deputy, William Aronwald,
rejected one spinoff investigation after another, David's exasperation
rose to the surface, and it finally boiled over when, in the summer of
1974, they decided to shut the operation down altogether.

Shaw and Aronwald dismissed many of Goldfarb's tidbits as speculative. The possibility of nailing a judge here or a politician there,

they argued, had to be balanced against the possibility of failure, the high expense of maintaining the operation, and the problem of security. They had been particularly troubled on this last count (they said) since Les Wolff's arrest. Although they had kept his picture out of the newspapers, they continued to worry that someone might make the connection or that Wolff himself might spill the beans. The time had come, they said, to present the cases that had already been made to a grand jury and to move Goldfarb into the federal witness-relocation program. They also proposed to shut down two related stings—a dummy fencing operation (Operation St. Louis) and a garment company (Operation Detroit) that actually made and sold a fake-fur coat known as the "Central Park Bobcat"; it sold so many of them, in fact, that the business wound up turning a small profit.

Goldfarb's protection had originally been a shared NYPD-FBI responsibility. But, as a result of some early lapses on the FBI end—compounded by the tendency of some members of the bureau's team to head home at three-thirty in the afternoon, regardless of what lay ahead (they didn't like to miss their car pools to New Jersey or Long Island)—Goldfarb had come to rely more and more on his NYPD backup team, and a close relationship had developed between him and David. In David's mind, the operation was just beginning. (There had been talk at the outset of keeping it going for five years—the statute of limitations on most of the relevant offenses.) He protested that Goldfarb himself wasn't worried about his safety and that, in any case, it was a police responsibility.

"No, he's an FBI undercover," he recalled Shaw replying.

"Well, ask him who he works for," David suggested.

"I work for David," Goldfarb volunteered.

"You stole him from the feds," Shaw said.

"I didn't steal him—I happened to be nicer to him," David countered.

The way David read the situation, Shaw and Aronwald were merely following in a long tradition of prosecutors who, when an investigation began to implicate high-powered suspects, insisted on seeing overwhelming evidence first—a "conviction kit," to use a phrase coined by David's longtime friend Robert Levinson, of the FBI. David and Goldfarb, who was equally determined to go forward, drew up a list of weighty cases and suspects they still hoped to pursue and launched a campaign to get the decision reversed.

McCarthy, who sympathized with David's frustration, might have been a valuable ally in this effort. (Or perhaps, just as valuably, he might have convinced David that it was folly for a cop to resist a decision that had the weight of the U.S. Justice Department behind it.) But the first deputy commissioner had gone into a second retirement, his departure being one of the minor aftershocks of another big shift in the city's political landscape: the inauguration of Abe Beame as mayor in January 1974. Beame, for his part, had turned over the management of the police department to one of the few traditionalists who survived the Murphy years, Chief Inspector Michael J. Codd. McCarthy decided that he would stay on only if asked. Not being asked, he submitted his retirement papers again and returned to the golfer's life in Pompano Beach from which Murphy had extracted him.

The new first deputy commissioner, James Taylor, was neither a dynamic leader, like McCarthy, nor a frightening one, like Walsh. He was "a man of much humility and the simple manners of an upstate farmer," in the recollection of one of his underlings. He was a surprise choice for the job; Taylor himself was surprised. "Why [Codd] asked me to be first deputy, I don't know," he said years later. Most people, on being appointed to such a position, would have been pleased to learn that it came with its own confidential investigating unit. This was a responsibility that Taylor could have done without, however. "This undercover business is too much to keep your hands on," he explained later. So when Shaw and Aronwald laid out their arguments to him, Taylor was not only receptive but secretly relieved, and he unhesitatingly cast his vote for the phaseout of Operation Cleveland.

—————

Respect for authority had never been one of the hallmarks of David's career, but in the wake of the decision to close down the Garment

Center investigation, his characteristic pluck and boldness crossed a crucial line, into the zone of blind folly. In certain large and pragmatically important ways, the situation that he faced at the end of 1974 was not favorable to blowing the whistle. His grievance involved a couple of law enforcement officials who did not share his determination to pursue some allegations that might or might not ever be proved. Had he paused to examine the battle conditions, he might have seen the advisability of yielding and surviving to fight another day. But he did not pause. He decided to hold a grand farewell dinner for Goldfarb on the eve of his and his family's entry into the federal witness-protection program. To this dinner David invited the members of his squad, who had become Goldfarb's daily intimates and were serving as Goldfarb's bodyguards that night, and representatives of NBC News, *The Village Voice,* and the *Daily News.* David's idea was to let them hear Goldfarb's side of things, so that when the feds officially announced the first set of indictments, patting themselves on the back for a triumphant investigation, the press would be in a position to raise questions about the operation and its unfulfilled potential.

One of the reporters—Jack Newfield, then of the *Voice*—took an immediate interest in a story he heard at the dinner. It concerned a Brooklyn trucker, convicted of tax evasion, who in casual conversation with Goldfarb had boasted that he wasn't worried about going to prison, because his lawyer had an "in" with the judge. The lawyer and the judge were buddies, he explained, and everything was arranged: if the trucker would buy the judge a racehorse, he would get off with a modest sentence. The trucker told this part of the story to Goldfarb in a tone of annoyance—he didn't mind paying the cash, but why a racehorse? "Let him pick his own racehorse."

The racehorse story was one of a number of leads that David and Goldfarb both believed had been neglected out of petty jurisdictional rivalry. Shaw later said that he had apprised his Eastern District counterpart of the allegation, and that they had agreed—in the interest of protecting Goldfarb's cover—not to take any immediate action beyond monitoring the trucker's sentencing. It seemed to

David, however, that the charge was one that had to be investigated immediately, or the opportunity would be lost.

Newfield, who was the author of an annual *Voice* listing of the city's worst and best judges, knew the chief judge in the Eastern District, Jacob Mishler. David thought that Mishler might want to know—and deserved to know—that an accusation had been made against one of his judges, and he thought that Newfield could get the information to him. The next morning, Newfield appeared in David's office (David was out at the time) and persuaded a sergeant who had attended the Goldfarb dinner to give him a copy of some police reports detailing the racehorse allegation.

The dinner and the Durk-Newfield link came to Shaw and Aronwald's attention when, not long afterward, the racehorse story and the larger dispute over the decision to halt Operation Cleveland erupted into the news. Goldfarb, who was angry about his relocation arrangements—his son, to mention just one of his grievances, had trouble getting into a school because he hadn't been provided with proper records—had taken his complaint to a Senate committee, and it had become public. In the Sturm und Drang that followed, the fact that David had not directly caused the disclosure was a fine point that people tended to lose sight of. He had, after all, confided in representatives of the press, one of them had obtained copies of confidential reports, and the story was out. David could not effectively defend himself because he refused to take the easy course (urged on him by some of his colleagues) of blaming the sergeant who had, unthinkingly, turned the reports over to Newfield.

What David's superiors saw was an ugly, headline-grabbing squabble between Goldfarb—an informant—and the U.S. attorney's office, with David supporting the informant. In one newspaper article Aronwald was quoted as saying of Goldfarb, "He is a witness for us. And he doesn't make decisions, although he thinks he is Dick Tracy." To which Goldfarb shot back, "At least Dick Tracy made cases, which is more than I can say for Aronwald." In another article, David commented that the operation had been terminated just as it was pointing toward judges and politicians, and accused Aronwald of "doing nothing" about the racehorse case. Aronwald, in the same story, called David "a cancer on all law enforcement."

Aronwald, who had just replaced Shaw as chief of the strike force, was a prosecutor who prided himself on his toughness (he had once coldcocked a defense lawyer in open court), and he and David had a lively mutual dislike. When Aronwald got wind of the Newfield business, he instinctively assumed that David had given Newfield the reports and began taking steps to have David indicted—a plan that ran aground only when it emerged that the documents in question were police rather than FBI reports, and thus not a federal matter.

In a rage, Aronwald demanded that the department suspend David for breaching the security of the operation and putting court cases in jeopardy. Taylor, according to one of his aides (Taylor himself did not recall this episode when he was asked about it long afterward), was inclined to think that Aronwald was overstating things, out of personal enmity, and for a time it appeared that David might escape punishment. But Aronwald refused to let the matter rest. He went to Police Commissioner Codd, and speaking in the name of the Justice Department, pressed him to relieve David of his command and have him brought up on charges. "I made it very clear to Codd," Aronwald said later, "that the Justice Department would have no further dealings with the NYPD in any investigative undertaking that David Durk was in any way connected to—that I could not trust David Durk, and I would not ask the people working with me to trust him."

David, meanwhile, drafted an angry memo with the title "Breach of Faith Between the Southern District Strike Force and the New York City Police Department." Judge Mishler, for his part, called Codd and Taylor to offer a statement of support for David, saying that he had performed a service for the court. Under the murky circumstances, the department was not about to bring charges against a cop widely regarded as a hero. But it was not about to take his side against Aronwald, either. When David submitted his memo, Taylor seemed horrified by the thought even of being known to have read such a document. "I'm not asking you to initial it and hand it back to me,"

David assured him. "I work for you, and I'm giving this to you. You can keep it."

Before long, the department announced that David's unit was being disbanded because it had completed "the investigation it was formed for." And, once again, the headquarters brass took up the question of what to do with David Durk.

The idea of a transfer to Coney Island enjoyed some support, Commissioner Codd being a devotee of the old practice of sending errant cops to commands as far away as possible from where they lived. According to another participant in the discussions, however, it was thought important not to make it obvious to the world that David had been "harpooned." In the end, the decision was made to send him to Queens, as the administrative lieutenant in charge of keeping records for the Queens detectives. In his new assignment, David would be placed under the close supervision of Deputy Chief Edwin Dreher, who was renowned for his no-nonsense ways. Aronwald was pleased to learn of the outcome, because he knew Dreher to be the sort of commander who, if David took the smallest step out of line, "would squash him like a bug." All this, however, was explained to the public—by First Deputy Commissioner Taylor—as a routine transfer. When a reporter asked Taylor why he had given David such a job, Taylor praised David for his "unique qualities" as an investigator and added that, regrettably, the department did not just then have an investigation worthy of his talents.

CHAPTER

FOURTEEN

⟶⊳●⊲⟵

The year 1975 was the beginning of a bleak period for the police department, and for the city. Abe Beame had run for mayor on the slogan, "He knows the buck," and he knew it all too well. Although John Lindsay took most of the rap for letting the city's finances get out of hand, it was Beame who, as city comptroller, had patched together the last-minute budget deals (sometimes scrawling the numbers on the back of an envelope) that permitted the city to pretend it had things under control. As mayor, he went right on doing the same thing—and now he was contending not only with the accumulated consequences of the city's own loose financial practices, but also with a global recession, brought on by a jump in the price of oil. Now, too, after years of profitable inattention, the banks became duly alarmed and demanded drastic austerity measures in return for further loans.

Beame proclaimed a "rigid hiring freeze" but shrank from actually imposing it. Then, a year into his mayoralty, the banks and the state (its own credit now imperiled) banded together, insisting on real cuts and placing the city's finances under a pair of watchdog bodies, the Municipal Assistance Corporation and the Financial Control Board. When the layoffs finally began, no agency suffered more than the police department. During the Lindsay years, the department had grown by nearly five thousand officers; now many of these men and women lost their jobs (police strength would decline, by layoffs and attrition, from 31,600 to 23,500 under Beame), and working conditions for those who remained became increasingly threadbare.

Anchored to a desk at a station house in Forest Hills, David Durk was a mirror of the city's pain. One of the duties of his new assignment was to assemble a list of police phone lines that could be disconnected to save money. Another was to draft a memo instructing detectives throughout the borough to use both sides of a piece of paper. He was also asked to make a small personal contribution to the city's financial-rescue plan: the commander's pay he had been receiving in his previous job was taken away from him.

This sort of thing, David told himself, couldn't happen to him. The press wouldn't let it happen. He had led a charmed life in the police department. Like a trapeze artist, he had become accustomed to mid-air leaps that carried him away from disaster, and the press had been the means of his rescue in the moments of greatest danger. This time, he had reached—and plunged.

After the dissolution of David's squad, a *Times* editorial urged the department to find him "a new assignment that will permit full scope for his investigative talents," but as David bitterly noted, the news pages of the *Times* treated the Operation Cleveland controversy as a murky affair, and there was even a column of news analysis questioning David's role as a "source" who had tried to control "the gathering and presentation of the story."

There had been a quarrel between David and Arthur Gelb concerning the Goldfarb farewell dinner and the fact that no one from the *Times* had been there. Burnham had been invited, but he was now working out of the paper's Washington bureau, so he had declined. David had then decided to go with a group of reporters he knew and trusted, and, as it happened, they worked for NBC, the *Daily News*, and *The Village Voice*. "I see you're traveling in new circles," Gelb noted with wry disapproval afterward. How could David have failed to include the *Times*, Gelb asked, "after all we've done for you?" David, who did not at all care for Gelb's phraseology, pointed out a few things he had done for the *Times* over the years. In any case, he said, "You don't own me."

Perhaps the *Times*'s ambiguous coverage of his current plight was, as David believed, retribution for his perceived ingratitude. Or perhaps it was less personal than that; perhaps the press, in its relentless quest for novelty, had simply grown tired of him. Youth confers a license to make trouble, and David was no longer young. He had turned forty—he had become a middle-aged rebel, and the world did not quite know what to make of such a character. Whatever the explanation, the coverage *was* ambiguous, and the police brass, David felt sure, read it as a signal that they could send him anywhere they wished, with impunity. "As long as the winds from West Forty-third Street were blowing at my back, no one would dream of touching me," he said later.

If he had become somewhat irrational about the *Times*, it may have been because his feelings on that subject were tied up with a larger, and more justified, orneriness about the media in general. Five years after the events, the Knapp Commission story was known the world over, through a movie. But it was not the movie that David had expected—the one with Paul Newman as David Durk. Like many Hollywood projects, that movie had come to naught, and a new team had staked a claim to the same literary territory. Then, with a few minor—and, by the movie world's standards, perfectly routine—exercises of dramatic license, David had been all but removed from the tale, and, in effect, robbed of recognition for his life's greatest achievement.

———

He had been uneasy about the movie idea from the start. Instant wealth was a concept that David appreciated as much as the next man, and he was far from averse to the notion of becoming a hero to millions of American moviegoers. But he couldn't help worrying about the reaction of one small part of the potential audience: his fellow cops. He told himself that the right kind of movie—one that captured the satisfactions and frustrations of the job as it was experienced by cops in general—would give them pleasure. But there was also the possibility of the wrong kind of movie: one that credited him with Hollywood-style heroics and celebrated him as an Ivy League idealist among evil companions. Such a movie would only make him an object of cops' scorn, and that was a thought David could not abide, for, as Sydney Cooper had said so derisively, he loved the police, and he wanted them to love him back.

Before he would sign a contract, then, he insisted on certain assurances—most important, the cast of characters had to include cops from more traditional police backgrounds who were just as dedicated, and just as honest, as he. He even helpfully introduced the producer of the would-be movie, John Foreman, to several such cops, and one of them, Frank Serpico, was at the exploratory dinner with Paul Newman. By the time Warner Bros. formally announced the production, in June 1971, it had two heroes rather than one: Newman would play a character based on David, and Robert Redford a character based on Serpico. (A large supporting role would be that of a reporter based on David Burnham.) It was the age of the buddy movie, and as a result of *Butch Cassidy and the Sundance Kid,* which Foreman had coproduced, Newman and Redford were the buddies everybody was after. Cops, corruption, Newman, Redford—it was a package a producer could take to the bank. Unfortunately for Foreman, however—and for David—Serpico was not at all sure he wanted to be part of it.

He and David had been through a series of crises over the course of their five-year friendship, and at times they had cooked, shopped, eaten, and drunk together. After Serpico's shooting, David was one of the first people at his bedside. (He and Arlene took care of Serpico's pet rabbit for the duration of his hospital stay.) David had pestered everyone he could think of—Cooper, Burton Roberts, Robert Daley—about promoting Serpico. ("If you can get your brother a judgeship, where's Frank's gold shield?" David asked Roberts on one occasion. Roberts claimed he had been trying.) Like many people who have been badly treated, however, Serpico tended to be sweeping in his judgments. The NYPD, the law-enforcement fraternity in general, and City Hall were, in his eyes, dens of thieves and hypocrites; the presumed corruption fighters—people like Patrick Murphy—did not rank much higher in his estimation; and he reserved some of his most intense anger for the man who had been in his corner the longest.

There had always been a large element of tension between them. David was forever dragging Serpico places, and Serpico did not enjoy being dragged. "He had an air of superiority about him," Serpico recalled. "He would throw off big words. I always felt him looking down at me."

"Dave was a very persuasive sort of individual," Paul Delise observed. "He had an influence on Frank, and I think Frank began to resent it."

Many people inside the police department thought of Serpico as David's disciple, and the press, too, tended to treat them as a twosome. After Daley's article in *New York,* however, Serpico began to achieve a measure of independent celebrity, and as he became a figure of interest to journalists, lawyers, prosecutors, community activists, and political reformers, they heard him speak with startling bitterness about David Durk.

"To me, they were both good men—I admired both of them," Paul Delise has said. Delise, along with others who were close to them, tried to soften Serpico's anger. But in the summer of 1971, Serpico met someone—a journalist named Peter Maas—who listened to his put-downs of David with greater sympathy. Stocky and muscular, Maas cut a Hemingwayesque profile. He had made his mark with a book, *The Valachi Papers,* that was an imprisoned mobster's inside look at organized crime, and in his other writing there was a pattern of finding honor and courage among the commonfolk. Although his knowledge of David was based on a few fleeting encounters, he prided himself on his ability to size people up quickly, and to him it was obvious (Maas said years later) that David was a self-promoter who enjoyed "playing cop" and "hanging around a lot of chic liberal parties."

Serpico told Maas about the proposed movie and said he was not yet bound to it by a signed contract. He noted that Daley—David's

friend, not his—had been asked to write a story outline. Daley's article had been built around the Serpico-Durk friendship, and what
Foreman had in mind, Serpico suspected, would be similar: "*Butch
Cassidy and the Sundance Kid*, New York style," with Serpico as David's
lamebrained Italian sidekick. Maas declared that the truth could
never be told by treating the two men as fellow heroes. The real story,
he observed, wasn't Durk and Serpico. It was Serpico alone.

In saying this, he tapped a deep vein. Serpico wanted out of the
police department—it had become a prison for him. David, on the
other hand, was operating on a broader stage, traveling in circles
where his anticorruption work was appreciated. David had his parties, his speaking engagements, his network of friends and connections outside the department. He was getting something out of his
whistle-blowing. Burnham was, too. Serpico had learned about the
imminent publication of the *Times* article, in April 1970, not from
David or from Burnham, but from a hostile plainclothesman who
had confronted him with the rumor that "you spilled your guts to *The
New York Times*."

"It was like I didn't matter," Serpico said years later. "All they were
concerned with was their Pulitzer Prizes, their big stories, their pro-
motions. Serpico was expendable."

Maas gave shape—and respectability—to Serpico's grievances,
and together they made history: the history of the struggle to cleanse
the NYPD, as it would be generally remembered by those who did
have not much direct knowledge of the events. "Alone" was the operative word. Ads for the movie *Serpico*, a largely faithful adaptation of
the book that Maas went on to write, would describe its hero as "the
most dangerous man alive—an honest cop." The only other sympathetic police officers in the book or the movie were two bosses, Delise
and Cooper. Both had helped Maas out with their recollections.

Among the people who had followed the story at close range, David
was generally judged to have been the instigator. ("He masterminded
the whole thing," Thomas Reppetto has said.) But in *Serpico*—movie
and book—David was reduced to a walk-on and lumped in among
the many people who had failed to deliver on their promises to Ser-

pico. Even in the decision to go to the *Times*, his labors, and Burnham's, were made to seem inconsequential. The "bulk" of the *Times* article, Maas wrote, was "supplied by Serpico." The movie would show Serpico giving the go-ahead and then, without further ado, the papers rolling off the presses. One reviewer described the Durk-like character, renamed Bob Blair, as "an over-achiever who knows that the top is gained as easily over the backs of crooked cops as of crooked crooks." Tony Roberts, who played the part, was helpfully instructed to take his inspiration from the familiar war-movie scene in which an officer tells one of his men "to go in and break up a pill-box while 'I cover you from here.' "

Maas had told Serpico that his story was the real story. If by that he meant that it was a strong story—a story for its times—he was correct, for it was a version of events that served him well not only in winning Serpico's cooperation but also in reaching a large public. Richard Nixon was president; the Watergate scandal was mushrooming; the gulf between law and order as practiced in the land and as long depicted in cop books and cop movies had become impossibly wide. The kind of movie that David had imagined and Foreman had promised—with good cops, bad cops, and in-between cops, operating in an oppressive system—might not have suited the contemporary mood. *Serpico*, under the direction of Sidney Lumet, gives its hero, played by Al Pacino, a Christ-like aura, and the audience is even led to believe (a notion Maas resisted, for want of evidence) that his fellow cops have elected to have him killed. Although he does not literally die, his hope of remaining a cop does, and he has to leave the country as well as the police department. "Serpico is now living somewhere in Switzerland," an end title declares.

The real Serpico not only left the country for roughly eight years but conducted a staged withdrawal from humanity. After Switzerland came stays in Holland and Wales, where, with some of his book and movie earnings, he helped establish a New Age collective. Then he returned to the United States, resurfacing in 1981 as a defendant in a paternity suit brought by an airline stewardess. (He advanced the novel but unsuccessful claim that he had been unwittingly "used as a sperm bank" by a woman who had led him to believe she was using a contraceptive device.) Eventually, he moved to a cabin in the woods of the Hudson River Valley; he kept an apartment in Brooklyn, though, and continued to visit it regularly. In the summer of 1993, when I asked him how he was spending his time, he mentioned two activities—"foraging" and "watching man make a fool of himself." He and David hadn't seen each other in twenty years.

After *Serpico* came out, a couple of local reporters wrote articles raising questions about the movie's accuracy. But when David himself raised some of those questions at a screening, Sidney Lumet refused to be engaged in what he dismissed as a childish debate. (One of his subsequent projects would be *Prince of the City*, about Bob Leuci, in which David would be stripped out of the story completely, leaving the impression that a federal prosecutor based on Nicholas Scoppetta had turned Leuci by himself.) Lumet declared that his field was entertainment, not literal truth. "I refuse to descend to this level," he told David.

For many people, however, *Serpico* became the truth—not only about Serpico's life, but about David's. Even on the campus of Amherst College, where his role was better known than in most places, the facts could not compete with the legend. A decade later, when Julie Durk was a freshman at Amherst, she found that classmates, hearing her name, would ask about her father. Then they would leap to the key question: did he—did she—actually *know* Frank Serpico?

———⟶◆⟵———

Police Commissioner Michael Codd was a tall and imposing man who filled his uniform well. After the slight and bookish-looking Murphy, he was instant reassurance to cops of the old school, and his performance lived up to the promise of his appearance. "Never a no. Never a yes. Just an endless round of maybes and perhaps" was how former assistant chief Anthony Bouza summed up Codd's response to unorthodox ideas and the people associated with them. Like William McCarthy, Bouza left the department during the Codd years, and he went on to serve as the chief of police of Minneapolis.

Another independent-minded boss who decided to depart was Paul Delise. He had been promoted to deputy chief and placed in command of the Public Morals Division by Murphy, but now he fell into disfavor for having the temerity to write a paper challenging a plan by the city's Off Track Betting Corporation to greatly expand its network of horse-betting parlors. Mayor Beame and Howard Samuels, the state's "off-track czar," took the convenient, if implausible, position that it was possible to create a vast new government-supported gambling operation, backed by an expensive campaign of publicly financed advertising, and to thereby produce hundreds of millions of dollars for public purposes (education in particular), without attracting any new gamblers; all the money, they insisted, would simply be "diverted" from organized crime. Delise sought to demonstrate that the OTB parlors were attracting people who had never gambled before, and that some of them were subsequently transferring their patronage to old-fashioned, and still illegal, bookmakers, who offered bigger payouts and easier credit. Soon after presenting his conclusions, Delise was given a desk job in the Bronx. "That was my demise, more or less," he recalled. When he retired, in 1974, he was the only deputy chief in memory to do so without a testimonial dinner.

David remained in Queens for seven months before he negotiated an escape. He was teaching a class at NYU, and the man who had hired him—Gerhard Mueller, a professor of law—had a long-standing relationship with the United Nations. Through Mueller, David secured a temporary assignment to the UN as part of a team that was to draft an international code of ethics for law enforcement officials. He spent a year at the UN laboring on a code that, in the end, was rejected by the General Assembly, although it won the enthusiastic backing of Amnesty International; then he returned to the department, and his career picked up where it had left off.

At the beginning of 1977, David was sent to what was called the Safe, Loft, and Truck Squad, as the commander of an antihijacking unit operating out of the 72nd Precinct, near the South Brooklyn waterfront. David and a team of five detectives had to make an office out of a piece of hallway adjacent to the ladies' room, and their furniture consisted of a desk, four chairs, and a single aging typewriter. Jimmy Lanzano, a highly capable detective who tended to hide his talents and good intentions under a blanket of raunchy humor—and who later would become a friend of David's—was working there at the time, and he got precise instructions about how to handle him. "I was told, 'Show him around, get his feet wet, and stay in Brooklyn,' " Lanzano recalled. "Basically, my job was to keep David away from headquarters."

Many, if not most, hijackings were prearranged affairs, or "give-ups." It was a crime that seemed to call for undercover work, but instead, the detectives in David's unit followed a routine of driving around the city looking for hijackings; and, as David commented later, their cars, while unmarked, were unmistakable. "We had cars in lime green—I'm talking about a real bright lime green," he said. "All the colors that nobody else bought, the PD bought." The detectives made a point of putting plenty of mileage on their odometers every day, so that no one could say they hadn't been out looking. They worked a strict daytime shift, in spite of the fact that most hijackings occurred at night. (Permission for overtime was all but impossible to obtain. Their superiors had to be presented with compelling evidence that a hijacking was about to occur and that the unit would be in a position to make the collar.) David himself, however, was told to work a permanent four-to-twelve shift, because, as Lanzano later explained, "That way headquarters was closed by the time David started working."

Lanzano, like David, rarely bothered to say the polite thing to his superiors—and this became a bond between them. One day, on a visit to headquarters, David was taken to task for wearing sandals. "Only faggots" wore sandals, an inspector pointed out to him.

"Inspector, say 'gay person,' " David retorted. "Can you say 'gay person'?"

On another occasion, David was reprimanded by a superior who had observed him driving, with Lanzano in the passenger seat. Lanzano was a detective, and David was a lieutenant. Therefore, Lanzano should be doing the driving. David, his superior earnestly warned him, was "undermining the rank of lieutenant."

It had been impressed upon David that he was not supposed to be making any arrests; his job was to interview the victims of any hijackings that came to light on the four-to-twelve shift and turn over his reports to the day shift for investigation. But David was not content to be a report-taker, and neither was Lanzano. Late one afternoon, they drove up to the South Bronx to look into an armored-car heist in which $25,000 in cash had been taken. After locating an eyewitness to the crime, they ascertained that the thieves were members of a youth gang, and further investigation led them to a woman who identified the key suspect as her boyfriend—one Blackie the Snake.

With their eyewitness in tow, David and Lanzano moved on to the Bronx borough robbery squad, hoping to find a mug shot of the suspect for possible identification. The robbery squad had gone home for the day, though, and no one in the station house knew (or would admit knowing) where the key to the office was kept. David, who found this sort of thing infuriating, was raising a ruckus about it with the station crew when Lanzano whispered, "David, back off!" Lanzano had been casing the building from the outside, and he explained that he had figured out a way to penetrate the robbery squad office from the roof.

"Do you realize what we are doing?" David asked as they proceeded to put Lanzano's plan into action. "We're burglarizing a police facility!"

Once inside, they found mug shots of sixty of the Bronx's most active holdup specialists hanging on the wall, and the witness (who was let in through the door) had no trouble making an identification. A few hours later, David arrested the suspect, and his coup was reported on one of the local radio news shows the next morning.

That same day, the Durk-Lanzano partnership was terminated, and David was told to concentrate on administrating rather than investigating. One of the things he had abhorred about the movie *Serpico* was the suggestion that a police officer who fought corruption had no future in law enforcement. Now his own career seemed to bear out the thesis. The situation was bad enough in itself; what hurt even more was the knowledge that other cops were looking at him and drawing conclusions. To some, he was a satisfying example of a rat who had been put in his place. To others, he was simply a living reminder of what remained the first rule of survival in the NYPD: Stay off the radar screen.

PART
FOUR

CHAPTER

FIFTEEN

❧

In the fiscal crisis of the mid-1970s, New York City slammed the door on a political era, rejecting not only the social experiments of the early Lindsay years but the whole idea—which reached back to Wagner and LaGuardia—that it was government's job to bring a sense of opportunity to the city's have-nots. Indeed, many New Yorkers concluded that the money the Lindsay people had spent on such programs was the very money the city now lacked for paying its bills. Yet, if people were no longer in a mood to ponder some of the city's deepest problems, the hot issues of the moment—the depressing arithmetic of laying off workers, cutting back services, and rolling over debt—were no fun to talk about either. Nor was there much point, since the decision-making power had largely passed from the city's elected leaders to shadowy conclaves of financial overseers. (The city's leaders pointed with pride to their success in avoiding bankruptcy, but in the process they had accepted arrangements that were not so far different from those that a bankruptcy court might have ordered.) And so New York's political discourse became increasingly removed from reality, and increasingly vitriolic—and along came Edward I. Koch.

He had started out, in the Wagner years, as a reformer, and a far-out figure even by the standards of Greenwich Village, where he lived and had a law practice. As a candidate for the state assembly in 1962, he loudly promised to push for repeal of the laws against sodomy. One of his major legislative achievements in the House of Representatives, to which Koch was elected in 1968, was the creation of a commission to study the decriminalization of marijuana. In a floor debate in 1969, he compared Ho Chi Minh with George Washington—two great patriots in the eyes of their people, Koch explained to his startled colleagues.

He broke with his party to support John Lindsay for mayor in 1965. But six years later (after Lindsay failed to repay the favor by endorsing Koch for Congress), Koch came out against a Lindsay proposal to build "scatter-site," low-rise public housing in the Forest Hills section of Queens. Although he presented the issue in class terms (the right of a middle-class neighborhood to stay middle-class), and though he was not against the project per se but was just asking for it to be scaled back, many of his friends and supporters were horrified. There was no obvious reason for a Manhattan Congressman to take a stand on such a question, and Koch—a onetime civil rights worker (and lawyer for other civil rights workers)—had identified himself with the "pro-white" position in a debate that was widely seen as a test of where people stood on race. It was, as Koch himself later observed, his Rubicon.

At the time, however, few people on either side of the East River were greatly stirred. In 1973 Koch took his new persona on a test ride—a brief run for mayor that ended when he realized its futility. Forest Hills and a newfound enthusiasm for the death penalty notwithstanding, Koch was still, in the outer boroughs, a hopeless Manhattan liberal. That was the perception of him, anyway, among the small minority of people who knew his name.

When he announced his second campaign for mayor, in 1977, he ran (as he had in 1973) as a law-and-order candidate. At first, it looked like a poor choice of a campaign theme, for crime had gone into one of its periodic downward cycles. (It had done so despite the city's loss, through layoffs and attrition, of some five thousand police officers—a seeming paradox that might have been an interesting debate topic.) Then, close upon each other, came two frightening episodes that made Koch's judgment look prescient: the Son of Sam case—a series of shootings and killings of young women and men by a maniacal postal clerk from Yonkers who claimed to be acting at the behest of a neighbor named Sam, who supposedly conveyed his instructions through his dog—and, in the darkness of a power failure caused by a lightning storm upstate, a night of riots and looting in ghetto neighborhoods of Brooklyn, Manhattan, and the Bronx. In harness, crime and Koch charged to the front of the race.

Koch captured the mood of the city at a particularly ornery moment in its history. The two remedies that he urged most frequently were more cops on the street, at a time when the city couldn't possibly afford them (police strength would actually decline by nearly three thousand during Koch's first term), and the death penalty, which was a matter to be decided in Albany, the state capital. (The governor, Hugh Carey, was strongly opposed.) Koch flogged the law-and-order issue relentlessly, even conducting death-penalty plebiscites in nursing homes and senior-citizen centers. (He seemed to acknowledge the hypocrisy of it all in a remark—which he later denied—to a friend, Congressman Ben Rosenthal of Queens. "I was a little troubled one day at an old people's center in Queens when Ed was doing his death plebiscite," Rosenthal told Nat Hentoff of the *Voice*. "You know, 'How many here are for the death penalty?' he says as he raises his own arm. Something must have shown on my face because Ed leaned toward me and whispered through his teeth, 'Listen, this is the only way I can get in.' ") In 1977, unlike 1973, New Yorkers took heed. They did so, in part, because of the feverish coverage that Koch received in the pages of the *New York Post*, whose Australian owner, Rupert Murdoch, had seen an opportunity to be a kingmaker in New York City politics and was not at all fussy about the distinction between the editorial columns and the news pages. The editorial in which the *Post* endorsed Koch ran on the front page, and the early editions, by a curious oversight, failed to identify it as an editorial.

It was no coincidence that Koch, who won the election, had fought the Forest Hills project, while Mario Cuomo, who finished second, had helped negotiate the eventual settlement that allowed a modified version of it to be built. Cuomo had established a reputation as a soother of differences. What the city seemed to want was a champion of its gripes—a spokesman, in particular, for the hurt feelings of the white middle class. And, on the level of raw emotion, Koch's campaign persona was not an act. His constituency might have changed, but the sense of outsiderly resentment was the same, and it was perhaps the most authentic thing about him.

Few New Yorkers—certainly few police officers—followed the election campaign of 1977 more closely than David Durk. In the early seventies, he and Arlene had been part of a circle of journalists, lawyers, and public servants who periodically got together for mass dinners with Koch, usually at restaurants in Chinatown. "Let me tell you about something perfectly wonderful I did in Washington this week," Koch would say, and then plunge into the tale of a confrontation with some Nixon White House operative or congressional bigwig. Invariably, he was the hero of his narratives, and, to his dinner companions, a charming hero: a plainspoken New Yorker who had gone to Washington and kept his head.

Koch, for his part, picked David's brain for ideas about the police and law enforcement. During the 1973 mayoral campaign, Koch even went as far as to suggest (it was never clear to David how seriously) a small favor that David could do for him: take him along on a sort of informal street patrol, find an incipient robbery, and arrange for him to play a heroic part in apprehending the robber.

After David's transfer to Queens, Koch had shot off a letter to Commissioner Codd complaining that David was "not being given a chance to use his exceptional talents. . . . Instead of pushing pencils, he should be collaring criminals," Koch had written. Codd had ignored the letter, but David had remembered it.

Koch had not forgotten David, either. That became apparent when, in the 1977 campaign, TV and radio ads for Koch began including, as an almost subliminal footnote, variations of the message "Ed Koch is the only politician trusted by Lieutenant David Durk." David had not been consulted about the use of his name. He learned of it when a police superior summoned him to a tête-à-tête, played a tape of one of the offending commercials, and reminded him of a rule barring cops from taking an active part in elective politics. When the dressing-down session was over, David called up Koch's media advisor, David Garth.

"Why didn't you tell me you were going to do this?" David asked.

"We didn't tell you because we wanted to protect you," Garth replied. "Besides, it's true."

If the election felt like good news for David, Koch's choice of a police commissioner firmed up the feeling. The job went unexpectedly to a lawyer (and former assistant U.S. attorney) named Robert McGuire, who, as it happened, had represented David, as well as Serpico, during the early stages of the corruption scandal. With Koch's election and McGuire's appointment, David began to think that his long exile from Police Headquarters might soon be over.

On the eve of McGuire's swearing in, David met him for drinks at the Carlyle Hotel and, emboldened by their friendship, made his job pitch. A number of past police commissioners had had special intelligence units—teams of detectives to act as their eyes and ears. It seemed to David that McGuire, as an outsider, would feel a particular need for such a unit, and David was volunteering to head it up. He offered to give McGuire "a straight count," whatever he might be called on to investigate.

McGuire, however, had a message of his own to deliver. If he were to give David such a job—if, as police commissioner, he were to intervene in the personnel process to arrange *any* assignment for David—it would smack of favoritism. Since they were friends, McGuire declared, it was important that David be treated as an ordinary lieutenant.

This concern about appearances was all but unheard-of in the NYPD: connections were the way that all policemen routinely got ahead, and a new purity did not suddenly take hold of the department with McGuire's appointment as commissioner. But, as he acknowledged afterward, he had another motive (one he did not share with David) for withholding assistance. Precisely because he was an outsider, he was reluctant to do anything that would mark him as suspect in the eyes of the permanent police bureaucracy.

"A very interesting thing happens when you are thrust into a position of authority," McGuire explained, years later. "You see things differently. I'm a collegial person in terms of management style. I didn't want people with rough edges. David is not the kind of guy who sits there in a room listening to other people's thoughts and occasionally contributing his own thoughts. He was outside the pale in terms of his relationships. The senior people in the department— I'm talking about honest people—respected David for what he had done. Their attitude was 'This guy enabled me to go to work in the morning and feel respected as a police officer.' But there's a big difference between that feeling and wanting him in your office every day. Their attitude was 'Who needs this guy? He acts like nobody's honest but him.' I figured I had enough problems as it was. I couldn't go in there with his baggage."

Of course, McGuire might have found a role for David that didn't involve bringing him into high-level staff conferences, but standing on principle, he recused himself, leaving David's future to be decided by the new first deputy commissioner, Joe Hoffman. By the time of his interview with Hoffman, David had lowered his ambitions. He was hoping to persuade Hoffman to send him, as a lieutenant, to a citywide decoy unit known as Street Crime. (The chief of detectives had approved the idea.) But this, too, was not to be. Hoffman greeted him by rising from an impressive high-backed leather chair and remarking, "You know, if there were any justice in this world, this would be *your* chair." Then, moving on from the theme of justice to the theme of the here and now, he informed David that he would be running a squad of detectives and plainclothes cops operating out of the 25th Precinct, in East Harlem. When David asked if he could expect the restoration of the commander's pay he had earned under McCarthy, Hoffman told David to "win your spurs" first.

His new assignment, David was quick to realize, would keep him uptown. (There were people at headquarters, Hoffman had remarked, who felt it would be a mistake to give David "a license to wander the city again.") It would also place him under Inspector Francis X. Smith, a hard-bitten boss of the old school, who served as zone commander for the 6th Division. David had run across Smith before. As a guest lecturer on ethics at the police academy in the early seventies, David had asked recruits what they would do if they ever received an illegal order. He had been banished from the academy after Smith—then a captain assigned there—denounced him for "inflaming the passions of the troops against their lawful superiors."

Smith was no happier than David about their renewed proximity. The department's organized-crime intelligence group had heard that there was a contract out on David's life—an aftereffect of his role in the arrest and imprisonment of scores of East Harlem drug traffickers a few years earlier. Smith, it seemed to David, was fixated on the possibility of his being killed. "They were crazy to send you here!" Smith exclaimed, in the course of a long introductory conversation (later reconstructed by David). "If you get shot, do you have any idea of the amount of paperwork we'd have to do?"

If *he* had anything to say about the matter of commander's pay, Smith commented, David would never get it. "You don't belong in this job," he explained. "On the outside, with your drive and zeal, you'd be a millionaire. But we're bureaucrats here. This is the Sixth Division. You keep looking for truth and justice. There is no truth here. There is no justice. This is the asshole of the world."

This was roughly the attitude of most of David's detectives—as downtrodden as any group of cops he had ever encountered. "The community despised them, and they despised themselves," he recalled. "Some of them would deliberately flatten the tires on their own cars to avoid going out on calls."

One detective, on meeting David, remarked with a snarl that "we used to eat great"—meaning before the Knapp Commission. Another detective brought a pet python with him to work every day. When David suggested that a python was not compatible with the "comforting atmosphere" people deserved when they reported a crime to the police, the detective countered that pythons were a "very docile" species.

"You know that and I know that," David replied. "But some people have another image of a python, and we have to respect their image."

The Kriegel connection had helped David become a detective. The Burnham connection had helped him land his grant from the Justice Department. By rights, the Koch and McGuire connections should have produced something better than this. And yet, he had a squad to command, and a neighborhood to police. Notwithstanding his barbed reception, David was soon returning home at night full of stories about small victories he had won in motivating his troops. "Wherever you put him, he'll get totally absorbed in the work—as long as it has something to do with crime," Arlene Durk has said. One successful innovation of his tenure at the 25th Precinct was the detective-for-a-day concept: if a uniformed cop developed a lead, he was allowed to work on it with the detectives instead of being forced to surrender it (and the credit) to them. The precinct also became a laboratory for David's belief that decoys were often the best answer to a pattern of recurring crimes. The squad's clearance rate, which had been among the department's lowest, quickly became one of the highest. Commissioner McGuire, hearing good reports, concluded that David was "flourishing" and that the decision to treat him like any other lieutenant had been vindicated. The next step in his career, McGuire assumed, would be the captain's exam.

But David was getting a very different message from his immediate boss. On the night before Thanksgiving, 1978, Inspector Smith cited several cops for taking their meal in an unauthorized area of the station house—the muster room, which had the station's only working TV set. "How can you do something like this?" David said. "Do you have any idea what this does to morale?"

Smith smiled wearily. "David, David, David, when are you going to understand? I'm evaluated on how many complaints I give out. I'm not evaluated on morale." He added that it was only a matter of time before he caught one of David's subordinates in a violation of some rule—"and you understand, David," Smith added, "we may have to give you a complaint for failure to supervise, even if you're off duty."

In his first term as mayor, Ed Koch confounded the expectations of critics by dealing forthrightly with another budget crisis, winning a series of management reforms, and as Senator Daniel Patrick Moynihan commented approvingly, giving the city back a measure of its former esprit. He also gained a reputation for integrity by taking patronage (at least temporarily) out of the process of appointing judges, instituting a lottery for summer jobs that had previously been awarded through connections, and creating an inspector-general system to watch for corruption in city agencies. He was "almost obsessively fearful of scandal," the journalists Arthur Browne, Dan Collins, and Michael Goodwin wrote in their "decidedly unauthorized" biography, I, Koch—so fearful that he fired one old friend after the Department of Investigation unearthed a case in which he had allegedly bilked some legal clients years earlier.

One of those caught up in the clean-government spirit of the first Koch administration was Deputy Commissioner of Investigation Philip Michael. Late in 1978, Michael got wind of financial irregularities in the city finance department, particularly in the section devoted to the collection of cigarette taxes. According to an internal study, the city ought to have been pocketing about $33 million a year more than it was. The finance department had a small squad of investigators assigned to cigarette tax enforcement. It was, to put it politely, not a very professional unit, and Michael had a suspicion that its problems went beyond ineptitude.

As the police department's trial commissioner in the post-Knapp years—the chief judge of its internal court—Michael had decided the departmental fates of crooked cops, and he had spent enough time with them to have heard David's name often, usually with expletives attached. Michael figured that anyone capable of arousing such violent emotions in cops who had used their powers to extort, steal, or traffic in drugs was probably a useful resource. Now, pondering what to do about the cigarette situation, his thoughts turned to David Durk.

The mayor was also thinking about him, for Garth—of all the members of Koch's circle, the one most sympathetic to David—had recently brought him up. "David is being hung out to dry—they keep transferring him from dustbin to dustbin," Garth had said, reminding Koch that he owed David a debt. Koch had muttered his agreement and agreed to look for something.

When Michael put forth the idea of sending David to the finance department, Koch endorsed it enthusiastically. David had done great things in the past, he told Michael, and would be sure to make the most of the opportunity. Koch did not say (but could well have thought) that this was the perfect solution to the Durk problem: removing him from the police department altogether and sending him to a low-profile area of city government where, as yet, he had no enemies.

But Koch had one large reservation. "I have great confidence in you," he told David. "But I don't want you dealing with anybody from the press."

Asking David to give up his right to talk to reporters was like asking an ordinary cop to give up his revolver. He hemmed and hawed, attempting to make a distinction between "working with the press," as a useful and symbiotic activity, and "leaking," which he promised not to do. But Koch stood firm. He insisted on a blanket embargo, and, boxed into a corner, David agreed. And so, in February 1979, he reported to the finance department, in the capacity of assistant commissioner for criminal investigation, at an annual salary of $39,300—a raise of $11,600 from what the police department had been paying him.

CHAPTER

SIXTEEN

⟹⟸

N ew Yorkers were paying the highest cigarette taxes in the country—twenty-three cents a pack, of which the city got eight cents and the state fifteen. (Cigarettes were also subject to a general city sales tax of 8.25 percent.) So tax evasion was very tempting. To prevent it, a small group of licensed "agent-wholesalers" had been given a statutory monopoly over the distribution end of the business. It was their responsibility to collect the tax from retailers and, using a stamping-and-metering machine made by the Pitney Bowes company, to apply a black ink tax stamp to every pack that passed through their warehouses.

The cigarette-tax enforcement unit was informally known as the bodega squad, because the daily routine of its twenty-five members was to walk designated beats, inspecting the grocery stores, newsstands, drugstores, bars, tobacco shops, and other businesses (upward of ten thousand retail outlets in the city as a whole) where cigarettes were sold, and issue the occasional summons for failure to display a cigarette retailer's license or some other petty infraction. They worked on foot because there were no cars for them. They worked a strict nine-to-five shift because there was no money for overtime. Any retailer who was of a mind to, then, could sell unstamped cigarettes with impunity on evenings and weekends.

A few days after he assumed his new post, David called this ragtag group together and gave them one of his "bleeding in front of the troops" speeches. They had every right to be cynical, he said, about working for a city that gave them as little support as it did, while it spent over a hundred million dollars rebuilding Yankee Stadium in order to (as David saw it) appease George Steinbrenner, the Yankees' owner. He paid tribute to the value of the wild-goose chase, and promised never to punish anyone for an honest mistake. "You're not getting paid much," he said. "You deserve more. But I'm going to give you your pride back. I can't give you your virginity, so we'll start with your pride."

He was looking for allies; what he encountered was hostility. The Commissioner of Finance, Harry Tishelman—a career civil servant —insisted that the department didn't have a corruption problem and didn't have a need for David Durk. When David ordered an audit of the vaults where contraband cigarettes were held, four of the five supervising investigators quit on the spot, without waiting for the results. Among those who remained, there were bitter feelings for the man who, as one of them said behind David's back, had "made us all suspect."

While the city concentrated on the retailers, the state (which had its own squad of tax investigators) was responsible for policing the wholesalers. Shortly before David's arrival, however, a member of the cigarette squad had detected counterfeit tax stamps on a high proportion of the cigarette packs for sale at a group of Merit gas stations and Woolworth stores, and he had traced them to a Brooklyn wholesaler, Nu-Service Tobacco. Now, investigators from the finance department and the Department of Investigation were preparing to raid the place.

The objective was to come up with three hundred cartons of untaxed cigarettes—three hundred being the minimum needed to charge Nu-Service under the newly enacted Federal Contraband Act. This did not appear to be a very lofty goal, since thirteen hundred cartons of contraband had already been identified in inspections of retailers supplied by the company. When the raiders struck, however, the Nu-Service people stood calmly by while thousands of cartons of cigarettes were examined in a fruitless search for irregularities.

Later, a quarrel broke out between the investigator who had found the counterfeits and a sergeant from DOI. The investigator, Tom Stanton, was tall and lanky, with shaggy blond hair and a shaggy blond beard. The failure of the raid infuriated him. "We were burned— somebody tipped them off that we were coming!" Stanton declared. "The volume coming out of that place was so heavy, day after day— and there was no way it was coming out of any other place!"

The DOI staff consisted mainly of cops on loan from the NYPD. They did not have a high opinion of the finance people, who were not cops. "Okay, so you blew it," the sergeant said, dismissing Stanton's complaints of a fix. "It's the breaks."

David, who had been standing on the perimeter of the conversation, didn't like the sergeant's attitude. "This case was given up—you know it and I know it," he interjected, but the sergeant denied knowing any such thing.

Turning away from him, David started talking to Stanton about how they might yet prove that Nu-Service was up to no good. Stanton, as it happened, had an idea. More than once, he had visited the headquarters of Pitney Bowes, in Stamford, Connecticut, seeking information about counterfeiting. Most of the people he had met there treated his inquiries as an affront. "Counterfeiting? Impossible!" was the company line on the subject. But one Pitney Bowes employee—an engineer—had broken ranks, acknowledging not only that counterfeiting was possible but that he had his own suspicions of some of the wholesalers. Stanton's notion was to go back to the engineer, ask how much ink Nu-Service had been buying for its machine, and seek to show that the amount was more than it should have been, if you looked at the number of cigarettes the company claimed to be selling. "He's kind of a buff," Stanton told David— meaning a law-enforcement buff. "He'd help us—if we went to his house, so he knew Pitney Bowes wouldn't come down on him."

It was a Friday afternoon, getting on toward evening, and Stanton wasn't expecting immediate action; he didn't even know the engineer's address or first name. But, having run into him once in the Pitney Bowes parking lot, Stanton did know the make of car he drove, and at David's suggestion, they did a computer check on the last name and the car, and came up with an address. Then, much to Stanton's surprise, David proposed that they head there forthwith.

As soon as they set out, David set to work on Stanton. In pre–Knapp Commission days, he said, the police department had been full of cops who had tried to remain personally honest while doing nothing to interfere with the dishonesty of many of their colleagues. "They kept their mouths shut because they felt just the way you do, Tom. They felt that they had no place to go." The Nu-Service raid suggested that the cigarette squad had a problem with what David euphemistically called "office security." He said he was prepared to offer rank-and-file investigators "de facto amnesty" for past offenses, as long as they weren't too egregious. But he wanted to know "what's going on."

Even in the most beaten-down of bureaucracies, there is usually at least one employee who goes about his job as if something depended on it. In the cigarette squad, Stanton was that sort of employee. He put in long hours (though he rarely got paid for more than forty a week); he studied the history—a long, sordid, and occasionally violent one—of cigarette smuggling and tax fraud; and he had a knack for spotting counterfeit tax stamps. But, although David had been quick to size him up as a kindred spirit, the feeling was not exactly mutual.

Sometimes referred to around the office as an "overage hippie," Stanton was a product of the antiwar movement and the counterculture, layered over a serious Catholic schooling. He loved Frank Capra movies; he drove a Volkswagen Beetle; and he could not abide cops. At the reference to de facto amnesty, he let out a scornful laugh. David was talking about people Stanton had worked with for years, and he was not about to turn against them in order to get in good with the new boss. When David mentioned some names—not asserting anything, just asking—Stanton defended them all. He even gave a fiery defense of a few people he actually couldn't stand.

His attitude toward David improved after they stopped at a police precinct for directions. They spent only about fifteen minutes there, but those fifteen minutes made a deep impression on Stanton. David introduced himself in a normal voice, and the desk sergeant responded in a needlessly loud one—"*Lieutenant Durk, how are you?*"—gaining the immediate and undivided attention of the half-dozen cops working in the station at the time. Word of David's appearance spread quickly. The main lobby of the station was rimmed, school-corridor style, by doors with small windows in them, and within minutes Stanton saw curious and agitated faces pressing up against the glass, two and three faces to a window. It seemed to him that he had never seen a more discombobulated bunch of cops.

It was after eleven that night when David and Stanton arrived at the engineer's house, and just by coming unannounced at such an hour they threw him into a state of shock. In hushed tones worthy of a spy mission, Stanton introduced David, making much of his rank—assistant commissioner—and of his history as the hero of the Knapp Commission inquiry. "If anybody offers him a bribe, it will be the worst thing that ever happens to them," Stanton said. He had told David, he explained, that the engineer was someone who could give them the inside dope on the Pitney Bowes system and its vulnerabilities. Anything he said on that subject, Stanton added, would be held strictly in confidence.

The immediate cause of their visit—the Nu-Service case—was soon forgotten, for in the course of a long and emotional conversation in his kitchen, the engineer acknowledged that counterfeiting was common and that high-ranking people at Pitney Bowes had covered up the problem, apparently in order to protect the company's image and its relations with the wholesalers. As a case in point, the engineer recounted his experience as a witness in a counterfeiting trial. His role had been to perform a courtroom demonstration of the use of the Pitney Bowes machine to produce a lawful tax stamp—a stamp that could then be compared to the counterfeit stamp. But the demonstration had gone awry, producing an image so blurry that the judge had been unable to distinguish the real from the counterfeit. The defendants had been acquitted as a result.

David asked him why the image had come out blurry.

The engineer explained that he had deliberately flooded the machine, on orders from his superiors.

As the interview progressed, Stanton was struck by David's unusual style of questioning. Most law-enforcement officers recognized only one category of informant: the no-good one in search of a reward—if not money, then leniency. A confession of wrongdoing, such as the engineer had now made, would normally be treated as a signal to get tough with him. David did not like the term *informant*— he preferred the more respectful *source*—and his interviewing technique owed as much to psychiatry as it did to law enforcement. He appealed to the engineer's idealism (and his natural desire to unburden himself) as well as his fear. Stanton was impressed by David's sense of when to press an issue and when to back off, and by his use of seemingly pointless digressions that allowed him to circle back to a sensitive question from an unthreatening angle. "The most important talent a detective can have is to direct the conversation," Stanton said later. "David is brilliant at this. He has this knack for never letting the conversation reach a dead end—for keeping it going until people tell him what he wants to know."

Cigarette tax fraud was hardly a new or an unknown phenomenon. For years, however, it had been conveniently blamed on "buttleggers"—smugglers who plied a trade between the low-tax, tobacco-growing states of the South and the high-tax, tobacco-consuming states of the North. Such people existed, but as David soon discovered, they were small-scale operators who generally carried their contraband in the trunks of their cars—a modus operandi that could not begin to account for the tax shortfalls the city had been experiencing. The tobacco industry itself had a lot to say about the evils of buttlegging. One reason it did, David began to suspect, was to distract attention from a far more serious problem: the activities of some of the so-called legitimate wholesalers.

In theory, the law required them to be people of high probity and financial stability; in practice, as Stanton explained, many of them were fast operators, and some had a definite moblike aura. For years, the business had been dominated by a Bronx company whose owners enforced a regime of assigned territories, payoffs, and fixed prices. For a hefty admission fee, a wholesaler could join the club and be insured against competition. Or he could buck the system by, say, cutting prices and invading someone else's territory—and run the risk of having a Molotov cocktail lobbed into his warehouse. After one such fire-bombing, the victim complained to Philip Ruta, a close friend of a man who later pleaded guilty to arson in the case. Ruta (in a conversation tape-recorded by law enforcement authorities) warned him to "stop drawing these filthy, dirty pictures because . . . it's going to get to the wrong people and you're going to have a problem."

The previous summer, as a result of Stanton's vigilance, city and state investigators had conducted a highly publicized raid on a group of stores served by a Bronx wholesaler, Joseph A. Schrager Candy and Tobacco. (The state's tax stamp featured a seascape with sailboats; the waves were missing in the stamp Stanton had spotted.) The raiders had seized thousands of cartons of cigarettes with counterfeit stamps—cartons conveniently labeled "bad" to distinguish them from the noncounterfeit stock, which was labeled "good." But the case went nowhere. In what Stanton described as an outcome fairly typical of cigarette investigations, the responsible officials refused to charge anybody, since, they explained, they had been unable to identify the individuals in the company who had actually done the counterfeiting.

With Stanton as his escort, David began visiting wholesalers. One of their first stops was Globe Tobacco, in the Bay Ridge section of Brooklyn. Stanton described the owner, Leonard Schwartz, as one of the most powerful figures in the business. Schwartz was a curly-haired, muscular man with a fondness for gold medallions and purple silk shirts, which he wore unbuttoned halfway to the waist, exposing a large expanse of deeply tanned chest. When David complimented him on his tan—it was the middle of February—Schwartz launched into an enthusiastic discourse on his tanning technique, which was to lie in a quarter-inch-deep tub of water and rotate his body as though it were a piece of meat on a spit.

"If somebody wants to fool around, he can fool around" was Schwartz's response when David brought up the issue of counterfeiting. At another point in the conversation, he asked, "Why shouldn't I counterfeit?"

"Well, there are a number of reasons," David replied. "For one thing, it's against the law."

"Nothing ever happens to anyone who gets caught," Schwartz said. "The worst thing they do is make you pay the back taxes."

David said he intended to adopt a policy of "full enforcement" of the tax laws.

Schwartz laughed. "Try and get me," he said.

"I'm going to try," David said.

(Schwartz enjoyed this sort of banter with the law. When two city investigators came to interview him about a minor irregularity, he complained about their "nickel-and-dime" questions. "If I'm going to do anything, it's going to be for the big money," he said. "Catch me for the big money.")

A counterfeiter might, in fact, be caught. But counterfeiting was not the only way to evade the tax. A far simpler technique, it soon emerged, was simply to rig the Pitney Bowes machine to generate stamps without recording them on the meter. Pitney Bowes officials liked to talk about the breakaway screws, the self-destructing fuses, and the other built-in security devices that supposedly made their machine all but tamperproof, and most of the relevant law enforcement authorities echoed the company's grand claims. In a typical encomium to the brilliance of the Pitney Bowes technology, Richard Brunella, chief of forensics for the Federal Bureau of Alcohol, Tobacco, and Firearms, told a reporter for the *Daily News* that "any attempt to enter the machine will result in damage . . . that could not be corrected." But when David and Stanton took a Pitney Bowes machine to a Brooklyn engraver for an evaluation, they got a very different picture. Using only a paper clip and a Phillips screwdriver, he quickly managed to make the stamping mechanism run independently of the meter. As an added touch, he had the machine run backward, so that, as David pointed out later, the city would owe the wholesaler money instead of the other way around. (These experiments had implications that went beyond cigarette taxes, for Pitney Bowes also made machines, utilizing similar technology, for the stamping and metering of business mail.) Finally, the engraver restored the machine to its original condition, leaving no apparent trace of his work. The machine was "so badly put together," he told them afterward, "you'd almost think it was *designed* to be tampered with."

Drawn to each other by a shared determination to get to the bottom of these matters, David and Stanton became a duo, and the duo expanded into a trio with the hiring of Barbara Bishop as the office's legal counsel. Bishop—a vibrant, extremely direct twenty-six-year-old who liked to chew bubble gum and referred to herself as Miss Innocent—was recruited from the Consumer Affairs Department, David having met her there two and a half years earlier, after calling to complain about a head-gasket problem on his 1976 Honda Accord. He had blown the gasket late one night on the FDR Drive, and, as he told Bishop, the car was still sitting at the dealership a month later, awaiting a replacement part. Bishop gave David her standard consumer-affairs speech, which concluded with a question—what was he after? A new car, a repair, or his money back?

"I want a national recall," he told her. It was an answer she had never heard before, and though her immediate response was to idly write the word *psycho* across his complaint form, she gradually developed an admiration for his all-engines, full-speed-ahead approach to injustice. (David's case had wound up as one of the more successful in Bishop's tenure at Consumer Affairs. From a Honda mechanic—a gun buff with a strong interest in police weapons and ammunition—he had learned that his complaint was far from unique. Although he didn't get a national recall, Honda USA eventually agreed to the next best thing: it would send letters to all owners of '76 Accords, alerting them to the problem and inviting them to bring their cars in for preventive maintenance.) David told Bishop that she would be doing God's work if she came to finance. As a further inducement, he offered her a $2,000 raise.

With Bishop and Stanton as his aides-de-camp, David brought new life to what had been a stagnant backwater of city government. His office—on the ninth floor of a building sandwiched between Centre and Lafayette streets, a few blocks from City Hall—faced a large open area where some forty auditors toiled listlessly, pencils in hand. They sat down in unison at the beginning of the day and rose in unison at the end. Into this enervating scene was now introduced the spectacle of Durk, Stanton, and Bishop—the three musketeers of tax enforcement—sweeping, tornadolike, through the ranks of auditor-filled desks.

A great believer in food, drink, and conviviality as aids in the intelligence-gathering process, David began setting up lunches and dinners with people in the cigarette world and gently drawing them out about the curious ties binding the wholesalers, Pitney Bowes, and city and state tax authorities. For years, the city and state had made a practice of bestowing large amounts of unsecured credit on many of the wholesalers, giving them the right to defer payment of taxes on cigarettes they had already sold to retailers. Such was the cash flow in the cigarette business that some of the larger wholesalers, Stanton calculated, could turn a profit on the float alone. What roiled him even more was a habit that the wholesalers had of going bankrupt and leaving the city and state holding the bag for, in some cases, hundred of thousands of dollars in uncollected taxes. Owners or officers of the bankrupt firms would then resurface with new corporate aliases, to build up their tax debts all over again. Stanton had often complained to his superiors about the bankruptcies, but, until David came along, his superiors had seemed mysteriously indifferent.

The mystery cleared up considerably one night in November 1980, when David, Stanton, and Bishop had dinner with a wholesaler and his wife—the Levys, let them be called here—at a restaurant on the Lower East Side. Dinner with the Levys was a social occasion. The talk, although it involved cigarettes, was mainly anecdotal and historical, and the Levys were only too happy to reminisce about how things had been done in days gone by. Under that rubric, they were soon confiding that they had repeatedly bribed a high-ranking finance department official (passing cash-filled envelopes to him in one of the office men's rooms) in return for extra allotments of credit. When Stanton asked whether any of the other wholesalers resented being put at a disadvantage, Mrs. Levy laughed and said no one would think of complaining— because everybody did it. There was even a fixed price schedule: for a hundred dollars, the Levys said, you got a thousand dollars in credit. (The official they implicated was still in office; he broke down under questioning by David and, shortly thereafter, submitted his resignation.)

The wholesalers seemed to take the corruptibility of city and state tax people for granted. "Are you here to take some more of my money?" a Yonkers wholesaler named Joe Farano inquired, when Stanton called on him in October 1980.

"What are you talking about?" Stanton said.

Farano had been caught a few years earlier supplying New York City retailers with cigarettes on which he had paid only the state's portion of the tax. The city slapped him with an assessment of $80,000, and on a friend's advice he went to John Calandra, a state senator from the Bronx who had a law practice on the side. Farano, to his surprise, also found himself meeting Mario Procaccino, a former state tax commissioner and city comptroller, who had been the Democratic candidate for mayor in 1969. After listening to Farano's problem, Calandra and Procaccino conferred briefly, then told him that for a $25,000 fee—in cash—he could sleep peacefully.

The amount was far more than Farano had bargained for. He said he would think about it.

A week later, he got a call from Procaccino, who wanted to know why Farano hadn't gotten back to him.

Farano explained that his offense—selling state-stamped cigarettes inside the city limits—had been an innocent mistake, and $25,000 was a lot to pay for a mistake.

Procaccino proposed a simple solution to Farano's problem: he could forget about Calandra's share of the fee, and just give Procaccino his $12,500. Farano agreed, and when his case came up for a hearing the assessment was reduced, he said later, from $80,000 to $1,200. But the legal fee had still seemed too high to him, so Procaccino had been forced to sue to collect. Now, state tax authorities were inspecting Farano right and left in what he interpreted as an effort to harass him into paying Procaccino's bill.

Stanton and David went to the finance department that evening to look for the records of the case Farano had described. Assessments and appeals were handled by a division that was kept separate from investigations. But Stanton knew where to find a key that opened a filing cabinet containing another key that opened another cabinet, and so on, until they found the file they were after. The story it told matched Farano's story: his company, Briker Tobacco, had been hit with an $80,000 assessment, which had been reduced, on appeal, to $1,200.

The wholesalers had a trade association, and David began to establish a relationship with its managing director, a former wholesaler named George Elicofon. Steeped in the tobacco industry's ways of doing things, Elicofon nonetheless saw himself as a reformer. Under his leadership, he told David, the wholesalers were trying to bring the bankruptcy situation under control—by setting a limit of two bankruptcies per career. Short and barrel-shaped, with a wide mouth, gray-white hair, and eyebrows so thick and dark that they might almost have been drawn on with charcoal, Elicofon was a born talker who rarely missed a chance to mention his famous brother, the *Life* photographer Eliot Elisofon, who had traveled among the high and mighty of Hollywood (and had changed the spelling of the family name). David was trying to find out about the netherworld of financial ties between wholesalers and current and former public officials. This was a subject that Elicofon rather enjoyed discussing, and his disclosures were no less interesting for the fact that his purpose in making them, as a rule, was to justify arrangements that might not look kosher to an outsider.

Every fall the wholesalers' association held a three-day convention in the Catskills, where the agenda included such things as a lively talk by the president of General Cigar on the cigar's reemergence as "the male symbol of success, gentility, and virility," an uplifting report by the head of the Tobacco Institute on "scholars and thinkers in many parts of the world" who were "beginning to question the inflamed rhetoric of the anti-smoking zealots," and a continuous round of golf, tennis, bowling, bingo, after-dinner dances, lottery drawings, and banquets. And every year, the convention would be attended by officials of the State Department of Taxation and Finance and members of the state senate and state assembly who were there to be honored as "legislator of the year" or "elder statesman of the year."

"We're not giving them cash—we're just picking up the tab for their weekend," Elicofon would say. "You can't expect a man who's getting an award to pay for his weekend."

Elicofon assumed a paternal attitude toward David. He wanted David to understand that the world in which Elicofon operated—a world governed by what he called "the veniality" of people—was not of his making. David believed that a different world was possible; Elicofon had once thought so, too. David had to wise up, as Elicofon had. "You're not practical, David," he would say. "You're a straight arrow. You know only one path, and you don't deviate for a second. You're a man of ability—you've got brains, you've got personality. But you've got a path that you don't deviate from. You'd be more successful in life, maybe, if you learned to back off a little. If you were my own son, I couldn't give you more constructive advice."

The democratic process imposed high tax rates on tobacco products, but much of what government took away when it was operating in the open, it gave back when no one was looking. In periodic lunches with David, Bishop, and Stanton, Elicofon described a system of regular campaign contributions that were funneled through the speaker of the state assembly, Stanley Fink—S.F., as Elicofon insisted on calling him. ("Never say Stanley Fink—say S.F.!" Elicofon commanded, whenever David forgot himself.) Elicofon accepted the need for such contributions as a fact of life, but from time to time he would speak with sincere revulsion about some occasion when the demands had become excessive. There was the time, for example, when he had been ordered to turn over $10,000 on his arrival at Albany Airport, as a kind of landing fee, before being driven to an appointment with Robert Morgado, an aide to Governor Hugh Carey. There was the $120,000 kitty that Elicofon had helped put together for a group of key legislators—a contribution, a leading figure in the state senate had implied, that would facilitate passage of a "fair trade" bill for cigarettes; the bill had been defeated, and the senator had refused to return the money. Greed, Elicofon complained, was getting out of hand in Albany.

The full extent of the intimacy among wholesalers, legislators, and state tax officials became apparent when David and his team were summoned to a discussion of "legislative priorities" at the offices of the State Department of Taxation and Finance, in the World Trade Center. He found himself being asked to support a bill that would sweeten the credit terms for the wholesalers, giving them sixty days instead of thirty to pay their taxes, supposedly as a gesture of concern for the health of an important New York State industry. "I want everyone here to know that I love New York State," Stanley Fink, who acted as the host of the meeting, said at one point. Also present was Leonard Schwartz, the driving force behind the measure, and Fink introduced him as "my good friend," explaining that they had been classmates at New York University Law School. Fink, David said later, seemed to expect the state and city tax people at the meeting to give their immediate consent. When David demurred, inquiring whether he would have a chance to read the bill first, Fink glowered at him and asked, "Who are you?" When David gave his name, Fink looked nervously at his watch. "I'm running late," he said, and after one more brief appeal for support he excused himself and departed.

Not long into his time at finance, David got a phone call from a man who will be called Jerry. "You're interested in cigarettes," Jerry said. David agreed that he was. Jerry instructed him to stand on the corner of Walker and Lafayette streets, staring down at the sidewalk, until a car came for him. (David had done this sort of thing before. He had even gone to one such rendezvous unarmed—a condition that, he was glad to hear, wasn't part of the deal this time.) He was picked up by two men in a hopped-up Plymouth. They drove through the Battery Tunnel in silence, switching cars on the Brooklyn waterfront; from that point on, David had only a hazy idea where they went, because he kept his eyes closed, as instructed. Eventually, the car parked in front of a school playground, and the driver departed, leaving David alone with Jerry.

Jerry was an old-fashioned buttlegger who made a living driving carloads of cigarettes from the town of Rocky Mount, North Carolina, to various used-car lots in Brooklyn. (The cigarettes were then distributed to beauty parlors and sweatshops, among other outlets.) He claimed to have been paying off state tax investigators for years in what amounted to a modest version of the liquor-related corruption of Prohibition days. He had been moved to confide in David, he explained, by his anger over a recent episode in which a senior state tax supervisor had caught him bringing a load of contraband cigarettes into Brooklyn and had forced him to turn over the cigarettes as well as all the money he had on him. "I had to get down on my hands and knees and beg him for enough change to pay the bridge toll," Jerry said.

In all the tangled story of cigarette-tax evasion, the most confusing—and, for David, the most compelling—part was the role of the major tobacco companies, Philip Morris, R. J. Reynolds, and Lorillard. The manufacturers weren't directly responsible for paying New York City cigarette taxes, but by choosing to sell to some people and not to others, they effectively decided who could become a wholesaler, and their decisions, it seemed to David, showed a partiality to people of very questionable integrity. Moreover, the tobacco companies seemed undisturbed by blatant evidence of tax fraud. A substantial proportion (40 percent, according to one government estimate) of the cigarettes purchased by North Carolina wholesalers were diverted to the black market in other states, yet none of the manufacturers had ever suspended its dealings with a wholesaler, in North Carolina or anywhere else.

One Reynolds executive's remark to David neatly summed up the industry's attitude toward cooperation with law enforcement. The comment was made in response to a question about Schrager and its misdeeds. Schrager had grown from a $20-million-a-year company to a $70-million-a-year company in less than eighteen months. Reynolds had been suspicious of Schrager all along, the executive told David, because no wholesaler could have expanded so fast by legitimate means. When David asked him why he had failed to share this suspicion with the city, the executive replied, "We're cigarette men, not policemen."

Since the case-by-case approach to cigarette-tax fraud was obviously a losing game, David proposed a catch-all remedy: a tax stamp that would be placed beneath the shrink wrapper of the cigarette pack, and applied at the factory, with government agents watching over the process. It was a simple plan, he reasoned, with the potential to greatly reduce counterfeiting and other forms of tax evasion. But when he put the idea to the tobacco companies' tax people, they turned him down flat. Nor was the reaction any better when Mayor Koch laid out the plan in a one-on-one meeting with George Weissman, the CEO of Philip Morris. Koch suggested that the tobacco companies try an under-the-wrapper stamp for six months, with the city paying the cost of the experiment. If revenues didn't increase as a result, Koch promised, the city would drop its cigarette tax altogether, as the industry had long been urging.

"It would slow down our whole process," Koch quoted Weissman as saying in reply.

David was enraged—the more so when he and Bishop visited a Philip Morris factory near Richmond, Virginia, and, while taking an escorted tour of the plant, noticed a machine putting a stamp under the cellophane. It was a tax stamp for Yemen—one of a number of foreign countries for which the tobacco companies, it turned out, already supplied this service. "They said it couldn't be done, until we went down and saw it," Bishop recalled.

What with one thing and another—the response to the under-the-wrapper stamp idea; mysterious truck hijackings that the tobacco companies didn't seem very interested in solving; export cigarettes that somehow found their way into domestic distribution; trucks that, when inspected, were revealed to be carrying unrecorded over-shipments of certain leading brands—David became convinced that the tobacco companies, which made no secret of their belief that cigarettes were overtaxed, had crossed a line between opposition and subversion.

His appointment had been a hasty attempt to solve two problems (what to do about cigarette taxes, what to do about David Durk) at once. He had hoped for something better, and there were people in the Koch administration who had wondered if, embittered by years of penance in Queens, Brooklyn, and East Harlem, David was up to the job. By the fall of 1979, however, he could say that while the industry was reporting a decrease in sales and tax collection at the state level was down, the city's revenues for the first half of the year were up $2.6 million. He received a note from the mayor congratulating him on "the superb job you are doing in rooting out incompetence, and collecting taxes heretofore uncollected." David had found a niche for himself, and his investigations were leading him into levels of possible subterfuge beyond anything contemplated by those who had hired him.

CHAPTER

SEVENTEEN

For a city in dire financial straits, New York had a curiously laid-back attitude toward collecting taxes. The finance department had several hundred employees who were supposed to look for cases of possible tax fraud, and they did so mainly from behind their desks—by, for example, mailing out letters of reminder to businesses that had paid taxes in past years but not in the current one. If the recipient fessed up and sent in a check, the city would gratefully deposit it; if not, that was generally the end of the investigation. But there were people in various nooks and crannies of the department who longed to go further, and as the word spread that something out of the ordinary was happening in the cigarette squad, they started coming to David with their ideas.

Anna Paulson, a white-haired woman who had been at the finance department in various capacities for thirty-seven years, would periodically comb the yellow pages for businesses that hadn't paid their commercial-occupancy taxes; when she found one, she would mail the suspected violator a form letter requesting answers to certain questions, including when it had commenced operations. She had noticed, she told David, that with suspicious frequency these businesses claimed to have only just been established. Paulson thought that the city should look into the truthfulness of their statements, but office policy was to take them at face value.

With David's encouragement, Paulson and others in her traditionally desk-bound unit began visiting the Forty-second Street library in order to consult its collection of old phone books. There they found evidence that many of the businesses in question had been going strong for years—in a few cases, for decades. Because there was no statute of limitations for failing to file a return, Paulson's efforts led to some very large settlements. In her perusals of the yellow pages, Paulson was also struck by the number of foreign airlines with offices in New York City. Quite a few of them, she discovered, had never paid commercial-occupancy taxes, while others had paid them on only a fraction of the space they leased. Most of the airlines pleaded ignorance when Paulson contacted them, but they wound up paying large bills for past as well as current taxes. (Among the fruits of this investigation was a check from South African Airways for $178,674.68, covering the years 1969 through 1978.)

Jack Burnescu, who had been a collection agent in a prior life, was upset about the nonpayment of commercial-motor-vehicle taxes. According to the law, the tax applied to any commercial vehicle used predominantly within the city, but the law was widely ignored by truck-rental firms, package delivery services, dial-a-cab companies, and the like. David helped Burnescu conceive an investigation that produced settlements with a long list of violators, including a major truck-rental company with a fleet of untaxed vehicles on long-term lease to one of the city's daily newspapers. With his bill collector's experience, Burnescu persuaded some of the violators to pay up without being hauled into court. Besides educating them in the possible legal consequences of nonpayment, he liked to point out that the city needed their money in order to repair the damage their trucks were doing to the streets.

David got the idea for another investigation—of the underpayment of sales and gross income taxes by bars and nightclubs—from Ed Murphy, a former con man and, until two recent heart attacks sidelined him, the manager, under the aegis of Matty "the Horse"

Ianniello, of a string of gay bars and clubs with names such as the Purple Onion, the Gold Bug, the Turntable—and the Stonewall, scene of the famous Stonewall Uprising, in which Murphy had been a prominent participant. (Ianniello had been acquitted of his Operation Cleveland charges, and he still had a hand in operating more than a hundred establishments in lower and midtown Manhattan.) David won Murphy's cooperation with the argument that gays should control their own bars rather than patronizing establishments run by organized crime.

After signing on as a $350-a-week consultant—under no circumstances was anyone to refer to Murphy as an "informant," David insisted—Murphy briefed the finance investigators on a variety of tax-evasion techniques that these bars and clubs employed. Some had separate cash registers, for reported and unreported income. Some would charge an entrance fee entitling a customer to several drinks, but pay taxes only on the drinks they sold in excess of that number. At Murphy's suggestion, David sent in undercover agents with silent clickers—like the ones that bus inspectors use to count passengers—to check on how many drinks were served, and to see how the tally squared with the place's tax records.

Susan Thomas, who had been a student of David's at Yale before he hired her as an investigator, took up watch one evening in a disco called Melon's, on Sixteenth Street, wearing chains and a gauzy dress that looked like something out of the Arabian Nights. After monitoring the place for a few hours, Thomas went to a public phone, called the number of a second public phone on a nearby corner, and gave a prearranged signal: "We're all here, and we're having a great time!" It was the cue for David and a couple of dozen investigators from the finance department and the NYPD to enter. They turned up the lights, sent the patrons on their way, seized the cash and records, arrested the principals, and shut the place down. There were about a dozen of these raids in all.

When people speak of the underground economy, they think of illicit businesses like narcotics, prostitution, and fencing. David's job had evolved into a crusade against the underground economy in a broader sense, encompassing legitimate businesses that systemati-cally failed to pay a significant portion of their taxes. It was a crusade in which, it seemed to him, every success—every business caught and compelled to pay—had a ripple effect on the many other mer-chants who had told themselves, "Why should we pay, when nobody else does?" And when a case involved a powerful industry such as tobacco, it sent a message to ordinary New Yorkers that the law applied to everybody equally.

This was a theme well suited to Ed Koch's early years as mayor, when, as Ken Auletta wrote in *The New Yorker,* he was "at war . . . with the city's entire political-financial-business-labor establish-ment." In his first term, Koch took a surprisingly close interest in David and his activities. They communicated often, by note, by phone, and face-to-face. Few other assistant commissioners became as familiar as David with the mayor's office at City Hall, or with the inside of Gracie Mansion. Few others addressed the mayor, even in private, as "Ed."

One of the early coups of David's tenure at finance was getting the cigarette companies to pay the taxes they owed on samples that they regularly gave away to promote new brands. By law, samples were taxable, but the tobacco companies had ignored the law for years. Then, in May 1979, an irate phone call from David to R. J. Reynolds about one such giveaway produced, a day later, a check for nearly $136,000. When Mayor Koch heard about it, he invited David over to City Hall, asked to see the check, gave it a kiss, and did a little dance around the office, waving it in the air.

A phone message from Anna Quindlen, then a reporter for the *Times,* was waiting for David when he returned to the finance depart-ment building.

"I'm not allowed to give interviews," he told Quindlen.

"The mayor's office told me to call you," Quindlen said. Her story, headlined CIGARETTE MAKER PAYS UP, appeared on the front page of the Metropolitan section the next day.

David was generating some very good press for the Koch adminis-tration. He was also stepping on a dangerous number of toes. Within months of his appointment, he had come across evidence of corruption in Albany, and the FBI had been brought in. Soon enough, the people at the State Department of Taxation and Finance figured out that they were being investigated, and who was responsible—and relations between the city and state tax authorities became openly belligerent.

The two agencies almost got into a shooting war in June 1979, over 2,500 unstamped cartons of cigarettes that had been deposited in the basement of a house on Staten Island. After staking the place out, federal Treasury agents—members of the Alcohol, Tobacco, and Firearms Bureau—and state tax investigators had reluctantly concluded that they didn't have enough evidence for a search warrant. The cigarettes were in large cardboard cases, and though some of them were visible through a basement window, there was nothing about their appearance to establish that the contents were contraband—not as far as the state tax people or their friends from Treasury could discern. The same cases that said nothing to them, however, spoke eloquently to Tom Stanton. They had coded dates printed on them, indicating that they had left the factory two days earlier. Any *lawful* shipment of cigarettes, Stanton explained, would have to have passed through a truck terminal in Hoboken, New Jersey—the Elk warehouse—that served all the tobacco companies as a point of entry into New York City. Elk could not possibly have gotten them in and out that quickly, Stanton said; besides, Elk put markings of its own on the cases it handled, and these cases had no such markings.

If there were a book of etiquette for law enforcement officers, it would advise against the practice of serving a warrant on a site already commandeered by a rival law enforcement agency. But etiquette had never been David's forte. Drawing on Stanton's observations, Barbara Bishop prepared an application for a warrant (the evidence was so complicated that the application ran eighteen pages), and she and David took it to the Staten Island DA's office, which was about a quarter of an hour away. (The state tax and Treasury agents had been unsuccessfully conferring with prosecutors at the federal courthouse in Brooklyn, more than an hour away.) When they returned, and David announced that he had a warrant, the state tax people went slightly berserk, and their legal counsel, Steve Somerstein, told David there was *no way* he or his team would be allowed to touch "our cigarettes." When David persisted, Somerstein—addressing his troops in the manner of a commander on the eve of battle—called on them to "secure the perimeter." Before cooler heads prevailed, several Treasury agents actually ran to fetch the shotguns they kept nestled in purple velveteen in the trunks of their cars.

Some weeks later, the state special prosecutor's office informed David that it was looking into a charge, leveled by state tax officials, that the finance department staff had made false statements in their application for a search warrant. The case was dropped for want of evidence—Philip Michael called the accusation "unfounded" and "absurd"—but not before somebody had leaked the information to the *News*, resulting in a story that made it look as if it were David and his unit that were suspected of being corrupt.

The Commissioner of Investigation, Stanley Lupkin, was a big man on the horizontal as well as the vertical axis, but there was a love of neatness and propriety in his crewcut, his bowtie, and his steel-rimmed glasses. He smoked a pipe and had a fish tank in his office, and he had a habit of sprinkling food into the fish tank during meetings. Lupkin was a lawyerlike man who admired "solid," "realistic" men who could "think dimensionally" and "map out a plan and follow through." He expected subordinates to lay out the facts coolly and await instructions. He had been dubious about David from the start, and his doubts grew with time. "Why did I subject myself to this?" he would sometimes ask himself when a session with David came to an end.

Lupkin considered David an "unguided missile," because, among other things, his cigarette-tax investigators—now outfitted with cheap tape recorders, which David had bought for the purpose—were making bribery collars when retailers offered them money to overlook violations of the law. David regarded these arrests as a declaration of independence from the ways of the past: the squad was announcing to the cigarette industry and to the rest of city government that it couldn't be bought. But bribery, Lupkin pointed out, was his department's lookout. If a finance department employee received a bribe offer, his duty was to report it to the Department of Investigation. David countered that Lupkin's people made every bribery case an elaborate production. "You had to make an appointment with them three days in advance," he said later, "and by the time they were ready to do anything the possibility of making the case had vanished."

In the spring of 1980, Stanton discovered counterfeit tax stamps on packs of cigarettes coming from a newly established wholesaler in East Harlem, Sea-Lar Tobacco. Stanton had had his eye on Sea-Lar, which had more than doubled the volume of its business in the space of a few months. A surveillance of the company's warehouse, at 112th Street and Second Avenue, revealed that although Sea-Lar had ostensibly been founded by two Chinese-Americans—a father and son, both named Fan—its principals also included two men who had just resigned their positions as regional sales executives for R. J. Reynolds. For a pair of tobacco-company officials to go to work in a graffiti-covered warehouse in Spanish Harlem was a very unusual job switch, and Stanton found himself wondering if they had not somehow known ahead of time that Sea-Lar would be such a runaway success. One of the Reynolds men, when asked by Stanton to explain the source of the company's extraordinary good fortune, replied, with a grin, "Dynamic sales leadership in the marketplace."

After several weeks of surveillance, Sea-Lar's warehouse was raided in a joint finance-FBI operation, and 90 percent of the cigarettes that had just been loaded onto an outbound truck turned out to bear counterfeit stamps. When the two former Reynolds executives showed up in mid-raid, David put them under arrest along with the Fans. (They were "former" inasmuch as they insisted—and Reynolds confirmed—that they had resigned. But they were driving a Reynolds-owned car, and one of them had a gun that was registered to the company. "How come you haven't reported the gun or the car stolen?" David asked a Reynolds official later.) After he had taken the four suspects to his office to be booked, two attorneys from

Kostelanetz and Ritholtz—one of the most prestigious law firms in the country when it came to tax matters—put in an appearance and made a flurry of phone calls. Then David got a call from Stanley Lupkin, asking him to put the arrests on hold while Lupkin pondered further. After hours of discussions involving Lupkin and a federal prosecutor who had helped plan the raid—discussions from which David was pointedly excluded—Lupkin told him to let the two Reynolds men and the younger Fan go, uncharged.

"By authority of who?" David demanded.

"Authority of *me*," said Lupkin.

The only arrest that stuck was that of the elder Fan, who spoke no English but comprehended enough to respond to David's and Stanton's questions about who controlled the company by drawing a pencil sketch of himself and his son as puppets. Exasperated, and determined to pursue the case through other channels, David went to a young assistant DA named Gavin Scotti. They agreed to try to make a deal with Mr. Fan, securing his testimony against the men from Reynolds. But the plan evaporated when, soon after the old man's arraignment, he jumped bail and fled to his native Taiwan. With the collapse of the Sea-Lar case, nine cigarette wholesalers— nearly a quarter of those licensed to do business in New York City— had been caught counterfeiting over a period of five years, and not one owner or manager of a company had been brought to trial, either by the city or the state.

In October 1980, Philip Michael was elevated to the job of finance commissioner (replacing Harry Tishelman). Michael was a slender, softspoken man with thinning reddish hair. It was he who had championed David's appointment in the first place, and in the early going he had been a sort of fourth musketeer with David, Bishop, and Stanton—an eager coconspirator, who took pleasure in their successes; shared their suspicions of Pitney Bowes, the state tax people, and the tobacco wholesalers and manufacturers; stayed up late with them writing progress reports for the mayor; and seemed as determined as they were to document a pattern of tax evasion and recover many millions of dollars for the city.

Now, as David's boss, Michael was responsible for the full range of his activities, and he began to regard them more warily. David was, for one thing, an unusually time-consuming subordinate. When he wasn't actually in Michael's office with some problem or other, Michael was often fielding "Did you hear what Durk has done now?" phone calls or struggling to restore some semblance of civility to the finance department's relations with the last person or entity David had alienated. Sometimes, Michael's dealings with the team of Durk, Stanton, and Bishop made him feel like a teacher facing a noisy claque of students in the front row. He took to calling Stanton and Bishop "your playmates"—as in "Don't bother to bring your playmates with you this time" when he was summoning David to a meeting. Not that he considered either of them lacking in brains or dedication. The main thing he had against them (though he once remarked that Stanton "dressed like a socialist") was the degree to which they seemed to be in David's thrall.

With Michael as finance commissioner, David hoped to get more support for the cigarette investigation. In particular, he was looking for Michael to help him bring a RICO (the acronym for the Racketeer Influenced and Corrupt Organizations [Act]) lawsuit seeking hundreds of millions of dollars in damages from all the parties involved. But first the investigation would have to go undercover, for there was no other way, David had decided, to get the necessary evidence.

On New Year's Eve, 1980, he found a likely undercover agent in the manager of a bankrupt Bronx distribution company who had blown the whistle on his boss for walking off with tens of thousands of dollars in cash just as his company was supposedly collapsing from debt. The manager, who was Hispanic, felt that he had shouldered most of the work of running the business, while being paid meagerly, and then had been left to face the authorities after his boss had fled. Playing on his resentment, David and Stanton persuaded him to turn over records documenting the fraud and to reveal, among other things, that his company had been receiving unlogged shipments of cigarettes from the Elk warehouse. When he agreed to act as a front if the city would set him up as a wholesaler, David was exhilarated. When Michael turned the idea down and, after a few weeks of further discussions, announced that he wanted David "out of cigarettes," David was dumbfounded.

He could only imagine that Michael—or someone above him— was yielding to pressure from the tobacco industry. "When we started out, everybody presumed that it was organized crime and Italians—a fly-by-night contraband operation," David said later. "As soon as they understood that there wasn't any caravan of trucks coming over the Verrazano Bridge at midnight—that we were going up against heavyweight companies with the money and the resources to really bat you around—City Hall had a heart attack!"

David would come to regard Michael as someone who had sacrificed his idealism on the altar of ambition. "In the beginning, he was as aggressive as could be," David recalled. "And then it was, 'Forget it!' He did a total flip-flop. You could see it in his clothes. He used to dress like a regular person, and all of a sudden he started looking like a banker."

Whether the tobacco industry exercised any influence, direct or indirect, over the investigation's fate is hard to say. That it would like to have had such an influence is clear. From time to time, tobacco-company people would run into David at some industry get-together, and—their tongues loosened by drink—give him a hint of their true feelings. At one such gathering, a pair of R. J. Reynolds officials cornered him in the hallway of an upstate hotel, and as another city official who was present recalled, "It started as chitchat—'Oh, how great to see you again.' Then it was, 'Get off our turf. You don't know what hardball is till you've played with us.' They made it plain that they would do whatever they had to do to take us apart personally, and to take the entire unit apart."

In the summer of 1980, Barbara Bishop was thumbing through a piece of proposed tax legislation when, in the fine print of a very long bill, she came across a clause directing the city to cease all activities "relating to the imposition, administration, collecting, and enforcement of cigarette taxes" and turn over its cigarette tax cases and files to the state. Bishop was never able to determine exactly who was responsible for the provision, which was quietly dropped after she began asking questions about it; nobody seemed to know how it had gotten there, or why the offending clause had been set in roman type, which was normally reserved for language that merely restated existing law. (New provisions were supposed to appear in italics.) But somebody, it seemed, had gone to considerable lengths to try to slip it through the legislative process unnoticed—as it might well have, if Bishop had been any less meticulous a reader of the papers that crossed her desk.

There were plenty of people in government, certainly, to whom the industry could appeal for help—people like Peter Solomon, the Deputy Mayor for Economic Development in Koch's first term and his chief fund-raiser in the 1981 reelection campaign. Solomon had been a member of the board of Philip Morris's parent company, Culbro, and his willingness to listen to former associates in the tobacco world became apparent when he called up David one day, and urged him to "be nice" to some wholesalers who were coming to see him. ("What does 'be nice' mean?" David replied.)

From no less an authority than Ed Koch, David knew that Philip Morris's chairman of the board, George Weissman, was greatly displeased. In a conversation with the mayor (later recounted to David by Koch), Weissman complained about the city's campaign of—for so Weissman viewed it—harassment against his company, and he spoke of possibly relocating Philip Morris's corporate headquarters from New York City to Yonkers. "Go ahead," Koch quoted himself as saying in reply.

A decade later, the idea that the tobacco companies were involved in large-scale tax fraud might not have raised so many eyebrows; at any rate, it would not have seemed very far out of line with other emerging discoveries about, for example, the industry's suppression of research findings on the dangers of smoking and its seeming manipulation of nicotine levels to ensure the addictiveness of the product. But in 1980, David was talking about companies that had worked long and hard, and very successfully, to establish their credentials as honored members of the American corporate establishment and benefactors of good works. Philip Morris, through various subsidiaries, manufactured Parkay margarine, Maxwell House coffee, Kool-Aid drink mixes, Log Cabin maple syrup, Breyers ice cream, Post Raisin Bran cereal, Jell-O, and Miller beer, as well as Marlboros, Benson & Hedges, Parliaments, Merits, Alpines, Chesterfields, and Virginia Slims. Weissman himself served on the board of Lincoln Center (he later became its chairman), and Miller was the underwriter of a summer concert program in Central Park. The company, moreover, was preparing to put up a new headquarters building at Forty-first Street and Park Avenue. Mayor Koch might or might not have told Weissman to "go ahead" and move to Yonkers. In the cold light of morning, however, Koch, like any mayor, would go to some lengths to dissuade Weissman from taking such a step.

To some in the Koch administration, the truth or falsity of David's suspicions was probably immaterial, in view of the political hazards of an all-out legal battle with the tobacco companies and the difficulty of prevailing in court against them. In explaining his decision, however, Michael made no mention of any such concerns. Cigarette taxes, he said, accounted for only $160 million of roughly $15 billion in annual city revenues, and David, in his preoccupation with them, was neglecting other tax problems no less deserving of the city's attention. "I'm not interested in cigarettes anymore," Michael told him. "And you shouldn't be. We've got bigger fish to fry."

For weeks, David continued to lobby for his undercover operation. It was absurd, he said to Michael, to balk at spending $35,000 (the startup budget for the operation) when the city had just agreed to pay a million dollars to the Washington law firm of Arnold and Porter for its services in writing a model cable-TV franchise agreement. "How can you reject this," he asked, "when Arnold and Porter is getting a million dollars?"

But the decision was final. "There comes a time when you have to move on," Michael told him.*

———⊶⊷⊷———

Six years had passed since David's ruinous confrontation with Aronwald and Shaw, and once again he had thrown his heart and soul into an investigation, only to see it cut short by people whose investment was less deep. Once again, his superiors claimed to be guided by the highest motives, and once again David suspected otherwise. Michael, an experienced prosecutor, had said that he wasn't persuaded that the cigarette investigation would ever yield results to justify the expense; in David's mind, one of the main things standing in the way of those results was Michael's lack of support. The tobacco companies had had a hand in the decision, he felt sure, and he was equally sure that they had plenty to hide. To abandon the investigation under such circumstances was almost unbearable for him. And yet, he stopped short of going to the press or threatening to quit his job. This time, David accepted the decision with what for him was a good grace—the good grace being attributable to the fact that, just as

* One clear upshot of David's two years on the cigarette beat was a decision by the city and state to abandon the Pitney Bowes ink stamp and go with a paper stamp developed by the Meyercord Company of Chicago. One by one, the other states also dropped their contracts with Pitney Bowes. The problem of uncollected cigarette taxes eased after 1985—but, it could be argued, largely because the wholesalers found another way of enhancing their earnings at the public's expense. That year, the legislature finally passed a "fair trade" law making cigarettes the only product in New York to enjoy a state-guaranteed profit—6 percent, or about fifty cents a carton. The wholesalers had retained a former deputy state tax commissioner, Alfred Donati, as their chief legal representative. One wholesaler later said that the industry had spent $225,000 to get the fair-trade bill passed; $200,000 had been allotted to a group of key legislators. When George Elicofon was asked about this, he adamantly denied that the association had paid anyone off; the legislature had passed the bill strictly on the merits, he said. But he was proud of his achievement on the wholesalers' behalf. "What I've done for these guys—I've made them millionaires," he said. "You can't buy a jobbing house for less than a million dollars today. Before I got 'em this bill, you could have bought one for less than half a collar button."

More than a decade later, many of the same people and firms still dominated the tobacco industry in New York.

Michael had said, there were other areas of tax fraud waiting to be looked into.

Ever since his transfer to the finance department, people had been coming to him with tales of tax shenanigans involving major New York City merchants and the purchasers of expensive clothing, furs, and jewelry. One common device for avoiding the city's 8.25 percent sales tax was for the store to send an empty box to an out-of-state address. The practice was so routine that, according to one of David's sources—a former saleslady for several clothing stores—customers would tell her, "I want this shipped, but I'll take it with me," and they expected their meaning to be understood. To test the waters, David went on an undercover shopping expedition, accompanied by a finance department administrator named Laura Weisel. With David, in a rumpled corduroy jacket, acting the part of a down-at-the-heels professor engaged to an heiress (Weisel), they visited a series of jewelers, supposedly searching for a wedding present for her mother to give her. At store after store, when David asked about sales taxes on the goods they were examining, helpful employees offered to send an empty box to his out-of-state home; when he said he didn't have such a home, they asked if he knew someone who did.

These undercover missions came in for heavy criticism from some key people at finance, including the department's general counsel, who argued that they were entrapment, pure and simple. To overcome the objections, Michael ordered a statistical survey of the problem. It turned out that more than 90 percent of the most expensive transactions—for $10,000 and up—were escaping the tax. (In one store, the figure was 98 percent.) "Basically, no one who lives in New York ever buys jewelry, art, or furs," Michael commented at the time. One major furrier was making shipments that consistently weighed less than five ounces. Finally, the magnitude of the tax revenues at stake—and an enthusiastic endorsement from Mayor Koch, whose sister had complained to him about the empty-box ploy—carried the day, and the operation, dubbed Big Ticket, got the go-ahead.

It was not easy to find plausible undercovers for such a purpose. David needed people with the right vocabulary, accent, and accoutrements—"You can't walk into Cartier's wearing a little Eastman quartz watch you bought on Fulton Street," one of his colleagues later pointed out. Finance had several female investigators who might fill the bill; the male side of the staff looked less promising until David recruited a recent graduate of Columbia named Nicholas Bache. Bache was short and mild-mannered and not at all actorly, but he came from the Prudential-Bache Baches, and he had no objection to using his own name as an undercover ID.

At Van Cleef & Arpels, a saleswoman who hoped to sell Bache a fifty-thousand-dollar necklace said the store was "honored" that he had chosen to shop there.

Bache was about to seal the deal on the necklace when his "wife"—a finance undercover named Merrie Gordon—popped the sales tax question by pointing out that "nobody pays taxes anymore."

"I really don't like paying New York taxes," Bache chimed in.

The saleslady promptly offered to hire a limousine and accompany them to the New Jersey end of the Holland Tunnel. There, she explained, she would formally hand over the necklace, and they would be free to take it anywhere they chose, including right back to Manhattan in the limousine.

With the undercover phase of Big Ticket completed, the finance department began a store-by-store audit of sales records. When one jeweler—Bulgari's, in the Pierre Hotel—balked at turning over its records, shotgun-armed police officers and city and state tax agents invaded the store and seized its files. (The raid, reported on the front page of the *Times*, was the finance department's way of sending a message to merchants contemplating a similar path of noncooperation.) Among the firms ultimately indicted were Cartier's, which agreed to pay the city more than $2 million in fines and unreported taxes, and Van Cleef & Arpels, which forked over $5 million—the largest amount the city had ever collected for sales tax delinquency. Perhaps as important as the fines was the finding of a post–Big Ticket survey that the proportion of tax-free transactions—originally 90 percent—had declined to less than 60 percent. When finance department undercovers made a new round of visits and again tried to get stores to resort to the empty-box ploy, they were turned down more often than not. "I can't do anything like that anymore," one horrified salesclerk replied, pointing to a news clipping about the indictments that had been posted on a nearby wall.

Mayor Koch was delighted with Big Ticket, and he insisted on having a press conference at City Hall to personally announce every indictment and settlement, instead of letting the prosecutors run the show, as they usually did. (He also began to say that he and his sister had thought up the investigation in the first place.) David was far from delighted. The audits had uncovered transactions involving some exceedingly well-known and well-heeled people, including (as a story in *Newsday* later characterized them, naming no names) "a former national security adviser, a billionaire arms dealer from the Arab world, a 'queen' of a hotel empire, a real estate developer now specializing in skating rinks, a famous azure-eyed singer who appears in casino ads, a casino owner who also appears in the ads, a liquor magnate whose family originally ran hootch out of Canada and a television interview personality with a slight lisp."

Big Ticket was an investigation dear to David's heart, and he saw it as a means of achieving a quantum leap upward in tax-law compliance, born of a growing faith on the part of taxpayers that others, especially the rich, were paying their rightful share. He assumed that at least a symbolic handful of the customers would be prosecuted, both as a matter of fairness and as a deterrent. He had even entered into discussions with David Garth about a possible public-service advertising campaign in which convicted celebrities would pose together under the message, "If they got us, they're gonna get you."

But the question of prosecution was for prosecutors to decide. Specifically, it was up to the New York State attorney general, Robert Abrams, and the Manhattan district attorney, Robert Morgenthau, and after months of interviews and deliberations, they resolved to give immunity to all the customers in return for their cooperation. A well-known owner of a baseball team, for example, was let off despite the fact that he had expressly asked for an empty box to be sent to an address in Florida. (David's outrage mounted when the team later

hired as its general counsel one of the prosecutors who had negotiated the deal.) The same approach was adopted (except in a single
case) with the owners and managers of the stores, including one jew-
elry-store manager who had offered his own Connecticut home as an
out-of-state destination for a $90,000 clock purchased by a publish-
ing magnate. Basically, it was companies that took the rap; their
executives got off scot-free. Turning the case over to Abrams and
Morgenthau had been "like sending it to the Bermuda Triangle,"
David said later. As for the impressive-sounding fines, he objected
that if you factored in the probability of getting caught, and the
prime rate, they were not much greater than the taxes that had been
evaded. "The lesson was that if you get caught you pay the back
taxes," he said. "So if you're willing to risk the embarrassment why
shouldn't you cheat?"

One night, David was working late at finance when he got a call on
the "bat phone"—an unlisted number set aside for informants. An
"unknown female," as he put it, told him in a hysterical voice that she
was a prostitute who had been beaten by her pimp after giving a
judge a social disease. (The judge had paid her a thousand dollars.)
She described a midtown bar run by her pimp that served as the
headquarters of a top-drawer prostitution ring.

Eager to conduct the investigation himself, David presented it to
Michael as a tax case. "The ultimate three-Martini lunch," he said,
explaining that many of the bar's transactions were, according to the
prostitute, treated as deductible business expenses. But Michael—
tired of David's efforts to expand his turf—saw it as a police matter,
and he brushed aside David's ardently expressed belief that the police
department could not be trusted with such an investigation. So David
and the head of the pimp squad wound up making a joint expedition
to check out the bar.

Once there, they were propositioned left and right, and David identified himself as a law-enforcement officer to the manager, who was
the pimp described by the caller. At the pimp's suggestion, the three
men proceeded upstairs, where the pimp opened an attaché case and
began counting out hundred-dollar bills; when the amount had

come to about $5,000, he slid the bills across the table to David. But before David could make any response, the pimp experienced a revelation. "Oh my God, I remember who you are!" he said.

"Relax," David said. "Why don't you call your lawyer and let me speak to him?"

The pimp made the call, and after the three of them had chewed things over for a while, he got off the phone, and began to explain the workings of a business that thrived on six- and eight-hundred dollar "lunches" that clients charged to house accounts or credit cards. The pimp was a convicted felon and thus legally barred from holding a liquor license, but that problem, he said, had been taken care of (as others had been) with a bribe to the State Liquor Authority. He identified the attorney who had handled his liquor license application as a prominent Queens politician, recently elected to Congress.

The pimp still owed a balance of $5,000 on the bribe, and he told David that, as part of a deal with prosecutors, he would be willing to wear a wire when he made the final payment. He also agreed to turn over a client list that supposedly included corporate executives, politicians, and officials of the UN.

The next afternoon, David escorted the pimp and his lawyer to the U.S. attorney's office for the Southern District. David wasn't happy about turning the case over to the feds in this unresolved state; he would far rather have given them the "conviction kit" that, in his experience, they usually required. But Michael had told him that his role was strictly to "make introductions," and that's what he did, with results that bore out his fears. When one of the prosecutors warned the pimp that *he* was the target of the investigation, his lawyer balked, and the discussion broke off. As for the client list, a couple of FBI agents were said to have accompanied the pimp home in order to fetch it, but they insisted later that they had never actually laid their hands on any records. "Two giant Rolodexes," David said. "That list made Sydney Biddle Barrows"—the Mayflower Madam— "look like an amateur."

In earlier years, Michael had often joked about David's tactlessness. "If you don't want to negotiate with me, you can negotiate with

David," he once told a tobacco-company official (gleefully repeating the line to David afterward). As time passed, he found the subject less amusing. "David was continually asking you to side with him against everybody else," Michael said, years later. "He kept denouncing people."

An investigation of several prominent banks for "parking" money in the Caribbean in order to reduce their New York City tax bills led to a confrontation between David and a group of bank officials with whom the city was trying to reach a settlement. "You guys are wearing expensive suits, but as far as I can see you're tax cheats the same as anybody else, and you should pay the same fines," David remarked during one negotiating session—the last one he was allowed to attend.

In 1984 Michael recruited a detective named Robert Gardner as "chief investigator"—a new post, which put him under David, and over Stanton. Gardner was good-looking, a snappy dresser, and an energetic office politician, and David disliked him intensely. Michael tried to minimize the significance of Gardner's coming. His role, according to Michael, was to handle the administrative duties for which David had no patience, freeing David up to be more of a planner and a catalyst—and to focus on Big Ticket. But by now, Michael had already nudged Barbara Bishop into a new job, and with Gardner's appointment he had broken up the Gang of Three that had so vexed him. (Bishop went on to serve a brief stint as an assistant DA in Manhattan, and a longer stint in Brooklyn.)

Michael's enthusiasm for Gardner was short-lived. His star plummeted after an incident in which a $17,000 surveillance van (which Gardner had allowed a female investigator to drive home) was abandoned on the Major Deegan Expressway and then stripped to a carcass after being left there overnight (again on Gardner's authority). By then, however, David had been relocated to an office in the Municipal Building—"closer to me," as Michael said, explaining the move, but far from the investigators.

In November 1985, Michael announced his own imminent departure from city government to go to work for Merrill Lynch, and the weakness of David's position became still clearer. At the time, he was laying the groundwork for yet another big investigation—of tax evasion in the sale of art, antiques, and Persian carpets. The idea had been sparked by a TV interview, in which David Bathurst, the chairman of Christie's—one of the country's top fine-arts auctioneers—had extolled "collectibles" as an investment on the PBS show *Adam Smith's Money World.* An advantage of collectibles over stocks and bonds, Bathurst explained, was that "we respect the underground economy." David took him to mean that dealers in collectibles didn't go out of their way to supply the authorities with records (or to create records in the first place) that would show when someone had turned a profit.

Here was a $10-billion-a-year industry that seemed to thrive on contempt for the tax laws. David showed a transcript of the Bathurst interview to Rudy Giuliani, the newly named U.S. attorney for the Southern District of New York, who reacted with an outrage akin to David's own. Then he took the proposal to Michael's replacement—commissioner-designate Paul Crotty.

Crotty, a Democratic party operative and fund-raiser, came from an important family in New York State politics. His brother was the counsel to the governor, and his father the Democratic boss of Buffalo. A getting-to-know-you session between David and Crotty went abysmally: "Oh, the famous David Durk!" Crotty exclaimed, by way of greeting.

David, seeking to explain what he did at finance, got to talking about his practice of cultivating sources by going to parties and engaging in conversation. Crotty, who had briefly served as an assistant U.S. attorney, was incredulous; in his experience, he said, the only really useful information—the kind you could go to court with—came from people who were "under the hammer" of the law. David countered that in *his* experience, such sources were chronically unreliable, and he mischievously asked if Crotty had ever won a case. Michael, who was sitting in on the conversation, "looked daggers at me," David said later.

Crotty made it plain that he was not going to go ahead with the art investigation, or, David concluded, with any of his other ideas about tax enforcement. Later, Michael, in what amounted to his parting words to David, warned him that the prospects for his continuing to play a significant role at finance were poor, because Crotty considered him a loose cannon.

David begged Michael to set the record straight.

"Believe me, I've tried," Michael said. "It's not that easy."

David took his grievance about the art investigation to Mayor Koch, who listened briefly, excused himself, and asked David to give the details to an aide. Somehow, word of this conversation got back to Crotty, who excoriated David for "going over my head" at a time when, as he pointed out, "I'm on a honeymoon here." In fact, David no longer had much clout with the mayor. Koch, like Michael, had grown impatient with the intramural disagreements. "It is . . . distressing," Koch had written in one of his memos (an unusually harsh one), "that notwithstanding your obvious talents you are constantly in conflict with every agency and official with whom you come into contact. . . . I am not interested in a lengthy dialogue as to why you cannot work with or get along with this person or the other."

If there was any doubt about where the mayor stood, it vanished a couple of days before Michael's official departure. "I have some bad news for you—there may be a problem with your line," Michael told David, referring to the civil service line on which his job was classified. The mayor's personnel people, taking cognizance of the fact that David was no longer supervising people, were "reclassifying" him from assistant commissioner to staff analyst—an adjustment that would bring his annual salary, then in the $60,000 neighborhood (it had reached that level partly as a reflection of the money he had made for the city), down to less than $40,000. Since there was obviously nothing but grief in store for David if he remained at finance, he began to look elsewhere. He made inquiries about returning to the police department, but he was told that too much time had passed. The department did not by law have to take him back, and it wouldn't. Checking around with other agencies, David gradually came to understand that he was persona non grata with the entire Koch administration, and he decided to take his pension—only to find that it, too, was going to be far smaller than he had supposed. Because of a technicality (the kind that mayors had been known to straighten out for appointees departing on good terms), his seven years at finance would be disregarded for purposes of calculating his retirement benefit. If he had remained a police lieutenant through those years, he would be due to receive about $34,000 a year. As it was, he found himself forcibly retired, at fifty-one—after twenty-two years in law enforcement—on a pension of less than $17,000.

CHAPTER

EIGHTEEN

⟶⇒❧⇐⟵

By the mid-eighties, Ed Koch no longer had much patience with the reformers and apolitical figures he had welcomed into his first administration, and most of them had moved on—either physically, to new jobs outside city government, or mentally, to a no-nonsense pragmatism about what could be accomplished and what couldn't be (and therefore wasn't worth discussing). The city, meanwhile, had not only rebounded from the crisis of the seventies but was in the throes of an unexpected economic boom. It was a boom that some people found troubling, inasmuch as it never reached far beyond Wall Street, the real estate business, and the executives and professional dependents of some of the city's richest corporations. Homelessness, which had become an issue at the start of Koch's mayoralty, grew worse rather than better, and so did conditions in the inner city. The mayor, however, did not seem to concern himself much with these matters. Like the young financiers who made millions during his years in office, Ed Koch was enjoying the moment.

John Lindsay had crossed party lines, from Republican to Democrat. Koch all but endorsed Ronald Reagan for president in 1980 and 1984, and sought and won Republican backing when he ran for reelection in 1981. He also negotiated a rapprochement with the big financial and real estate interests he had once disparaged, and it became difficult to discern where political fund-raising left off and the exercise of the city's regulatory authority began. It was a time when, as Jack Newfield and Wayne Barrett observed in their account of the Koch years, *City for Sale*, "campaign contributors got tax abatements and zoning changes to invade the heavens and block out the sun." Giant office towers (many of them fated to remain half-empty years after their completion) would stand as the most obvious monuments to Koch's mayoralty.

He won election to a third term with nearly 75 percent of the vote, and his inauguration, on January 1, 1986, was attended by Donald Trump, Carl Icahn, Henry Kissinger, George Steinbrenner, and Ivan Boesky. "The city's symbol is no longer the Statue of Liberty," the columnist Jimmy Breslin wrote, "but instead is a limousine double-parked on a Manhattan street, as the police dare not tell it to move."

———

David felt the change in Koch as a cold wind. "In the beginning, he was sending me notes and inviting me over to Gracie Mansion—he thought the attitude of the tobacco companies was outrageous," David said later. "By the end, if I tried to talk privately to him about something, he got furious."

If Koch seemed to turn a deaf ear to David's talk about the art industry as a large potential source of uncollected taxes, he was intensely—excessively, in David's view—keen on the issue of street peddlers and *their* taxpaying practices. By law, only food and (as a result of a quirky reading of the First Amendment) books could be sold on the streets of New York, but on major commercial thoroughfares throughout the city there were peddlers selling clothing, jewelry, and other goods as well. The various merchants' associations had long complained about the peddlers as unfair competition, since they were assumed to be paying neither taxes nor rent. Each year the complaints mounted in the months leading up to Christmas, when merchants and peddlers alike did a disproportionately large share of their annual business. And when the merchants got after the mayor, the mayor got after David.

"What am I charging them with?" he asked Koch, in response to one of these directives. To move in on the peddlers and seize their wares without hard evidence, he said, would be tantamount to robbery. David thought that City Hall was doing the bidding of the Fifth Avenue Association—a body whose influence he had resented since his days as a uniformed cop in midtown. "Do you realize we have fifty-three uniformed cops, plus supervisors, assigned to nothing but peddler control from Fifty-ninth Street south?" he asked Koch at one point. "And we have maybe nine cops assigned to senior-citizen robbery, and three cops for rape."

David's idea, instead of arresting and prosecuting peddlers, was to franchise and regulate them, insuring that they paid taxes as well as a fee for their use of public space. But this was a policy question, and the policy had been set by others. At City Hall's behest, David and Barbara Bishop put together an elaborate antipeddler operation in 1981, and they were proud of the care with which they dotted every *i* and crossed every *t*, legally speaking. They went to some lengths, also, to implicate the peddler suppliers (for most of the peddlers belonged to organized commercial networks), not just the peddlers themselves. But David continued to argue the issue with Koch, and their arguments fed a growing sense on the mayor's part that David could not be counted on.

One of the powers of his office, Koch reasonably believed, was to be able to get on the phone and tell an appointee to take care of something. He would get on the phone with David—and get an argument. One holiday season, Koch called from his limousine to indignantly report that he had seen a Christmas-tree vendor operating on a city-owned pier along the Hudson River. Koch told David to lock the man up.

"It's four o'clock on the day before Christmas, Ed," David pointed out. "How would it look in the newspapers: two Jews arresting a Christmas-tree vendor on Christmas Eve?" After a protracted debate in which the mayor threatened to replace David with someone who knew how to follow orders, Koch relented. But, as David was to discover, an assistant commissioner could not afford too many such victories.

————

During his first two terms, Koch gave a convincing impression of being his own man—the rare politician who owed nothing to anybody. His third term taught New Yorkers that he was considerably less independent than he had made out. While Koch had appointed highly qualified people to major, visible offices, it became apparent that he had quietly ceded to the Brooklyn Democratic machine control of a number of obscure agencies that were characterized by a heavy cash flow. The Brooklyn boss, Meade Esposito, and, later, the bosses of Queens, Donald Manes, and of the Bronx, Stanley Friedman, became, in effect, subcontractors responsible for administering a large swath of the administration that bore Koch's name. (Why Koch entered into these arrangements, from which he never sought to derive any personal profit, was never clear. He was evidently motivated, in part, by a desire for the sort of overwhelming voter approval that comes most easily when you have every party organization working for you. Another factor may have been a longing to be accepted by people who "knew things about real life that he did not," as Newfield and Barrett observed.) Under Koch, the government of New York City proved to be riddled with profiteers and bag men: people like Transportation Commissioner Anthony Ameruso, who wound up being convicted for lying about a secret real estate partnership he had formed with a developer to whom he had awarded an interest in a ferry concession, and Geoffrey Lindenauer, a onetime quack sex therapist who spent the greater part of his time as deputy commissioner of the Parking Violations Bureau pocketing bribes and repaying them with city business. Manes—Lindenauer's patron—stabbed himself to death with a carving knife after he came under suspicion in January 1986. Less than a year later, Friedman was convicted and imprisoned for his role in dispensing a $22 million contract for a handheld parking-ticket computer to a dummy company whose only obvious asset (it had never made a computer of any kind) was Friedman himself.

The police department was an agency that Koch sold short in more subtle ways. His first police commissioner, Robert McGuire—the son of a retired deputy chief inspector—was an intelligent, articulate, and well-intentioned man. But, as his explanation for not giving David a job suggested, a desire to preserve amity turned out to be perhaps his most distinctive quality as a leader. "Flexible," "moderate," and "a skilled mediator" were some of the words used by his friends to describe McGuire's style. Through the first two years of his tenure, the department continued to shrink, crime rose, and McGuire struggled to contain the damage. He instituted saturation foot patrols to "stabilize neighborhoods," and he launched a program to target career criminals—especially robbers. Otherwise, he left a surprisingly faint imprint on the bureaucracy he headed. "Some people don't know how powerful they are," one police official said of McGuire afterward.

Detective Jimmy Lanzano was working at Safe and Loft when McGuire was commissioner. Lanzano by then had spent twenty years on the job and had a bundle of medals, despite his reluctance to apply for them. (If a New York City cop did something heroic, he was required to submit his own name for recognition—a procedure that, naturally, undermined the value of whatever recognition ensued. But cops could also request an alternative form of reward—a day off—and Lanzano generally went that route.) He was a canny, tireless, and utterly dedicated detective—one of the countless good men and women whose services went largely unappreciated by the New York City police department.

He and his wife had raised six children, and in addition, they were "shelter parents" who took in neglected and abused infants while they awaited placement in foster homes. One little girl—a cerebral palsy victim who lacked the power of speech—had spent four years in the Lanzano household when the city took steps to send her to Willowbrook, a notorious institution for disturbed children. Rather than let that happen, the Lanzanos decided to raise her themselves, and over the objections of child-welfare officials who told him he was asking the impossible, Jimmy Lanzano ultimately got the city to pay for her to attend a special school, where she learned to communicate with a visual-identification device.

Lanzano's superiors tolerated his lack of diplomacy because he knew more than anybody in the department about the role of organized crime in hijackings. He had spent much of his career searching for "drops"—places where organized-crime people kept stolen goods. For ten years straight, he led Safe and Loft in arrests, and he was frequently called in to help homicide detectives with mob murders that had them stymied.

In 1981 a former partner of Lanzano's—now a sergeant—asked him to look into a fraudulent company in which the sergeant's driver had become an unwitting participant. The company was stealing gasoline from a Long Island refinery (while paying refinery employees to overlook this fact) and then selling it, at a discount, to local gas stations. Another participant, it developed, was the son-in-law of a second sergeant of Lanzano's acquaintance, and after a preliminary investigation, Lanzano resolved to persuade the sergeant's son-in-law to cooperate, with the aim of nailing the mastermind of the operation—a retired transit cop. Unknown to Lanzano, however, the son-in-law was already cooperating—with investigators from the Internal Affairs Division (IAD), who were looking into the role of yet another police officer in the scheme. The Internal Affairs inquiry shifted its attention to Lanzano, and to the fact that *his* investigation had not been authorized by his commanding officer.

Lanzano was called downtown for an interview at IAD. Having no idea what it was about, he appeared in his usual attire, dungarees. "Is this how you dress?" an IAD lieutenant asked him. Then the interrogation moved on to the central question: "Who authorized your investigation? Did your commanding officer know?"

A decade after the Knapp Commission, Internal Affairs once again had a reputation for letting serious corruption cases fizzle, and homing in, instead, on procedural violations. And the department was rife with procedural violations. Lanzano had to admit that his CO had *not* known. His CO was fully aware, however, of the fact that Lanzano routinely commenced investigations without authorization. Lanzano's practice was to spend weeks searching for a drop, and only when he found it (sometimes closing eight or ten cases at one fell swoop) would he make an official record of the investigation. The point was, of course, to make Safe and Loft's statistics look good by reducing the number of unsolved cases, and Lanzano was far from the only detective who operated this way.

"Holy shit, I've got a problem," Lanzano's CO told him. "If you tell them what you've been doing for the last five years, we'll all be in trouble."

Since the inquiry had already cast a cloud over Lanzano's chances for promotion to second-grade detective (a long-sought goal), he decided to retire, without mounting a defense against the charge. "It would have caused a lot of problems," he said later.

Any sane law enforcement organization would have gone all-out to keep someone like Lanzano. But in the NYPD, people would spend years building up precious expertise, and then, when they were forty or so, put in for retirement. The Brain Drain was perpetual, and the department never seemed to lift a finger to slow it. And so, in November 1982, Lanzano left in order to launch a new career as a jewelry and clothing salesman. (Later he was to start a private investigation firm, specializing in insurance fraud.)

To the public, the police commissioner is New York City's "Top Cop"—a figure of awe-inspiring prestige and importance. To many in the trenches of the NYPD, however, the identity of the commissioner is a matter of relative indifference. Lanzano, when he was reconstructing the events leading up to his retirement, had trouble even remembering who the commissioner was.

————

In April 1982, a black divinity student complained that he had been hauled out of his car and beaten by white cops in Harlem, and the incident led Congressman John Conyers, Jr., of Michigan, to convene a series of highly emotional public hearings on the problem of brutality in the NYPD. Robert McGuire, who had already been preparing to leave, resigned in order to become the president of the Pinkerton security and investigation firm. And Koch turned to Ben Ward.

Ward brought an imposing résumé to the commissioner's post. He was a magna cum laude graduate of Brooklyn College, with a law degree to boot, and after a long, slow climb up through the ranks of the department in the fifties and sixties (when black superiors were a rarity), he had served as Deputy Police Commissioner for Community Affairs, and, later, as the city's traffic commissioner, under Lindsay, and corrections commissioner, under Koch. He looked very good—on paper. Almost immediately after his appointment as police commissioner, however, the Department of Investigation issued a report criticizing him for "late night and weekend meetings with a female guest" in the corrections commissioner's office, and it became apparent that he had a drinking problem. Sometimes a big piece of police news would break (such as the Palm Sunday massacre of ten people— including seven children—in Brooklyn), and Ward was nowhere to be found. At other times, he was present and accounted for—and people wished he hadn't been. At a PBA convention in the Catskills in August 1984, Ward made a giggling, incoherent appearance, accidentally tearing down a curtain as he stumbled to the podium. "We had about a thousand delegates, and here's the PC cockeyed," one police official recalled.

"I daresay I shall never have another drink while in public office," Ward said after that episode.

On another occasion, he seemed about to trade blows with the fire commissioner at City Hall. On still another, he told a Queens woman who had expressed alarm about a serial rapist who was then at loose that she might be better off staying at home, since she was "the kind he's looking for."

Although Ward rarely acknowledged specific error, he liked to point out that he was "human" and might from time to time require forgiveness. But he presided over an organization with exacting rules of behavior, and he was a stern enforcer of those rules. In April 1985, five police officers assigned to the 106th Precinct, in Ozone Park, Queens, were indicted for using stun guns to compel several suspects to confess to selling marijuana. Ward removed or transferred no fewer than eighteen people whom he deemed to bear some responsibility for the episode. "Accountability is the name of the game," he explained, but as Peter Blauner wrote in *New York* magazine, "Some people felt 'hypocrisy' was the more appropriate word."

Mayor Koch always denied the obvious explanation for hiring Ward—that, in the heat of the political moment, he had needed a black police commissioner. He insisted that Ward had been chosen exclusively "on the merits," but no one else believed it—not even Ward. And whatever the motives for hiring him, it was hard to imagine that, except for Koch's vulnerability on matters of race, he would have kept him in the job as long as he did. As it was, Ward served as police commissioner for nearly five years, and he was a figure of contempt for much of the force.

Late in 1985, a cop from the 75th Precinct, in East New York, began telling David about coworkers who were robbing drug dealers and, in some cases, dealing drugs themselves. "If they got a call for a man with a gun, or a man selling drugs, they would radio back not to send any assistance," David recalled. "That was their code language—their way of telling their buddies to join in the fun, and the straight cops to stay away, so they could rip the guy off in peace." At one of David's last public appearances in his role at finance (a press conference involving untaxed beer), he sought out the mayor and, in a brief private conversation, told him that a corruption problem was brewing involving cops and narcotics. Koch reacted furiously. "I *have* a police commissioner!" he replied. In other words, if David had something to say about the police department, he should say it to Ben Ward.

David wound up passing his information, through an intermediary, to Ward's chief of Internal Affairs, Daniel Sullivan. But, as Sullivan would later testify, his boss had a powerful dislike for "bad press," and it was part of IAD's mission in the Ward years to contain and curtail corruption inquiries so as not to upset the commissioner's peace of mind. The only apparent result of David's tip—and of other tips about the same group of cops—was a decision to reassign them to new units, where they started up their criminal activities anew, free of the suspicion they had engendered in their former commands. Six years passed before they were exposed, and the case was broken, in the end, not by the NYPD, but by the police department of Suffolk County, Long Island, where several of the drug-dealing cops lived.

CHAPTER

NINETEEN

In the summer of 1990, as New York's first African-American mayor, David Dinkins, settled into office, the life of the city took a scary turn. The last week and a half of July saw the seemingly inexplicable shooting deaths of nine-year-old Veronica Corales, as she slept in her parents' car after a family expedition to the Great Adventure amusement park; one-year-old Yaritimi Fruto, shot by gunmen whose intended target (also successfully dispatched) was her father; three-year-old Ben Williams, who was at home asleep when a person or persons unknown pumped eighteen bullets through the steel door of his family's apartment; and nine-month-old Rayvon Jamieson, who died in his walker, another victim of a blast of gunfire through an apartment door.

Four such incidents in the space of nine days was something out of the ordinary. But the phenomenon of children killed by stray bullets was becoming alarmingly routine, and youth was also a distinguishing characteristic of the suspects in most of these "drug-related shootings," as the police decreed them. There had been a change in the personnel practices of the drug trade. With the rise of crack cocaine, the torch had been passed to a new generation of street-level dealers: teenagers armed with the latest semiautomatic weapons—a combination that had proved to be even more potent than crack itself.

Although violent crime was concentrated, as ever, in the city's poorest neighborhoods, there were headlines that fed a broader sense of peril that summer. John Reisenbach, a young advertising executive, was shot to death in an apparent robbery while using a public phone in front of his Greenwich Village apartment building. (His own phone was out of order.) Sean Healy, a young assistant district attorney, was killed when he entered a bodega in quest of a box of doughnuts and accidentally stepped into a turf war between drug dealers—less than a block from the Bronx courthouse. Hugh Harley, an eighteen-year-old who was working at a shoe repair shop in order to pay for college, was stabbed in the heart after apologetically informing a would-be robber that he had no money.

Brian Watkins, a tourist from Provo, Utah, was stabbed to death while defending his mother from a gang of muggers in a midtown subway station. Watkins was killed, according to the police, by members of a Queens gang called FTS (the letters stood for "Fuck That Shit"), which had made mugging or beating someone a prerequisite for admission. The Watkinses were tennis buffs. They had spent the day at the U.S. Open, and they were on their way to dinner at the Tavern on the Green. As the love of tennis had brought them to New York, the love of dancing had brought their son's killers to Manhattan. The Watkins family crossed the path of the gang just as it was seeking a source of spending money for an evening at the Roseland Ballroom, a once-dowdy dance hall that had successfully reoriented itself to the youth trade. It was there that transit police arrested five of an eventual eight suspects, just a few hours after Brian Watkins was pronounced dead. They appeared to be enjoying themselves.

The murder of Brian Watkins was every tourist's nightmare of a visit to New York, and it led the national as well as the local press to ask whether New York had become not only unlivable (an old question) but unvisitable. *Time* weighed in with a cover story on "The Rotting of the Big Apple," featuring a poll in which 59 percent of the city's population seemed to express a preference for some other hometown.

The elected leaders of New York city and state, and those who aspired to replace them, responded to the crime wave with an anti-crime bidding war. Leader A: "Here's my plan to put five thousand new cops on the street." Leader B: "I call your five thousand and raise you another two thousand." The high bidder, in the end, was Mayor Dinkins. His race and liberal views having fed doubts in some quarters about his anticrime mettle, Dinkins seemed to feel obliged to promise the most new cops of all, and to pay for them with a pot-pourri of new taxes that, by law, could not be touched for any other purpose. (This police hiring and spending spree would wind up being the major policy initiative of Dinkins's mayoralty.) Not since the days of the Knapp Commission had there been so much public discussion of the police and their problems, and David Durk watched it all from the sidelines.

He was fifty-five—an age when, if things had gone better for him, he might have had an imposing title, a secretary, and an office with a panoramic view of Manhattan. Certainly, a lot of his contemporaries and former associates had those things. Twenty years after the Knapp Commission's inquiry, the people associated with it were doing well for themselves. Whitman Knapp was a federal judge, emeritus. Michael Armstrong had become the defense attorney of first resort for politicians accused of being crooks. (Donald Manes had consulted Armstrong shortly before taking his life. Alfonse D'Amato was a longtime client.) Nicholas Scoppetta, after parlaying the Robert Leuci operation into a job as a special assistant U.S. attorney, had served as a deputy mayor and Commissioner of Investigation under Abe Beame, and had gone on to hold a series of law enforcement positions in subsequent administrations. (Leuci himself had embarked on a new career as a writer of police novels, and an anticorruption consultant.) The Bronx district attorney, Burton Roberts, had become that borough's chief administrative judge—and a model for a character in Tom Wolfe's *Bonfire of the Vanities*. Cornelius Behan, Serpico's inspector-confidant, had left the NYPD to become the police commissioner of Baltimore. Patrick Murphy was an honored elder statesman of law enforcement, after a decade's service as president of the Police

Foundation, a Ford Foundation offshoot (with its offices in Washington) that doled out grants for police-related research and experimentation. Jay Kriegel had served for years as a high executive at CBS. Of all the important figures in the Knapp Commission story, only David Durk—arguably the most important—had failed to derive any lasting material or professional benefit.

One of the questions I hoped to answer, as I began that summer to research the story of David's life in law enforcement, was how a city in such straits could cast aside someone of his talents. Still, I assumed that his situation was temporary, and so did he, after the failure of Ed Koch's campaign for a fourth term. Almost invariably, when I talked to David in the months following the 1989 election, he seemed to be dickering with some agency or other over the details of his imminent return to law enforcement. But then, one after another, the prospects evaporated, and it became apparent that his employment problems were not confined to any one mayoral administration.

New York, like a number of other cities at the time, was flirting with an idea called community policing. Since World War II, progress in the police world had consisted of putting more and more cops into radio cars and linking those cars with more and more sophisticated systems of communication, in the name of reduced response time. But while there had been plenty of progress by these yardsticks, crime had kept on increasing, and an ominous gulf had developed between the police and residents of minority neighborhoods. In 1975 the Police Foundation conducted a simple but influential experiment, in collaboration with the Kansas City police department. In some police beats, patrol levels were doubled or tripled; in others, patrol was eliminated altogether, with radio cars allowed to enter only in response to citizen calls. Then the researchers waited for the consequences—only to find that, as far as anyone could measure, there were none. Preventive patrol didn't seem to prevent anything.

The Kansas City study fueled a quest for a new model of policing, and the quest gained momentum in 1982 with the publication of an *Atlantic Monthly* article, "Broken Windows," in which the political scientist James Q. Wilson and the psychologist George Kelling theorized that the crime increases of recent years had something to do with a police fixation on emergencies. Wilson and Kelling called on the nation's police departments to recognize the discretionary power of officers and turn them into problem solvers—people who, instead of simply responding to incidents after the fact (and writing reports), would be encouraged to address the crime patterns and other chronic conditions that put neighborhoods on edge. There was an element of nostalgia in this analysis that David Dinkins, among other people, responded to. Like many city-dwellers of his generation, he had fond memories of the old-fashioned beat cop—the kind who, as Dinkins noted longingly, would spot a boy running with the wrong crowd, and tell him, "Jamaal, go home" (Jamaal was the name of a grandson of Dinkins's). But the community police officer of Wilson and Kelling's imagination was innovative as well as tough, not thumbing his or her nose at missions that law-and-order types might deride as "social work"—helping local residents establish a community garden in a vacant lot that had been taken over by undesirables, for instance.

In September 1990, David accompanied me to a City Hall press briefing where Dinkins and his police commissioner, Lee Brown (the two of them together looking like a poplar and an oak tree), proclaimed their intention to effectively add, by a complex mathematical calculation, ten thousand new cops, to reorganize the department from top to bottom, and, in Brown's words, to "change the whole philosophy" of the NYPD. The reporters in attendance—perhaps somewhat overwhelmed by the two giant briefing books that had been distributed to them—reacted favorably. Their questions had less to do with the basic merit of the proposals than with the means to pay for them and the amount of time it would take to get so many additional cops on the street. Only David, it seemed, had deeper doubts.

A major element of the Dinkins plan was the idea of confronting "quality-of-life problems" on the streets. "What do they mean by a quality-of-life problem?" David said to me as the briefing broke up; it was the start of a long putdown. "They mean, for example, a gang of menacing kids hanging out on a corner. Well, it's not a crime to act menacing. The reality of a case like that is that even if a cop acts within the law and makes a legitimate collar for a minor offense—disorderly conduct or simple assault—the DA's office will say, 'Get out of here!' Either that or, when the case is called, the judge will have Legal Aid and the prosecutor approach the bench, and without consulting the cop, he'll dismiss the case, and the prisoner will laugh at the cop. 'You're chump change, Jack,' he'll say. He'll have the effrontery to do it in open court, and believe me, he will not be held in contempt. Now the cop has been humiliated, and when he goes back to his post he has lost his credibility. The system is telling him that his best efforts are worthless, so the really important quality-of-life problems are ignored, and you get cops spending their time on things like a corner that needs a traffic light. The cop calls up the traffic department, and six months later they put in a light, and everybody pats each other on the back. Considering what a cop costs the city—fifty, sixty thousand dollars a year—do you really think he should be acting as a referral service? But that's what it boils down to, a lot of the time. Community policing won't work unless you have good people and you tell them, 'We're going to give you a license to do the right thing.' If that happens, you don't need the façade."

For many of the city's politicians, the point of community policing was simply to satisfy a cry for greater "police visibility." Some of its proponents implied—or came right out and said—that the mere presence of more uniformed cops on the street would deter crime. "In my experience, the only thing a uniformed cop will deter is a fight outside of a bar, if he happens to be there at the time," David told me. "The crimes people are really worried about are street robberies—muggings. That's what New York City is number one in. If a uniformed cop has any effect on a street robbery, it's to move it a couple of blocks, or delay it a couple of minutes. Nothing short of wall-to-wall cops would have a significant deterrent effect on the overall number of street robberies. This city is talking about a program that will cost big money, but, even so, the cops will be spread thin. Some of these posts will be a quarter of a mile from one end to the other! If there's a robbery in progress, and you're on foot, there's no way you'll get there on time. What we're going to wind up with is a lot of widely spaced scarecrows.

"When I was in uniform," he continued, as we proceeded down the stairs, "kids would say stuff to me like 'Hey, Mr. Cop, man, give me a cigarette.' These guys *laugh* at uniformed cops. The only thing that scares them—the only thing that deters street robbery—is decoys. They're terrified of decoys. I've been a decoy, and I made collar after collar. When I was running the Twenty-fifth Precinct anticrime unit, I put one guy out on crutches and I gave another guy a double-breasted green blazer and a squash racquet, and had him get off the train at a Hundred-and-Twenty-fifth Street and Park Avenue, looking as if he were bombed. He hardly ever made it down the block without being held up. There was a time when decoys made up five percent of the patrol force, and they were responsible for twenty-five percent of the felony arrests. Now they're down to almost nothing."

"What happened?" I asked.

The main thing that happened, according to David, was a series of incidents in which decoy cops were accused of perjury and other offenses. For example, a decoy would lie down on the Bowery with a dollar bill sticking out of a pants' pocket, and the decoy team would charge the guy who took the money with robbery instead of the proper offense, grand larceny. Notwithstanding these abuses, the operation had a conviction rate of roughly 90 percent, and more than 80 percent of the arrestees had significant criminal records. "So clearly they were taking the right people—they were not locking up divinity students and virgins," David went on. We were outside now, and the sun had set on all of lower Manhattan but the rooftops and the Brooklyn Bridge, which shimmered in the distance. "Definitely there were abuses, but the concept was sound. The problems could have been corrected by picking the right people and giving them the right kind of training. But the Manhattan DA's office got very upset, and they leaned on the PD to cut down on the use of decoys. And then someone came up with the bright idea that we should be making 'jump collars' instead, which means looking for citizens who fit the profile of a typical victim, and waiting for *them* to be held up.

Well, it becomes a lot more difficult to make a collar that way, and there's plenty of room for abuse, because when the cop finally sees a person being robbed there's a temptation to wait until he gets really hurt, in order to make sure the case is taken seriously. I think it's an unconscionable idea. But it's typical of the way the police department operates. If someone objects to something, you abolish it."

The department, in promoting the virtues of community policing, liked to cite inspiring examples of cops who had won the respect of the local citizenry—"neighborhood heroes," as David put it, adding, "Well, we've always had these people. They exist with or without community policing."

But surely, I said, it was a step in the right direction for the department to support them and hold them up as role models.

He refused to concede the point. "The danger of puffing all this up," he replied, "is that cops see those stories on the TV news too. They know there's light-years of difference between the claims and the reality. They've lived through too many of these programs. They've been lied to too many times."

It was an occasion—by no means the first in my conversations with David—when I wondered if his judgment had been skewed by bitterness about his long exclusion from the profession he loved. I had talked to a few community-policing enthusiasts, and they struck me as sensible and well-meaning people; indeed, they seemed to be aiming for a style of policing much like the one that David himself had long advocated. By the end of the Dinkins years, however, I couldn't help noticing that the press and even some police insiders had adopted a view of community policing that was scarcely more approving than David's. An article in the *Daily News*, based on the leaked findings of an internal department study of the experiment to date, described the program—"hailed as the most ambitious overhaul of the Police Department in a generation" and "funded with $500 million in new taxes"—as a "shambles," with many cops "working bankers' hours" and "fudging reports about how much time they actually walked their beats." According to the study's author, former assistant chief Aaron Rosenthal, there was "a serious chasm between the showroom sales spiel used to sell community policing to the public, and the actual on-the-street product their tax dollars purchased."

Even without Rosenthal's comments, the allure of community policing would have faded as the NYPD fell under the shadow of a new corruption scandal. In September 1992, the city watched raptly as a panel of distinguished members of the legal profession, headed by a white-haired chairman, Milton Mollen, held court in a hallowed hall decorated with flags and historical portraits, and a series of crooked cops and inattentive superiors trooped through, describing a new style of police corruption that had arisen with the new style of drug dealing. The TV cameras were smaller than the ones that had been trained on David Durk, Frank Serpico, and the other witnesses of their era two decades earlier. New voice- and image-disguising technologies had been developed, making it possible for honest cops to testify anonymously, on videotape. Otherwise, it was all very familiar.

As the scandal unfolded, Mayor Dinkins and Police Commissioner Brown made much of the fact that they were talking about "pockets" of corruption rather than a department-wide phenomenon, as in pre-Knapp days. What the new corruption lacked in pervasiveness, however, it made up for in insidiousness. There was testimony about cocaine-dealing cops, cops riding shotgun for drug dealers, cops committing stickups and murders, and cops failing to give evidence in the murder of a fellow cop. Michael Dowd, the archetypal crooked cop of the new age (the Mollen Commission's answer to William Phillips), stood accused of receiving as much as $15,000 a week to protect the citywide operations of a Dominican drug kingpin, and, on one occasion, of using his police shield to lure out of hiding a cocaine dealer whose rivals then took the opportunity to assassinate him.

The pads of the sixties were a tradition that cops fell into, more or less effortlessly, and they involved relationships upheld by payers and payees alike. The corrupt cops of the nineties—who made a habit of robbing drug dealers and extorting money from them, and who in many cases became drug dealers themselves—were after "thrill and power," in the Mollen Commission's words. Unsystematic this latter-day corruption may have been. But it was not any less destructive.

Dowd—a cocaine user himself, pale, flabby-featured, and without affect, Hannah Arendt's "banality of evil" in the flesh—had a "crew" of fifteen or so other cops who had made a "till death do us part" pact. They would get together periodically by an inlet of Jamaica Bay ("the pool," they called the site) to drink, laugh, fire off their guns, and plan their freelance drug raids, which amounted to armed robberies of dealers and bodegas.

Just about everyone involved in the Mollen Commission's hearings paid tribute to the dedication, valor, and effectiveness of the "vast majority" of the force. But the commission heard evidence of many presumably honest cops—and supervisors—who had had plenty of reason to suspect what Dowd and his crew were up to, and who had either done nothing to stop it or had taken active steps to help them elude detection. As the scandal spread, the pattern of crooked cops operating in teams, with the tacit support of colleagues and superiors, was repeated in precinct after precinct. In the 30th Precinct, in upper Harlem, nearly a quarter of the command came under suspicion. And, of course, the neighborhoods that had the worst problems with drugs and violence were also the ones where the police had, in effect, stopped policing.

Dowd's testimony was a guide not only to corruption—the official subject of inquiry—but, between the lines, to other aspects of police life that were hard to square with the vision of a force that had, as Mayor Dinkins liked to say, "reinvented itself." A summer-long detail in Coney Island—when Dowd was one of a group of cops patrolling the boardwalk to make the summer crowds feel safer—was "one drunk day after another," he told the commission. His drinking was an open secret among his coworkers, but he was never punished or, for that matter, offered help. (Eventually, he got sent to an alcohol rehabilitation center; that, however, was after an incident in which Dowd pulled his gun on a sergeant and threatened to kill him. By then, the precinct brass suspected him of being on cocaine. When they tried to make him submit to a urinalysis, the police union, the PBA, rode to his rescue and got him enrolled in an alcohol abuse program—evidently a standard ploy for officers facing drug tests.)

During a two-week period when Dowd was planning a raid on a major drug dealer, he spent long stretches of time, in his radio car, three miles outside his assigned sector. "Did any supervisor ever say to you, what are you doing three miles outside your sector?" a Mollen Commission attorney asked him. No, Dowd replied, and the supervisors in his own precinct apparently didn't notice his absence, either. Dowd passed one whole year of his police career with no arrests and no court appearances—and no complaints from his superiors. "They were happy that I wasn't making any arrests," he explained, "because I wasn't costing the city any money."

That Dowd could get away with this conduct suggested that it was not drastically different from the norm that police bosses, for all their protestations of a new philosophy, expected. Chief Rosenthal's study reminded me of another impolitic theme of David's—the "Kitty Genovese phenomenon among cops," which he traced back to Patrick Murphy and his anticorruption measures. "At the sound of the crash, they run the other way," he explained. "Ever since Knapp, the real problem with the police department has been massive malingering, and it's totally justified, given the disciplinary policies of the department. If a cop makes an off-duty arrest, the first question he gets asked is 'Were you drinking?' and the second question is 'What did you get involved for?' "

It was sad, I thought, that David could not proudly acknowledge the achievement of liberating cops from the pressure to take graft—of making it possible to have a career in the NYPD without being a crook or burying one's head in the sand. This was a significant change, for which David and, for that matter, Patrick Murphy deserved credit. Yet David saw, as few others did, that there was a large missing element in the Murphy program, and in community policing as well. The great mass of cops simply didn't believe in them.

Since the Knapp Commission days, under Murphy and his successors, uniformed cops had been showered with a stream of orders intended to keep them away from bars, gambling establishments, and other "corruption hazards." They had been all but ordered not to make drug arrests by a headquarters brass that cynically assumed that when a drug dealer was locked up by a uniformed cop, it was because he had refused to pay the cop off. Off-duty arrests, and arrests made close to the end of an officer's shift, had also been discouraged, lest cops be tempted to make arrests solely to generate paid overtime—collars for dollars, as they were called. For years, law-and-order types had railed against the "handcuffing" of the police by the courts. But one legacy of the Knapp Commission was the handcuffing of the police *by* the police.

On a Monday evening in August 1991, a car belonging to the entourage of the Grand Rebbe of the Lubavitchers—a proselytizing group of Hasidic Jews—went out of control and killed a seven-year-old black boy, Gavin Cato, in the Crown Heights neighborhood of Brooklyn, where blacks and Hasidim lived in sometimes uncomfortable proximity. Three hours later, a mob of young black men attacked a twenty-nine-year-old Australian Lubavitcher, Yankel Rosenbaum, who had come to New York to study the Holocaust. Rosenbaum died later that night.

Two more days of violence and vandalism followed, and when the troubles ended, the recriminations began. Soon the city was caught up in a feverish effort to find out just who was responsible for ordering the police to do nothing until the press coverage became too intense to ignore. When a commission appointed by Governor Mario Cuomo released its report, Mayor Dinkins seized on the finding that *he* had issued no such order. (A disengaged leader by nature, he sounded a little like the Emperor Nero proudly pointing out that nobody had unearthed a memo on his letterhead saying "Let Rome burn.") Of course, no one had issued any such order—no one had to. The governor's report was a two-volume affair that carefully reconstructed the comings and goings, physical and mental, of a large cast of potential decision-makers. In all that verbiage, however, there was no insight into the situation as telling as the words (quoted in the *Daily News*) of a "law enforcement source" defending the senior police commander on the scene, Assistant Chief Thomas Gallagher. It would be unfair to blame Gallagher, said the source (who appeared to speak from a thorough knowledge of the department), because "if you're not being told what to do, you're not going to do anything."

The image of the police in pop culture is one of constant action. In cop movies and TV shows, station houses teem with snarling felons and their victims, and every tour of duty is a nonstop series of emergencies. The characteristic pose of hero-cop and villain-cop alike is the chase, the fight, the dogged pursuit. The image is so powerful that city-dwellers tend to doubt what they can see with their own eyes, which most of the time is far different: police officers standing around, if not in massed formation, then in pairs or small groups, talking, if at all, mainly to each other. In the wake of the Mollen Commission scandal, the police department launched an advertising campaign designed to regain New Yorkers' confidence. COPS CARE was the message emblazoned on a series of posters that showed uplifting pictures of New York City police officers engaged in helping citizens. The deep, dark open secret of the police world—the subject of a cover-up in which the police and the media were engaged in a long-running conspiracy—was that many cops did not care, because they weren't convinced that anybody who counted wanted them to.

———

In the latest scandal, as in the last one, corruption was not the only issue; the scandal was also about an official reluctance to act against it. When Police Commissioner Lee Brown was asked how Michael Dowd and his crew had so long eluded the department's Internal Affairs investigators, he explained that there had been nothing in Dowd's record to indicate that he was corrupt. This, about a patrolman who, on a take-home paycheck of about $400 a week, drove a $30,000 red Corvette and lived in a $300,000 house (one of four that he owned or co-owned) at the end of a cul de sac in Port Jefferson, Long Island—a house that, as the columnist Mike McAlary observed, "no honest cop" could have afforded. "You can indict on the house alone," McAlary added.

Brown's successor, Raymond Kelly—assuming office with the scandal in full bloom—was more honest in acknowledging the weakness of the "field internal affairs" units that Murphy had established in the name of decentralized responsibility. In this "bifurcated structure," Kelly observed, important cases had been left to units that were badly short of equipment and manpower. The Dowd case had been dumped in the lap of a single well-intentioned detective, Sergeant Joseph Trimboli, with thirty or forty other cases in his portfolio at the time. Dowd himself was the subject of a whole series of accusations over the years, and in October 1988, after a federal informant (a "Mr. A") linked Dowd and other cops in the 75th Precinct to payoffs, sex-and-drug parties at hotels near Kennedy Airport, and stickups, Trimboli pleaded—in vain—for Internal Affairs to take over the investigation, since, as he eloquently explained to the Mollen Commission later, "You're talking something far beyond the ability of Joseph Trimboli to investigate."

What the department needed, in Kelly's view—what he now promised—was an "expanded and centralized" Internal Affairs, outfitted with "advanced surveillance equipment" and "a new computerized information system," and raised to the status of a bureau answerable to the commissioner directly.

"What's wrong with Internal Affairs has nothing to do with its size or equipment," David told me, after Kelly announced his reforms. "And God knows how many times it's already gone back and forth between being a division and a bureau. The problem is, if you're an honest cop—or an honest citizen—with information about corruption, you still get the same lousy set of choices you did before Knapp."

He was speaking from fresh experience, for Dowd's name had been one of those he had tried to blow the whistle on, as far back as 1986. "We gave IAD everything they needed to catch those guys," David recalled. "All they had to do was invent a call—three Hispanics dealing drugs on the corner of wherever—and then put an undercover out there with a wad of bills and let him be ripped off with the videotape running. But they wouldn't do that; they wouldn't do anything unless the cop agreed to come forward, identify himself, and wear a wire. Since time immemorial, that's been the attitude; either you stand up and say, '*J'accuse*,' and your career is over, or you go away."

CHAPTER

TWENTY

———⟫●⟪———

In the middle of a job negotiation, David would sometimes discover that the official with the authority to hire him was a friend of a former nemesis of his, and when the job failed to come through, he would glumly conclude that he had been blackballed. Whether anything of that sort happened in any particular case is difficult to say. That he had plenty of grounds for concern I can testify, from interviewing his former bosses. Paul Delise and William McCarthy remembered him fondly; some of the others could hardly speak at all, such strong emotions had I summoned by asking them to describe the experience of having him as an underling. They sputtered. They slammed down the phone. They spewed out damning adjectives. "Why would you want to write about *him?*" one former supervisor of David's demanded.

I thought it best not to go into one of my reasons: a desire to understand how someone who was not a criminal—who had made a career of apprehending criminals—could generate so much hostility among so many well-situated and otherwise sober officials and former officials of government, and how that hostility could endure with seemingly undiminished intensity for (in a few cases) fifteen or twenty years. Since I was anxious to persuade these people to cooperate, it behooved me to explain my aims in unthreatening terms. So

I talked about whistle-blowers—about what unusual and sometimes contrary people they are, and where they spring from, and why they often come to no good in the end. But this, too, proved to be dangerous ground. David's ex-bosses did not like to think of him as a whistle-blower, and they were almost unanimous in attributing his career problems to other causes.

"David Durk is a malcontent," William Aronwald, the former strike-force chief—lately a lawyer in private practice in Westchester County—said to me. "He could never accept the idea that other people were as honest as he was. He's the kind of person who is just incapable of participating in any kind of collective enterprise in which there is going to be disagreement. If he thinks the investigation should continue, and you don't think it should continue, he is going to say you're corrupt."

"David's problem is he had a moral fervor so powerful that it tended to shut down all other body systems," another former adversary of David's—a prosecutor who has since become a judge—told me. "He said he was an investigator, but he was really a tub-thumper, a chest-beater. He was like an evangelist—he wanted to drive out the evildoers with his sword by sundown. And you never knew when this guy was going to accuse you of somehow being in league with the malefactors.

"I don't have the slightest doubt," the judge continued, "that if he had been more circumspect, if he had been more skilled at—I won't say toadying, but at functioning in a collegial setting and carrying on a civilized discussion, he would probably have a significant position in law enforcement today."

———————

In November 1993, Rudolph Giuliani became the first former law enforcement officer to be elected mayor of New York City in four decades (since the questionable William O'Dwyer). Giuliani achieved his victory with the fervent support of the PBA and of the city's police in general, David Dinkins having alienated much of that constituency with his response to a police shooting in Washington

Heights in September 1992—a shooting initially portrayed as the cold-blooded murder of an innocent man, and later shown to have been the desperate act of self-defense that the police officer, Michael O'Keefe, had said it was all along. Dinkins, seeking to keep the peace in a volatile neighborhood, rushed to the home of the victim's family and offered to send the remains back to the Dominican Republic for burial at city expense. He thus became the mayor who had "paid for a drug dealer's funeral," and allowed Giuliani to become the candidate who would "never pay for a drug dealer's funeral."

Giuliani made the most of the distinction. Early in the campaign, he denounced Dinkins as "antipolice" (one of the milder things Giuliani said, actually) before a rally of protesting cops at City Hall—a rally that later erupted into what *Newsday*, in a headline, labeled a "blue zoo": a miniriot of cops shouting racist epithets and obscenities, and briefly blocking the Brooklyn Bridge, where they cursed out motorists who challenged them, including one woman who was trying to deliver her seriously ill son to a hospital.

In other settings, though, Giuliani displayed a subtle understanding of the police and their failings, and in contrast to some law-and-order candidates, who shifted their attention to other issues once in office (perhaps because, campaign oratory notwithstanding, they didn't really think there was much to be done about crime), he seemed prepared to have his mayoralty judged by his success in making the city safer.

Giuliani's police commissioner—a Bostonian, William Bratton, who had come up through the ranks of that city's department—brought an attention-getting bluntness to an office long known for evasion and pomposity. The NYPD, as Bratton assumed command, was still unearthing more pockets of drug-related corruption. In April 1994 it got out that at least a dozen cops at a precinct in upper Harlem—soon to be dubbed the "dirty thirty"—had been providing paid protection to local drug dealers and beating and robbing any who were slow to appreciate the need for such arrangements. The usual drill for a police commissioner in these situations was to call a press conference at headquarters, denounce the cops who had actually been charged, heap praise on the remaining 99.9 percent of the force, and wait for the story to go away. Bratton showed up at the precinct along with the arrest team, personally collected the shields of two of the accused, and at the next morning's roll call, gave a stunned group of their coworkers a talking-to. They could expect plenty of ugly looks from the citizenry, he warned them. And with reason: some of them had in all likelihood committed similar crimes ("We're probably not going to be able to get all of you—that's unfortunate"), while others had surely known what was happening and had kept the knowledge to themselves. "I've been disappointed—being quite frank—that more did not come forward. . . ." Bratton said. "We need to think carefully about that."

Although Bratton was more honest than his predecessors about the extent—and the consequences—of the problem, he plainly understood that a heavy-handed bureaucracy enforcing a million regulations was no way to deal with corruption (to say nothing of crime). As far back as anyone could remember, police commissioners had seemed to think that they could either come down hard on the department, and be applauded by editorial writers, good-government groups, civil rights organizations, and other outside arbiters, or strive to be liked by the rank and file. Bratton saw no conflict—he intended to do both things at once.

He and his appointees minced no words in describing the NYPD, before their coming, as an agency whose "business was to stay out of trouble, not to police the city," as one Bratton aide commented. The new team gave the strong impression that their main business, in fact as well as theory, would be fighting crime. JUST ASK posters went up in precincts around the city, reminding patrol officers and detectives of a new, department-wide effort to question suspects more insistently—to ask everyone arrested with a gun, for example, where he got it. The top brass began holding twice-a-week "crime-strategy meetings" at headquarters, where commanders from all over the city got to boast of their successes, to exchange useful crime-fighting notes, and if they had let a problem go unaddressed, to be called on the carpet for it. Civilian anticrime patrols were created to police certain out-of-the-way areas of the city (bridges, for example), with the help of cellular phones preset to 911. Detectives began receiving regular computer printouts of their arrest records—and the Detective Division's productivity increased sharply. "There were people who hadn't made an arrest in years," Bratton said. An aide referred to them as "conscientious objectors."

"The very best way to deal with corruption," Rudy Giuliani told *Newsday* soon after the 30th Precinct episode, "is to give police officers meaningful, active work to do and to have high standards for them." He went on to decry the post-Knapp policy of discouraging uniformed cops from making drug arrests—a policy that, although motivated by fear of corruption, had left cops demoralized and perhaps, Giuliani suggested, more prone to break the law. "Maybe we got the worst of both worlds," he said. "We [were] not making arrests of street-level drug dealers by uniformed police officers . . . and we got corruption anyway."

If Giuliani sounded a little like David Durk, the resemblance was not necessarily coincidental. They had worked together on several cases during Giuliani's tenure as U.S. attorney, developing a rapport based on a strong common dislike for criminals in high places—and for law-enforcement colleagues who lacked the courage to tangle with such people. "Unlike some people in law enforcement, I have a very positive view of David," Giuliani told me, a year before his election as mayor. "He's a remarkably good influence. Organizations need people like him, even if he raises nine bad ideas for every good one. But some managers are frightened by him. They get so worried about being criticized—that's how organizations become dead bureaucracies."

In the background of Giuliani's campaign loomed David Garth—the Talleyrand of New York politics in the late twentieth century, and someone who, like the candidate, was willing to declare himself a friend of David's. "David Durk is a walking embarrassment to us," Garth said to me. He characterized David as a "hot potato" and "a guy who has to be handled," but added that "with all his mishegos, he's more trustworthy than the people who don't trust him."

It began to appear that David, like an old ship that had seen glory in past wars, was going to be brought out of mothballs and put back into service. During the transitional early months of the Giuliani administration, he held meetings with Garth, Giuliani, and Bratton. Meanwhile, from other sources, I heard a rumor that David was under consideration as a possible Deputy Commissioner for Intelligence—a job to be created expressly with him in mind. (It was a plan that reminded me of something that David's old friend Jack Ferguson—a veteran of the Intelligence Division—had said: "Give him a stack of legal pads, a bunch of sharpened pencils, a bank of phones—and he's dynamite. The department has never used him properly.")

But the spring and summer of 1994 passed without any announcement of his hiring, in this or any capacity, and I noticed that David became increasingly caustic in his comments on the police department's new leadership. As it happened, I had begun to write an article about Commissioner Bratton, and he impressed me. He was looking for ways to have an effect on crime, without reaching for the usual Constitution-be-damned proposals. He stood up for his officers, without falling into the us-and-them posture of a Darryl Gates or a Frank Rizzo. And—the thing I liked best about him—although he had been in the management ranks for more than a decade, he remained in close emotional touch with his years as a street cop and his early distaste for bosses who stayed away from volatile situations and weighed in with their criticisms afterward.

"When I was working District Fourteen, we had a brouha in one of the public parks, and every cop in the district was there," Bratton told me. "There were two sergeants, Pitts and Martin, back in the station, and we were calling for PS—patrol supervisors—and neither one of those bastards would come out. They were two cowards hiding at the station house. We had a lot of them like that in Boston. They didn't want to see anything."

David acknowledged some of Bratton's strengths but, characteristically, he wanted to be sure that I was aware of the holes in the record—among them, a certain close Bratton advisor who, at an earlier stage of his career, had been known for countenancing the beating of suspects; the pressure being exerted on cops to underreport crimes so that headquarters could claim sharper reductions; and the continued ineptitude (as David saw it) of Internal Affairs. My article appeared, and I had the feeling David didn't think much of it. I had this feeling because, for several weeks, I heard nothing from him. Finally, I called him up and asked him straight-out, and he told me where he thought I had gone wrong—in abundant detail. (He also told me that he had defended my honor against a fellow journalist of anti-Bratton leanings, who had theorized to David that I had been, in some manner, bought off. No, David had said, not bought off—just snookered.) It seemed to me David might be letting his resentment about not being offered a job color his views on other matters, and we argued about a few of them. But, recalling our similar differences about community policing, I didn't argue too hard.

———><®<———

One night, I gathered some friends and former coworkers of David's around a table at a Chinese restaurant on the East Side. As strongly as some of his former bosses believed that he had gotten his just deserts, this group held the view that he was entitled to something better. Thomas Reppetto, the president of the Citizens Crime Commission of New York City, approached the subject of David's recent fortunes via a short memoir of his own career, in the Chicago police department—a career that had dead-ended after he took a leave and obtained a doctorate in public administration from Harvard. "Some people might think it's a good thing to get a Harvard doctorate," Reppetto said. "But when I came back I was dropped down from commander to captain, and it was made very clear to me that I had no future. And I was by no means a Durk. When I look at him, I see what would have happened to me if I had stayed around in Chicago. I'd have started swinging wild."

As an ex-cop who knew what it was like to be trapped in an unfriendly bureaucracy, Reppetto could forgive David some of his resentments, and as a historian (the author of a book on the evolution of American policing, *The Blue Parade*), he knew that the NYPD had a tradition of ultimately rewarding its whistle-blowers. "Maxie Schmittberger—he was on the take, and that didn't prevent him from being rewarded," Reppetto pointed out to me, referring to one of the principal cooperative witnesses before the Lexow Committee, in 1894. "He squealed and he wound up serving a long term as chief inspector. A real reform administration would have made David a deputy commissioner."

I asked Henry Ruth—David's old Justice Department supervisor and, later, a Watergate special prosecutor—for his take on David's troubles. "David is someone who takes his dog for a walk, and comes back with two informants," Ruth said. "He could have made so many cases if people had just welcomed him into the scheme, but he didn't fit. Law enforcement lost a great opportunity over the last twenty-five years."

"He's a zealot, but a nonzealot would never have done what he did," Lawrence Goldman—one of David's oldest friends—observed. "In terms of the history of this city, he made a tremendous difference, and how many people can you say that about? It's societally wrong, what's happened to him. Somebody, somewhere, should give him some money and say, 'Durk, go be Durk.' "

Yet it gradually emerged that most of David's friends, in addition to being irritated with law enforcement for keeping him out, were irritated with David for not making more of an effort to get back in. Several people had stories to tell about how they had put in a good word for him somewhere, and David had failed to capitalize on it. He had developed a habit, in job interviews, of trying to head off possible problems by introducing them up front. He would startle potential employers by asking them to imagine delicate situations in which their expectations and his might come into conflict. One old friend of his, after greasing the wheels for an investigative position with a high official of New York State, was confounded to learn that David, in his interview, had raised the possibility of finding corruption in the official's own office. That was the last he heard about that job.

Sometimes he would feel a compulsion to bring up nettlesome issues from his past. He would tell himself that he was making a sort of preemptive strike against questions that were bound to arise sooner or later. But the effect, often, was to make people with little prior knowledge of his history feel suddenly uneasy about it. Friends would urge him to keep his presentations simple, but things wouldn't stay simple with David. No matter what people asked him, he seemed to detect another question emanating from them: why, at his age, with his accomplishments, didn't he already have a job in the field he loved? So every question triggered a sort of meganarrative that was, at bottom, nothing less than the story of his long and tumultuous law enforcement career.

Feeling a need to cram a great deal of information into what was, inevitably, too little time, David would dispense with the transitions and explanations that might have served to put his listeners at their ease. Characters, great and obscure alike, would enter his narratives unannounced and be referred to by their last names exclusively. "He rattles on about these events from fifteen years ago that even I can't follow," Reppetto complained. "I'm probably as familiar with the history of law enforcement in New York City as anybody around, and a lot of the time I lose him—I'm three paragraphs behind. He'll mention a name, and I have to say, 'Wait a minute! Who's that guy?' I tell him, 'Choose one or two points and make them—get in and get out.' "

David's recollections had a timeless quality, stemming in part from the fact that he often failed to say whether something had happened fifteen years ago or last week. A newcomer to the experience might feel like Dorothy traveling by cyclone in *The Wizard of Oz*: every so often, a familiar element would pass through the conversation (asbestos . . . Trump . . . gypsy cabdrivers . . . the Queens DA's office . . . Colombian hit men), but the connections between them were not always evident.

Even some of his admirers found his manner of discourse taxing. "You get crazed listening to him," Tom Robbins, a reporter at the *Daily News*, told me "and sometimes you want to shout 'Stop!' "

The columnist Sydney Schanberg—an old friend of David's, and the author of innumerable stories based at least in part on his tips—felt a need, at a certain point in their relationship, for a temporary cessation of contact. "He wore me out," Schanberg explained later. David obligingly stopped calling—until after six months Schanberg indicated that he was strong enough to resume their conversations.

———————

In the course of my interviews with the new police commissioner and the people around him, I asked what had happened to the idea of a job for David Durk. It was a subject they didn't much want to talk about, but after prodding—and with the assurance that I wouldn't quote anybody directly—a few high-ranking police officials told me that David had been adversarial and unfocused in his talks with them. One top Bratton aide confided that David was "crazy."

The word was meant as a conversation-stopper, I gathered. Certainly, the aide showed no interest in discussing what sort of craziness David might have contracted, or whether, crazy and all, he might still be of some service to the New York City police department. Nor did anyone in the new regime raise the possibility that the department, and the city, had a debt to settle with him.

CHAPTER

TWENTY-ONE

David and Arlene Durk live on a quiet road lined by trees and fields, in the rolling hills of Putnam County, an hour's drive, and worlds away, from Manhattan. Their house, purchased in 1976, is low-slung and modern in a jerry-built way, having started out as a playroom for a wealthy couple who lived up the road. There's nothing fancy about it as a piece of architecture, but it has a pleasing view of sloping meadows and thickly wooded hills. Deer cruise the bushes and flowers on the back lawn. Wild turkeys have been known to parade past the Durks' bedroom window.

Into this tranquil setting is introduced, on a more or less daily basis, the *Times*, *The Wall Street Journal*, the *Daily News*, the *Post*, and (when David can find it at the nearby supermarket where he does his newspaper shopping) *Newsday*. By ten on a typical morning, he is seated in his study—a crowded loft overlooking the living room—with the day's well-digested papers arrayed before him, and more often than not he is worked up over something. It might be a small item nestled in the ad-crowded inner pages of a tabloid: a letter to the editor of the *News*, say, from a citizen who tried to point out an armed drug dealer to a couple of plainclothesmen, only to be told that they couldn't do anything about it, because they were from another precinct. "The police department is constantly telling people they have a duty to come forward if they have knowledge of a crime," David says. "Here's someone who came forward and look how he was treated!"

Or it might be a bigger story, like Commissioner Bratton's announcement that in response to revelations of widespread police perjury, he has decided to require every New York City cop to take an annual refresher course in testifying. "A course is fine, but it won't mean anything unless the department starts backing up cops who tell the truth," David says. "Let's say you're on the witness stand and you admit you got distracted for a minute, so you can't positively say that the package you found on the ground is the same package the suspect was carrying earlier. We tell cops, 'Oh, honesty is great,' but what really happens to somebody who testifies like that? A superior is there with the thumbscrew saying, 'You let the guy walk!' And if the cop was up for detective, how much you want to bet he's not going to get the gold shield? You're talking about a total reversal of what has been the reward system inside the police department."

The medium of transmission for David's commentaries these days is the telephone. Through the magic of Call Waiting, he is capable of staying on the phone for hours at a stretch, and experience has taught those on the other end of the line not to be surprised when the business portion of a conversation with him is overwhelmed by a long and passionate discourse (combining elements of late-night talk radio and Sunday morning evangelism) on current events in law enforcement.

Friends of David's have suggested that for the sake of his mental health he should cut down on his newspaper reading. He acknowledges the wisdom of their advice but has been unable to follow it. One friend, Harold Hess, retired a few years ago as an assistant chief and now spends as much time as possible flying and maintaining an airplane that he co-owns with some buddies; the only contact with the police department that he welcomes is his pension check. "When I'm out, I'm out," Hess says. "David, he'll never be out of it."

Getting him into the city, on the other hand, can be a challenge. Call to make an appointment with him, and he will talk about his car, which has to go into the shop on Tuesday, or about his cat, who has to see the vet on Thursday—about anything, it seems, except when he can make the trip. Rarely does he respond to an invitation with an outright refusal, but often he has a reason why you'll have to check back with him in a few days about a date and time, and by then there is likely to be a fresh maze of contingencies to consider. It's a little like conducting trade negotiations with the Japanese.

The city is a world of busy and powerful people, and every encounter with them, even if it is not a job interview per se, represents a kind of audition, in which David's credibility and fitness for duty are freshly examined. By staying in the country, he tells the world: If you want me, you know where to find me.

When David was still employed by the city, he would invite friends and coworkers out to Putnam County for afternoons of camaraderie, fueled by food and drink. (Cops who came for a visit in those days would sometimes kid him about living on an "estate.") He doesn't see any of his old associates these days, and some of them now have an impression of him as a recluse, holed up in the country, nursing his disappointments and resentments. Actually, the new Durk is every bit as sociable, in his neck of the woods, as the old one. He gets around, he meets people, and, as always, they tell him things.

An employee of a local supermarket tells him, for example, about state inspectors who don't care one way or the other if a store complies with the applicable health, safety, and consumer regulations; what they want, he says, is to have the trunks of their cars filled with free groceries. Sometimes they hand the manager their car keys and a shopping list.

A hardware-store salesman, in the process of selling David a wrench, mentions that he has a second job, in the Westchester County prison system. Before long he is discussing a group of guards who have made a profitable sideline of bringing in weapons and other contraband for inmates.

The manager of a concrete supply business gets to talking about overbilling, watered-down cement, and other corrupt practices in the maintenance of the dams at various upstate reservoirs that supply New York City with drinking water.

"This is someone who just can't go into a store and buy something without getting into these conversations," Arlene Durk has said.

After three decades in law enforcement—three decades from which some might derive the lesson that it's foolish to get excited about what probably can't be changed anyway—David is still getting excited, and others are still getting caught up in his excitement. The stories people tell him start out, typically, as idle entertainment or the venting of steam, but quite often, as people unburden themselves, they become seized by the idea that there may be something to be done about the situation. And, not infrequently, there *is* something to be done. The upshot of the prison-contraband story was a federal investigation in which more than a dozen people were arrested.

"He's been through the ringer—emotionally, financially, professionally—and he still has more passion than most people start off with," Julie Durk told me, speaking both with a daughter's love and as a motion picture executive in Los Angeles who has seen her share of cynicism. "For all his travails, he has never lost sight of the idea that people and institutions can be better if they are given the chance. People think he's antiestablishment. In fact, he has more faith in the foundations of society—in institutions like the police—than anyone I know."

———<>———

Another source of David's recent aversion to appointments in the city is money. There's the cost of gas and midtown parking—no small matter to someone who hasn't held what the world would call a job for nearly a decade. There is also the issue of compensation for his time. What people want from him, quite often, is information. David has a reputation among journalists, prosecutors, and other information hounds for knowing things that the rest of the world doesn't know. He sometimes feels the need to explain to these people that such knowledge isn't acquired by magic—that there is labor involved. They sometimes feel the need to explain back to him that ethical considerations don't permit them to pay for information. What this boils down to, David has figured out, is that while *they* will be paid for it, he won't be.

When he does get into the city, he sometimes runs into former coworkers, and they ask him what he is up to.

"Consulting," he tells them. It's an evasion, but not an untruthful one. After losing his job with the finance department, David and his friend Jerry McKenna set out to create a center for whistle-blowers— an institution that would see to their professional, financial, and psychological well-being, in addition to getting their complaints acted on. The idea seemed to be headed somewhere after it received a public endorsement, in 1986, from then–U.S. attorney Giuliani. In the end, though, it died for want of funding, and the only tangible results of the discussions with Giuliani were a few press items that led to a spurt of inquiries from whistle-blowers, and thus to many hours of unpaid labor—and unreimbursed phone calls—for David. In effect, he has *become* the whistle-blower center.

What he does for a client, as a rule, is to broker a connection with a journalist, a prosecutor, or a law enforcement officer who is willing to act on the tip, while protecting the source. From his spider's lair of an office, he runs a kind of underground railroad for the delivery of whistle-blowers and their information to safety.

It is the rare client who is in a position to pay for these services. That consideration aside, business hasn't been too bad. There seems to be no shortage of civil servants (or private citizens doing business with the government) who have witnessed illegalities that they are burning to report, and who have been unable to find, in the profusion of agencies and officials lawfully charged with investigating such matters, anyone they feel they can trust. From David, they get a ready understanding of the mental stresses that whistle-blowers are prone to, and a lifetime of experience in the circumvention of channels.

One of his clients—Beth Rowton, a Republican party activist and former model from Oklahoma—gave me a fresh perspective on the matter of David and craziness. Not his but hers, from which David, she said, had rescued her. "He's the emergency room for whistle-blowers," Rowton told me. "I would have given up had I not gotten hold of David Durk. He kept me sane."

From January 1991 until July 1992, Rowton was the assistant treasurer of Oklahoma, under Claudette Henry, the first woman ever elected there to the office of treasurer. In September 1991, Rowton and her boss were on a staff retreat in the northeastern part of the state when a reporter for the *Daily Oklahoman* called to inquire about some state funds that the treasurer had invested through a New York brokerage house, rather than (as Henry had promised during her campaign) through a firm based in Oklahoma. It struck Rowton as a minor flap—until she saw its effect on Henry and another colleague, Patricia Whitehead, who was the office's chief trader. Henry, according to Rowton, clenched her fists and berated Whitehead, shouting, "Why did you let this happen to me?"

"One of them panicked, the other started crying, and I knew something terrible had gone wrong," Rowton recalled.

A month later, breezing through Rowton's office on the way to the room that housed a special tape recorder that monitored every investment transaction, Whitehead remarked that it had become necessary for her to remove the tape. This was the equivalent, Rowton said later, of destroying the black box after an airplane crash, but Whitehead made light of it. "It was kind of like, 'Oh, I know Beth won't say anything—we're all friends here.' " After anguishing about what to do, Rowton reported the incident to Henry. The result—the only apparent result—was a sudden diminution of Rowton's responsibilities. "Virtually all executive communication stopped," she recalled. A few weeks later, Whitehead—whose standing in the office didn't seem to have suffered—cornered Rowton. "Don't you ever call my hand again!" she warned her.

Nine months later, Rowton was fired. By then, she had already given a sealed statement to a friend who worked at the Oklahoma attorney general's office. She began making early-morning garbage-inspection sorties to the homes of the key officials she suspected of being involved, first replacing every bag with a similar one, to avoid notice. Rowton is six feet tall and a former model—"It's not like me to go through garbage," she told me. She found discarded documents that bore out her suspicions. Some of them had been put through a shredder, but Rowton and her mother reconstructed them, using a picture frame and Scotch tape.

In August 1992, she presented her findings to the attorney general's people, expecting a warm reception and some action. Instead, they advised her that they would look at her materials, and institute a formal investigation if and when they concluded that a crime had occurred—a point Rowton considered settled.

"The authorities make you feel as if there's something wrong with you," Rowton told me. "They don't give you any information. They eat like an elephant and, as we say in Oklahoma, poop like a hummingbird." Another year passed, without any formal follow-up.

Meanwhile, Henry was publicly denouncing Rowton as an incompetent and a malcontent ("I was slam-dunked in the press," Rowton said), and there were incidents that could just possibly have been intended to frighten her: repeated break-ins, for example, at her parents' home, where she and her daughter were living at the time. Her daughter's dog was found killed. A similar fate befell a pet rabbit.

Rowton came across an article I had written about David Durk in *The New Yorker.* "I thought, 'This is a man after my own heart—where is this man?' "

David would eventually get her legal advice and put her in touch with a correspondent at ABC's *Nightline,* David Marash, who arranged a story about her. But, as important as anything he did, in Rowton's telling, was talking her through her distress. Their first conversation lasted three hours. "I would tell him, 'I'm going to slip through the cracks. He would say to me, 'That's normal—that's how you should feel at this time. But no you're not, I won't let you. These other people won't let you.' "

In November 1993, *Nightline* aired its piece—and the authorities, according to Rowton, sprang to life. In September 1994, the U.S. attorney's office for the Western District of Oklahoma handed down a thirty-two-count indictment alleging conspiracy, bribery, kick-backs, and money laundering on the part of Whitehead and two former associates. (One of them escaped arrest by fleeing to Costa Rica.) According to the charges, some $6.7 million of Oklahoma taxpayers' money had been pocketed in illegal commissions, while the state appeared to have lost well over $100 million as a result of investment decisions driven by dishonest purposes.

In July 1995, Whitehead was found guilty on charges of bribery, kickbacks, and money laundering; she received a sentence of nine years in federal prison. One of her codefendants, William Pretty, got eight years. (The third, Patrick Kuhse, remained unapprehended.) It was, by common consent, one of the biggest public-corruption cases in Oklahoma history. "We owe them a great debt for coming forward," the attorney general of the state said of Rowton and an associate who had worked with her on the investigation. But Rowton continued to be the target of threats for months after the sentencing; she was forced to send her daughter into hiding after a paste-up note was left on her porch warning: "The sins of the mother shall visit the children."

There is no listing for David in the yellow pages or, for that matter, in the white pages. People manage to find him just the same. Eugene DeSantis, the president of the DeSantis Holster Company of New Hyde Park, Long Island, contacted him in the summer of 1993 to lodge a protest about the bidding on a contract to supply new police recruits with holsters suitable for the 9mm pistols that the NYPD was about to start issuing them. DeSantis was a successful manufacturer who already did business with the FBI and a number of other law-enforcement agencies, and he considered himself a leading candidate for this contract as well. Yet, as he told David, the department had kept him out of the bidding by the simple device of not sending him an application and specifications after he had requested them. He suspected (though he had no proof) that he had been excluded because of his failure to offer an under-the-table inducement—a postretirement job, for example, for one or another of the police officials involved in making the decision.

David alerted Walter Mack, the department's Deputy Commissioner for Internal Affairs, and after a meeting with DeSantis, Mack promised to investigate the matter. Another part of the understanding, in David's mind, was to put the bid-letting process on hold. But a few weeks later, David and DeSantis were stunned to learn that the department had gone ahead, awarding the contract to a Queens company, Cobra Limited, whose holster was both costlier and, DeSantis claimed, less safe than his. Fed up, David turned to the press (as he had warned Mack he would). He called Selwyn Raab, a reporter at the *Times*, who made some inquiries and wrote a story about the curious fact that the head of Cobra had been convicted a year earlier of trying to bribe his way out of a federal income tax investigation—a felony conviction that would normally have rendered his firm ineligible for a city contract. By law, the department had to do a criminal-record check of every company receiving a contract worth more than $100,000. In Cobra's case, the responsible officials had come up with a sophisticated argument that relieved them of that obligation: cops, they explained, paid for their holsters out of a $1,000 annual uniform allowance, so they, not the department, were the purchasers. After Raab brought this situation to Internal Affairs' notice, the Cobra deal was rescinded. The contract, however, wound up going to a third company, which had agreed to follow NYPD design specifications that, in DeSantis's opinion, made an officer's gun susceptible to being yanked away from the front. Indeed, a number of other police agencies rejected the New York holster, and in January 1995 the manufacturer recalled it, citing a defective trigger-lock that might prevent a police officer from drawing his weapon in an emergency. The NYPD soon followed suit with its own recall.

One of David's more grateful clients was William Acosta, who sought him out in desperation after being forced to resign from the NYPD at the end of 1991. Officially, Acosta had been charged with "falsifying police records." According to Acosta, however, his real offense had been to run afoul of a clique of cops in his precinct by, among other things, reporting the presence of illegal gambling machines in bars and restaurants that were frequented by his colleagues and telling an off-duty chief that he was too drunk to drive.

Acosta realized a boyhood dream when he entered the New York City police department in October 1990, and he fancied that the department, too, was getting something out of the deal. A short, thick-torsoed man with a brush cut of dusty blond hair—Colombian on his mother's side, Italian on his father's—he spoke seven languages, and he had won commendations for his work as an undercover agent for the U.S. Customs Service, running a sting operation that nabbed a ring of thieving inspectors and baggage handlers at Kennedy Airport. In the NYPD, however, no one much noticed his prior law enforcement experience until some of his fellow cops in the 114th Precinct, in the Astoria section of Queens, seized on it as supporting evidence for their belief that he was a "rat"—an epithet that occasionally rang out from the rear of the muster room as he was delivering his "Here, sir!" at roll call.

His rathood was proved when Internal Affairs investigators came to inquire about a roll-call incident in which a white policeman had struck a black policewoman with his nightstick and she had replied in kind. Assured that anything he said would be kept in confidence, Acosta answered the investigators' questions—only to find, the next day, that the whole precinct knew about his testimony. (The reaction suggested to him that he had been the only witness, in a roomful, to admit seeing anything.) From then on, he was treated with conspicuous disdain by a group of cops who had dubbed themselves the Massapequa boys, after the Long Island suburb of that name.

One day, while Acosta, a sergeant, and another cop were searching a dead man's apartment, Acosta found a stash of large bills, including hundreds and twenties in seeming abundance. No sooner had he handed the money over than the sergeant ordered him to leave. Later, back at the precinct, Acosta checked the report on the dead man's property and saw that the sum found at the scene was listed as several hundred dollars, although he believed it to have been in the thousands. Acosta called an Internal Affairs hotline that was supposed to take anonymous complaints, but as soon as he began to explain his purpose he was pressed for his name and badge number, and he hung up.

His police career lasted a little over a year. His final run-in, according to Acosta, was with an off-duty chief who was coming out of a convenience store, staggering toward his car. Acosta told the chief that he shouldn't be driving and offered to call a taxi or a patrol car to take him home. The chief cursed at him, pushed him away, and got into his car. As it happened, a minor disciplinary matter involving Acosta—he had miscounted the number of parking tickets he had written—had just reached the office of the same chief for review. Acosta had been told to expect a written reprimand or, at worst, a few days of docked pay. Instead, word came back that he would have to defend himself before a departmental trial board on the unexpectedly grave charge of "falsifying police records." Then he was ordered to report to his precinct commander's office and given an ultimatum to resign or else be fired and have his record blackened for life.

After resigning, in panic, Acosta looked for help. His search took him, successively, to the PBA, the police Hispanic and Italian societies, a lawyer, and a reporter for *Newsday*. The reporter wrote an article about Acosta's plight, and the article mentioned a number of incidents that did not reflect well on the 114th Precinct. Acosta began receiving threats on his life—and occasional gestures of reinforcement, such as five rats, their throats slit, left on the hood of his car. He consulted the reporter, who suggested that Acosta talk to a retired lieutenant he had never heard of—David Durk.

Acosta was a cop after David's heart, and, like him, a magnet for criminal intelligence. David had barely begun to look into Acosta's case when, in November 1992, Acosta gave the police information that led to the arrest of two brothers in the stabbing of an off-duty corrections officer and the theft of his gun. (They had been stabbed themselves during the assault, and, searching for a place to wash the blood off, had burst into the storefront school in Queens where Acosta now made a meager living as a teacher of tae kwon do.) Having assured Acosta that his identity would be safeguarded, the Queens DA's office proceeded to give the suspects' lawyer a report describing the informant, unmistakably, as a "former police offi-cer"—a thoughtless indiscretion (to put the best face on it) that placed Acosta's life in jeopardy. Then, according to Acosta, a relative of the two brothers came to his school and asked him if he knew "what happens to people who testify against other people." (In the end, he was not asked to testify, the DA's office having struck a deal in which one of the brothers pleaded guilty to attempted murder, the other to assault; both were sent to prison.)

David had developed a four-level classification system for whistle-blowers: good person/good information, bad person/good information, good person/bad information, and bad person/bad information. He placed Acosta in the first category and referred him to McKenna, who agreed to plead his case for reinstatement. David also enlisted the pro bono services of Detective (retired) Jimmy Lanzano—his good friend from the antihijacking squad—and together they set about gathering evidence on Acosta's behalf. In December 1993, after many months of what looked to David like foot dragging, the department agreed to rehire Acosta, assigning him to Internal Affairs. David had won for Acosta the kind of vindication he craved for himself.

David Durk is someone who gets under people's skin—the skin of his enemies and his friends alike. I have asked others, and I have asked myself: what accounts for his hold on us?

He made something important happen—that's certainly a part of the explanation. He exposed corruption, and, more than that, he helped changed the way we look at it. David Burnham, who long ago left the *Times* in order to write books about the Big Brotherly side of such institutions as the Internal Revenue Service and the Justice Department, pointed out to me that the Knapp Commission scandal had cut deeper than the police-corruption scandals of previous eras; this, he said, was in no small part David's doing. "From what I've read of the history of the earlier moments of alleged reform, with most of them there would be the scandal, and everyone would go 'Tsk, tsk,' and we'd go right back to where we were before," Burnham said.

"What Durk did was to insist on the political accountability of the city fathers. Today, when you read about a government scandal in the newspapers, people aren't usually satisfied with the rotten apple theory; they're looking at the system and at the people in charge. Durk made a big contribution to that."

He is a figure in the history of his native city. He is also an astute chronicler of that history—a repository of precious institutional memory in a forgetful world. There are times when listening to him is like trying to follow an overgrown path in a forest. But if you stick with it, sooner or later the way gets clearer, you reach the top of a rise, and a vista opens up. "He provides you with an education that you're not going to get—ever—from talking to the official police spokespeople," Sydney Schanberg says.

Dumping on New York City has been a favorite sport of American politicians and political commentators in the eighties and nineties, and even many New Yorkers take a perverse pride in the faith that they have it worse than anybody. In fact, police foul ups and scandals have become frighteningly routine occurrences lately, and some American cities have experienced disclosures that seem outlandish even by New York standards.

In Los Angeles, the Rodney King case—the beating itself; the racist language that (in the ensuing inquiry) turned out to be an everyday feature of the police-radio traffic; the intimidating tactics with which many LA cops sought to compensate for the comparatively small size of their department in relation to that of the city—revealed habits of mind and action greatly at odds with the image of steely professionalism so long cultivated by the LAPD. In Boston, when the manager of a fur shop—Charles Stuart—murdered his pregnant wife in 1989, the police not only helped spread his inflammatory tale of a black assailant who had abducted the couple at gunpoint, but proceeded to sweep the neighborhood, rounding up black men almost at random and threatening and terrorizing witnesses (even attempting to plant incriminating evidence in the home of one of them) in the hope of securing testimony against the innocent man Stuart had identified in a lineup. Until a commission of inquiry protested nearly two years later, none of the officers or supervisors involved was disciplined in any way.

Miamians discovered in the late 1980s that the drug traffic had spawned crews of crooked cops (much like those unearthed by the Mollen Commission in New York) who made a practice of robbing suspects, conducting vigilante searches of their apartments and stealing whatever valuables they found there. In two raids on small freighters in the Miami River, a group that came to be known as the river cops were alleged to have stolen (and resold) a thousand pounds of cocaine. Attempting to flee one of these raids, three men jumped into the river and drowned. (Three police officers were subsequently charged with murder in addition to racketeering and trafficking in cocaine.)

The Miami police blamed many of their problems on a single group of recruits hired in the early 1980s. Under the prodding of a "use it or lose it" allocation of funds by the Florida state legislature, the city had undertaken to add two hundred new cops to the force. In the effort to meet this goal within the allotted time, the department had foregone many of the usual screening techniques, and by 1988 more than a third of the two hundred members of the "class of 1980" had been dismissed for one offense or another. Washington, D.C., around the same time, was having a similar experience with more than a thousand new cops it had hired under a mandate from Congress. To make things easier, the passing grade on the entrance exam had been lowered to 50 percent, and many background investigations had been conducted exclusively by telephone. Several applicants were in prison when they received notices inviting them to report for duty as D.C. police officers. One man got his police acceptance letter and was almost simultaneously turned down for parole.

A fast cure for the delusion that New York has the nation's most troubled police department is a look at New Orleans, where, in a department one twentieth the size of New York's, four police officers were charged with murder between the spring of 1994 and the spring of 1995. One had apparently ordered the contract killing of a woman (the mother of three) who had dared to file a brutality complaint against him. Another—a policewoman—was convicted of holding up a Vietnamese restaurant where she had been employed, after-hours, as a security guard. In the course of the robbery, she or her accomplice (it was unclear which) shot and killed the owner's son and daughter—they were on their knees, evidently praying, when they died—as well as a fellow police officer, a former partner of the policewoman's, who had been taking over for her as security guard.

In the summer of 1993, the New Orleans PD vice squad was disbanded after a sergeant came under investigation for holding up bars and strip joints. In 1994 it got out that, as a fairly routine practice, New Orleans cops were taking stolen cars that they had recovered and appropriating them for their own use. At a press conference called to announce the indictment of twelve police officers on drug charges, U.S. Attorney Eddie Jordan described police corruption in New Orleans as "pervasive, rampant, systemic."

These other cities might also learn a thing or two from David Durk. What police scandals lead to, as always, are calls for greater vigilance. What they don't lead to, generally speaking, is an acknowledgment that corruption, brutality, and indifference to civil liberties are symptoms of deeper conditions, and that police departments with such troubles need to do more than beef up their internal affairs units; they need to seek out good people (whatever their backgrounds), lay down rules that those people can respect, and encourage the best in them. Nearly thirty years ago, David began saying that, in contrast to some urban problems, those of the police could be improved in the here and now, by relatively obvious methods. He painted a picture of what a big-city police force *could* be, and it was a beautiful picture. It has not lost its beauty with the passage of time.

Scattered about the law enforcement world are people for whom David, in his unlikely way, has been a mentor. Those who worked under rather than over him tend to have warm memories of the association; some speak of it as a high point of their careers. A few, like Jack Burnescu of the finance department, have volunteered to me that they would like nothing better than to join up with David again. Others have cited lessons that they learned from him and have continued to apply. Barbara Bishop, his former counsel in the finance department, told me that in her subsequent career as a prosecutor in Manhattan and Brooklyn she often used David's techniques for questioning people and cultivating sources, including a line of his: "I'm not asking you to trust me—just test me."

Ask these people what the most important thing they have learned from him is, however, and it has nothing to do with suspects or sources. Rather, it concerns those dicey moments in an employee's life when (whether he acknowledges it or not) he would like to do one thing and his agency expects him to do another. Bishop's tenure at finance, she said later, was the only time she ever saw law enforcement operate at "full capacity"—unchecked by political concerns. Susan Thomas, a finance department investigator who went on to a job as a special agent for a federal law enforcement agency, told me that whenever she was faced with an ethical dilemma she would ask herself, "What would David do?"

"There's still a core of people here who identify themselves as 'Durk people,' " Tom Stanton, who took over David's old job at finance, told me. One of the characteristics of a Durk person, Stanton added, is the readiness to challenge a supervisor who gives an order that is less than kosher.

In retracing David's career, I have often felt an urge to rewrite it—in particular, to supply a more comforting ending. Like Stanton, Bishop, Goldman, Reppetto, Garth, and lord knows how many other people who have known him over the years, I want him to set his grievances aside and be rewarded in this life rather than the next, even if that means learning to be "more skilled at—I won't say toadying, but at functioning in a collegial setting and carrying on a civilized discussion," as that prosecutor-turned-judge so eloquently put it.

But I am also cheering him on, and wishing that more people were like him. Most of us carefully measure each professional step, with a view to ensuring a steady income, the approbation of our colleagues, and the most comfortable position we have it in us to attain. Meanwhile, we long to plunge, heart and soul, into every mission. David Durk is a warning to us—and an inspiration.

ACKNOWLEDGMENTS

First and foremost, this book could not have been written without the cooperation of David and Arlene Durk. David gave me access to more than thirty years' worth of personal notes, tapes, news clippings, original documents, and other materials, and introduced me to informants, colleagues, and friends. In addition, he and Arlene spent innumerable hours answering my questions—sometimes the same question more than once.

David and I have agreed to share in the proceeds of this book, but the writing and the conclusions are mine. A commitment to omit names and identifying information in a few sensitive cases was the only contractual limitation on my ability to tell his story as truthfully as I knew how.

For reasons that the reader will quickly come to understand, certain people and institutions that loom large in this book did not respond warmly to my inquiries. I am all the more grateful, therefore, to those who did. Thomas Reppetto, of the Citizens Crime Commission, lent help that went way beyond the call of any possible duty. I began to rely on him after a series of journeys to nowhere through the channels of the New York City police department, and I'm not sure, in retrospect, that any amount of official assistance would have been more valuable. In the end, though, the department briefly let up its guard, and did help, after all. For that, I would like to thank Deputy Commissioners Peter LaPorte and Tom Kelly, Lieutenant Richard Lebron, and Commissioner William Bratton.

I am grateful to all those who agreed to be interviewed (see "A Note on Sources," page 370), and especially to Barbara Bishop, William Bonocum, Anthony Bouza, David Burnham, Richard Dillon, Jimmy Lanzano, and Thomas Stanton, who reviewed parts of the manuscript and offered corrections and suggestions. And, for sure, they are not responsible for any errors of fact or interpretation that remain.

—————

I owe a large debt of thanks to Random House and to two Peters. Peter Osnos was my editor when I began this book and he was still my editor (and still working for the same publisher) when I finished it— listen up, *Guinness Book of World Records*! In between, he gave clear-headed advice and never complained when things took longer than they should have. His colleague Peter Smith brought a fresh eye to the book when one was badly needed, and stayed in my corner addressing problems large and small from there on out.

This book grew out of a two-part profile in *The New Yorker*. Not all editors would have immediately appreciated David Durk's worthiness as a subject, so I am grateful to Bob Gottlieb, who did. Thanks also go to Kim Heron, who clued me in to what was and wasn't important, and to Daniel Hurewitz, who checked as many facts as a fact checker could, and then some. And to Bill Finnegan, who helped me shape the story and gave me some much-needed encouragement. And once again to Eleanor Gould, who did her usual astonishing job of unraveling tangles in the writing; she did it not only for the *New Yorker* articles, but, as a favor, for a large portion of the book. Bless you, Eleanor!

Much of this saga of big-city cops was written far from the city— in the Adirondacks, sometimes even in an Adirondack chair on a porch visited by chipmunks and butterflies, facing a sunlit lake and many varieties of swooping, floating, pecking birdlife. To all those creatures, and to Sheila and Ben and Harriet and the Blue Mountain

Center, love and thanks, and here's the book, finally. I also had the good fortune to spend time at the MacDowell and Yaddo colonies— wonderful places, but let us not say it too loudly, or somebody will shut them down.

Thanks beyond words to my wife, Natalie, and to my children, Emma and Nicholas.

A NOTE ON SOURCES

The following people were interviewed for this book: William Acosta, Alfred Anger, Michael Armstrong, Martin Arnold, William Aronwald, Nicholas Bache, Barbara Bishop, William Bonocum, Anthony Bouza, William Bratton, Arthur Browne, Jack Burnescu, David Burnham, Mary Chiu, Kenneth Conboy, Sydney Cooper, Paul Crotty, Robert Daley, Paul Delise, Lawrence Dempsey, Alan Dershowitz, Eugene DeSantis, Robert DeVito, Richard Dillon, Alfred Donati, David Dorsen, Edwin Dreher, Arlene Durk, David Durk, Joan Durk, Julie Durk, Jim Dwyer, George Elicofon, Jack Ferguson, John Foreman, Arnold Fraiman, Jerry Friedman, David Garth, Arthur Gelb, Herman Goldfarb, Barry Gottehrer, Rudolph Giuliani, Lawrence Goldman, Merrie Gordon, Marvin Gutlove, Harold Hess, Charles Kaiser, Ann Kemp, John Kifner, Peter Kline, Whitman Knapp, Ed Koch, Jay Kriegel, Jimmy Lanzano, Robert Leuci, Robert Levinson, Harvey Lippman, Stanley Lupkin, Peter Maas, William McCarthy, Robert McGuire, Jeremiah McKenna, David Marash, Philip Michael, John Miller, Milton Mollen, Ed Murphy, Patrick J. Murphy, Patrick V. Murphy, Jerry Nachtman, Shirah Neiman, Jack Newfield, Mary Nichols, Anna Paulson, Charles Piccoli, Gabe Pressman, Thomas Puccio, Thomas Reppetto, Burton Roberts, Sam

Roberts, Tom Robbins, Abe Rosenthal, Gregory Roth, Beth Rowton, Robert Ruskin, Henry Ruth, Sydney Schanberg, Frank Schiele, Leonard Schwartz, Nicholas Scoppetta, Irving Seidman, Frank Serpico, Edward M. Shaw, Ira Silverman, Joan Snyder, Steve Somerstein, Thomas Stanton, Larry Stephen, James Swain, James Taylor, Susan Thomas, Harry Tishelman, Martin Tolchin, Emmanuel Urzi, Laura Weisel, Clark Whelton, Tappan Wilder, Les Wolff, Robert Wood, Joanne Woodward, Peter Zimroth.

When dialogue appears in quotes, the words were recalled by a participant. They are, of course, only an approximation of what was actually said.

The following names are aliases used to disguise the identity of people who could not safely be named: Greene; Pagnotti; Gallagher; Carduccio; McManus; Ames; Maltby; Cheswick; Boyd; Dalton; Grainey; Jerry; the Levys; Poppin. In some cases, I have changed certain other particulars of their circumstances to afford them an added measure of anonymity. But in all cases, their recollections and the descriptions of the events they witnessed or participated in accurately reflect what they told me.

In addition to my interviews—the basis for most of the book—I relied on the New York newspapers, chiefly the *Times;* testimony before the Knapp and Mollen commissions; and the following books:

Browne, Arthur; Dan Collins; and Michael Goodwin. *I, Koch.* Dodd, Mead, 1985.

Daley, Robert. *Prince of the City.* Houghton Mifflin, 1978.

———. *Target Blue.* Delacorte Press, 1973.

Durk, David, and Ira Silverman. *The Pleasant Avenue Connection.* Harper & Row, 1976.

Ellis, Edward Robb. *The Epic of New York City.* Coward-McCann, 1966.

Gottehrer, Barry. *The Mayor's Man.* Doubleday, 1975.

Knapp Commission (Commission to Investigate Allegations of Police Corruption and the City's Anti-Corruption Procedures). *Commission Report.* 1972.

Maas, Peter. *Serpico.* Viking Press, 1973.

Mollen Commission (Commission to Investigate Allegations of Police Corruption and the Anti-Corruption Procedures of the Police Department). *Commission Report.* 1994.

Morris, Edmund. *The Rise of Theodore Roosevelt.* Coward, McCann and Geoghegan, 1979.

Morris, Lloyd. *Incredible New York.* Random House, 1951.

Newfield, Jack, and Wayne Barrett. *City for Sale.* Harper & Row, 1988.

Pilat, Oliver. *Lindsay's Campaign.* Beacon Press, 1968.

Reppetto, Thomas. *The Blue Parade.* Macmillan/Free Press, 1978.

Richardson, James F. *The New York Police: From Colonial Times to 1901.* Oxford University Press, 1970.

Riis, Jacob. *The Making of an American.* Macmillan, 1929.

Talese, Gay. *The Kingdom and the Power.* World Publishing, 1969.

INDEX

⟵►●◄⟶

ABOUT THE AUTHOR

JAMES LARDNER, a former Washington, D.C., police officer, has been a reporter for *The Washington Post* and a staff writer for *The New Yorker*. He is the author of *Fast Forward: Hollywood, the Japanese, and the Onslaught of the VCR*. He lives in New York City with his wife and two children.

A B O U T   T H E   T Y P E

This book was set in Photina, a typeface designed by José Mendoza in 1971. It is a very elegant design with high legibility, and its close character fit has made it a popular choice for use in quality magazines and art gallery publications.